S0-BSJ-162

NORTH DAKOTA
STATE UNIVERSITY
SEP 1 3 1988
SERIALS DEPT.
LIBRARY

WITHDRAWN
NDSU

MEDIEVAL CHRISTIAN LITERARY IMAGERY

A GUIDE TO INTERPRETATION

TORONTO MEDIEVAL BIBLIOGRAPHIES 11

General Editor: John Leyerle

Published in association with
the Centre for Medieval Studies, University of Toronto

R. E. KASKE

in collaboration with
ARTHUR GROOS and MICHAEL W. TWOMEY

Medieval Christian Literary Imagery

A GUIDE TO INTERPRETATION

UNIVERSITY OF TORONTO PRESS
Toronto Buffalo London

© University of Toronto Press 1988
Toronto   Buffalo   London
Printed in Canada

ISBN 0-8020-2636-2 (cloth)
ISBN 0-8020-6663-1 (paper)

Canadian Cataloguing in Publication Data

Kaske, Robert Earl, 1921-
    Medieval Christian literary imagery

(Toronto medieval bibliographies ; 11)
"Published in association with the Centre for
Medieval Studies, University of Toronto."
Includes indexes.
ISBN 0-8020-2636-2 (bound). – ISBN 0-8020-6663-1 (pbk.)

1. Literature, Medieval – Christian influences –
Sources – Bibliography.   2. Christian literature –
Bibliography.   3. Literature, Medieval – Themes,
motives – Bibliography.   4. Christian art and
symbolism – Medieval, 500-1500 – Bibliography.
I. Groos, Arthur.   II. Twomey, Michael W.
III. University of Toronto. Centre for Medieval
Studies.   IV. Title.   V. Series.

Z6517.K38 1988   016.809'023   C88-093819-6

PN
671
Z99
K37
1987

For Carol

Editor's Preface

The study of the Middle Ages has been developed chiefly within university departments such as English or History. This pattern is increasingly being supplemented by an interdisciplinary approach in which the plan of work is shaped to fit the subject studied. The difference of approach is between Chaucer the English poet and Chaucer the civil servant of London attached to the court of Richard II, a man interested in the Ptolemaic universe and widely read in Latin, French, and Italian. Interdisciplinary programs tend to lead readers into areas relatively unfamiliar to them where critical bibliographies prepared with careful selectivity by an expert are essential. The Centre for Medieval Studies at the University of Toronto takes such an interdisciplinary approach to the Middle Ages, and the need for selective bibliographies has become apparent in our work. The Centre has undertaken to meet this need by sponsoring the Toronto Medieval Bibliographies.

In his valuable guide, *Serial Bibliographies for Medieval Studies,** Richard H. Rouse describes 283 bibliographies; the number is surprisingly large and indicates the considerable effort now being made to provide inclusive lists of items relevant to medieval studies. The total amount in print is already vast; for one unfamiliar with a subject, significant work is difficult to locate and the problem grows worse with each year's output. The reader may well say, like the throng in *Piers Plowman* seeking the way to *Treuthe,* 'This were a wikked way but who-so hadde a gyde' (B.vi.I). The Toronto Medieval Bibliographies are meant to be such guides; each title is prepared by an expert and gives directions to important work in the subject.

* Publications of the Center for Medieval and Renaissance Studies 3, University of California, Los Angeles (Berkeley and Los Angeles 1969)

Each volume gives a list of works selected with three specific aims. One is to aid students who are relatively new to the area of study, for example Medieval Latin Palaeography. Another is to guide more advanced readers in a subject where they have had little formal training, for example Chaucer or Medieval Christian Imagery; and the third is to assist new libraries in forming a basic collection in the subject presented. Individual compilers are given scope to organize a presentation that they judge will best suit their subject and also to make brief critical comments as they think fit. Clarity and usefulness of a volume are preferred over any demand for exact uniformity from one volume to another.

Toronto, April 1988
JL

Contents

Appendix: Medieval Encyclopedias
(by Michael W. Twomey)

Abbreviations

AH	*Analecta hymnica*
BL	British Library, London
BN	Bibliothèque nationale, Paris
C	century
CCLcm	Corpus Christianorum: Continuatio mediaeualis
CCSL	Corpus Christianorum, series Latina
CSEL	Corpus scriptorum ecclesiasticorum Latinorum
DACL	*Dictionnaire d'archéologie chrétienne et de liturgie*
diss.	dissertation
EETS	Early English Text Society
MGH	Monumenta Germaniae historica
MLL	*Medieval Latin Liturgy*, ed. Pfaff
NUC	National Union Catalogue
PG	Patrologia Graeca, ed. Migne
PL	Patrologia Latina, ed. Migne
PLS	Patrologia Latina: Supplementum, ed. Hamman
SC	Sources chrétiennes

Author's Preface

In the tortuous development of this book, the most sustained and valuable assistance I have received has been from my colleague and collaborator Arthur Groos, of the German Department at Cornell University. As nearly as I can recall the details of our collaboration, it has gone something like this: During my first several years at Cornell I offered a seminar on 'research in medieval literature,' containing the nucleus of the bibliography and method presented here. This seminar was eventually taken over by Professor Groos, who greatly expanded the bibliography and distributed it to our students in bound form. After a few years I taught the seminar again, with substantial enlargement and revision of his bibliography; and when he then returned to teaching it, he subjected the bibliography to another major revision. Finally, of course, my putting the volume into its present form has included a great amount of revising of various kinds, including the addition of several sections that are virtually new; and Professor Groos's careful reading of the entire manuscript has produced several important corrections, modifications, and additions. The result is a book which, while its overall plan and method remain my own, is in many places so heavily and complexly indebted to Professor Groos that our respective contributions would be difficult to disentangle.

Only slightly less important has been the help of my other collaborator, Michael W. Twomey of Ithaca College, who undertook the demanding job of writing an appendix on medieval encyclopedias, read the entire manuscript with a productively critical eye, and compiled the index. Another contributor of special importance, though his name is not on the title-page, is Thomas D. Hill, my long-time colleague in the Cornell English Department, whose reading of the manuscript added a number of items I am delighted not to be without.

A work of this kind – miscellaneous in its coverage and extending over years in its composition – inevitably picks everybody's mind (or tries to), so that the attempt to acknowledge all debts is probably quixotic. Nevertheless, with apologies to whomever I may be forgetting, my thanks for various pieces of information to Robert Adams, John A. Alford, the late Judson B. Allen, Robert G. Babcock, Frederick M. Biggs, Robert J. Blanch, the late Morton W. Bloomfield, Emerson Brown, Jr, Robert G. Calkins, Alice M. Colby-Hall, J.E. Cross, Brian E. Daley, S.J., James W. Earl, Margot E. Fassler, Hugh B. Feiss, O.S.B., John Freccero, John B. Friedman, Patrick J. Gallacher, Creighton Gilbert, Richard H. Green, Rosalie B. Green, Michael Herren, J.N. Hillgarth, the late Alfred L. Kellogg, Robert E. Lerner, John Leyerle, Charles H. Lohr, S.J., Deborah MacInnes, Thomas W. Mackay, Giuseppe F. Mazzotta, the late Robert E. McNally, S.J., Jennifer Montagu, James H. Morey, Nigel Morgan, James J. O'Donnell, the late Edwin A. Quain, S.J., D.W. Robertson, Jr, Fred C. Robinson, Richard H. Rouse, John J. Ruffing, Edward C. Schweitzer, R. Mark Scowcroft, R. Allen Shoaf, Penn R. Szittya, M. Teresa Tavormina, Mary F. Wack, Siegfried Wenzel, Winthrop Wetherbee, James I. Wimsatt, Joseph S. Wittig, Charles D. Wright, the members of my National Endowment for the Humanities Seminar in the summer of 1986, and the two anonymous readers for the University of Toronto Press.

In the real world, I would like to thank Caroline T. Spicer and her staff at the Reference Desk of Cornell's Olin Library, for their skill and patience in handling questions and interlibrary loan requests that must sometimes have led them to suspect I really had taken all knowledge for my province; Elizabeth A. Rowe and Sandra McEntire, both then of Cornell University, for letting me participate in the blessings of the word-processor without having to learn anything about it; and Gayle Margherita and John W. Tanke of Cornell University for helping me read an unusually demanding body of proof. Special thanks are due to Anna Burko of the Centre for Medieval Studies at the University of Toronto, who edited the manuscript for the press (contributing many valuable additions and corrections), devised the system of boldface to help readers pick up authors and titles in the text, and eventually turned the whole thing into the best set of proofs I have ever seen.

This project has been supported at various times by a Guggenheim Fellowship, a Research Materials Grant from the National Endowment for the Humanities, and a National Endowment for the Humanities Fellowship for Independent Study and Research – for all of which, of course, my sincerest thanks.

My wife, to everyone's good fortune, has had nothing to do with the index; instead, she has contributed a number of valuable references, corrections, and suggestions.

November, 1987

REK

Introduction

During the past several decades, we have become increasingly aware of the allusive density of medieval literature, and of the extent to which much of its imagery depends on certain large bodies of traditional Christian learning – the Vulgate Bible and its voluminous commentaries, the liturgy, hymns and sequences, sermons and homilies, the pictorial arts, mythography, commentaries on major medieval authors, encyclopedias of various kinds, and so on. If so, it seems clear that this whole miscellaneous ragbag of traditional medieval lore is potentially of enormous value, as a kind of great awkward index to the connotations of a good deal of the imagery on which the meaning of medieval works partly depends. The difficulty, of course, is in finding one's way around in it. If, say, one suspects that an echo of a biblical verse in Chaucer or Dante may somehow depend for its meaning on traditional commentary on that verse, how does he go about finding the relevant commentaries? Or if one finds the word 'fire' in a context that suggests resonances beyond the literal without satisfactorily identifying them, how does he go about learning what the traditional associations of fire were?

There are of course many excellent studies which, while not focussing directly on such practical questions, provide a good deal of incidental help. One thinks, for example, of Friedrich Ohly's brilliant analysis of medieval figuration, 'Vom geistigen Sinn des Wortes im Mittelalter,' reprinted in his *Schriften zur mittelalterlichen Bedeutungsforschung* pp 1-31 – which, besides presenting a research programme that the members of the Münster Sonderforschungsbereich have been carrying out for decades under his leadership, includes a remarkable number of relevant titles in its footnotes and bibliography (pp 29-31); and of Hennig Brinkmann's *Mittelalterliche Hermeneutik*, which provides massive bibliography in many areas pertinent for the study of medieval imagery. A slighter but useful survey is Brian Murdoch's 'Theological Writings and Medieval German Literature: Some Bibliographical Comments,' *Neuphilologische Mitteilungen* 71 (1970) 66-82. None of these studies, however, is organized as an attempt to provide a method for dealing with specific problems of the kind mentioned above. There is in fact no generally available methodology for handling such problems, and a frequent way of confronting them seems to be to check a couple of commentaries or encyclopedias and make do with whatever one happens to find. The result is that scholarship of this kind, while it has made important contributions, has too often been forced into unconvincing interpretations by a simple lack of relevant information.

For the past thirty years I have been giving, in ever-expanding form, a lecture or series of lectures designed to equip my graduate students for dealing with just such problems. Having begun modestly enough as a single lecture for a fifty-minute class, it has now swollen to a marathon that fills most of a one-semester seminar; and the imagination quails at the number of copies, redactions, conflations, epitomes, and excerpts that must exist in varying degrees of coherence in student notes. Clearly, a pedagogical monstrosity; I have sometimes reflected that the only thing to be said in its favour is that it does, after all, seem to work.

The present volume, which is an attempt to expand these lectures into a usable printed bibliography, may require a few precautions. Most important, I cannot emphasize too strongly that its component chapters are not intended as 'bibliographies' covering the fields of medieval biblical exegesis, liturgy, mythography, and the rest in anything like the usual sense of the word, so that experts approaching them from that point of view will no doubt find all of them seriously defective. Rather, I have tried throughout to maintain the perspective of a literary scholar trying to interpret literary imagery with the help of first-hand research in these various fields, and so far as possible to be guided by my own past research (or by what I have learned incidentally about the techniques of such research) in selecting the items most likely to be of use; the subtitle 'An Essay in Subjective Bibliography,' whimsically suggested by one of my colleagues, would not be altogether inaccurate. I have also tried wherever possible to combine this raw bibliographical information with suggestions about the most profitable methods of using it – admittedly with rather mixed results, owing mainly to the differing degrees of intractability in the bodies of learning themselves. For example, biblical exegesis lends itself with uncommon readiness to the kind of systematization that can bring order to such research; and I think most users of the volume will agree that the chapter on it can be employed most directly and methodically of all. Mythography and the pictorial arts, though somewhat less docile, can still be managed with relative ease. At the other end of the scale are the liturgy and sermons, which – owing partly to the miscellaneous nature of the fields themselves, partly to a lack of systematizing tools – remain distressingly catch-as-catch-can; to a greater extent than I would wish, my treatment of them has been restricted to enumerative bibliography plus a few hopeful suggestions about possible methods of employing it. One should add also the obvious reminder that literary imagery can come from anywhere (including the author's own untutored imagination), and that the following eight chapters cannot pretend to cover all or even most of the possibilities. What they attempt is to sketch out approaches to seven large repositories of traditional material that I have found particularly rewarding, along with a miscellany of images that are in some way special (chapter 8), in the hope that this beginning may be expanded or augmented by others as their interests dictate.

A word should be said about that favourite question of reviewers, 'To what audience is this work addressed?' Primarily, I have tried to keep in mind the graduate student or young scholar who is interested in this way of interpreting medieval literature but has had little or no guidance in it – though I would be disappointed if more experienced scholars did not also find the volume at least sporadically useful. Like practically all worthwhile research on things medieval, the approach I am outlining presupposes some reading knowledge of Latin. With regard to modern scholarly languages (particularly German and French), I have tried throughout to cite the most useful studies, regardless of what language they are written in; to give undue preference to works that happen to be in English would, after all, be to discriminate subtly against those who *do* have an adequate scholarly preparation. I have ignored completely the problem of accessibility (citing in chapter 3, for example, the *Hymnale secundum usum insignis ac praeclarae ecclesiae Sarisburiensis* of Littlemore, 1850, which I have found only at the Union Theological Seminary in New York), partly because I can find no intelligent way of deciding where to draw the line between 'accessible' and 'inaccessible,' but mainly because the *National Union Catalogue*, interlibrary loans, microfilm, and photocopy have to a great extent rendered the problem itself academic. Finally, while I have for the most part omitted items that exist only in manuscript, I have occasionally broken this rule to include works of exceptional importance – for example several of the *distinctiones* and the *Liber de moralitatibus*, both in chapter 1.

I suppose it is obvious that my concern throughout is not with the venerable pastime of simple source-hunting, so dear to the hearts of scholars a few generations ago. For any literary artist using material in what may be highly original ways, exact sources for imagery and other imaginative details are notoriously difficult to pin down; and in the case of medieval literature, where we normally know so little about either the author's biography or the range of sources that may have been available to him, we would be almost helpless if our analysis of what he is drawing from previous works had to depend on a confident identification of his actual sources. Rather, I am talking about what might be called 'theme-hunting' or 'tradition-hunting': the study of motifs which presumably formed part of the cultural repertory of a medieval writer and his audience, and which could then be used by the writer in all sorts of original and oblique ways. This very concept, of course, carries with it an immediate further question: What kind of criteria do we have for establishing the existence of such allusion in an early literary work? Though there is no wholly satisfactory answer, I think the absolutely essential thing is that the allusion being proposed must really 'click' in context – that is, the proposed correspondence must be either precise or complex enough, and must carry an appropriate enough meaning for its context, that to consider it accidental would outrage probability. It is a criterion that admittedly leaves great room for disagreement, since one person's 'certainly' or 'probably' is often enough another's 'possibly' or 'hardly'; but it does at least provide a basis for thinking about this extraordinarily slippery problem. I would, incidentally, give this kind of close textual correspondence great priority over external historical probability, since, as I have said, in dealing with almost any early literary work we know relatively little about what may have been directly available to the author. Let us imagine, for example, that we are trying to interpret a particular passage of Chaucer; that on the one hand we have a letter signed by Chaucer, insisting that our passage is to be understood only in the light of a passage from the *Confessio amantis*, which after prolonged study turns out to have no possible relevance that we can see; and that on the other hand, a passage in the writings ascribed to Zoroaster offers an uncommonly precise and complex correspondence to our passage from Chaucer. In this admittedly improbable situation, it seems to me that we would have no choice but to reject the allusion to the *Confessio amantis* and assume some sort of connection – direct, or more probably indirect – between our passage and the works of Zoroaster.

I should add also the obvious caution that no mere *method* will supply the initial inspirations or hunches on which this kind of research often depends. Those, as always, have to come from one's own imagination, supplemented by the need for tenure, the direct inspiration of the Holy Ghost, or whatever else one happens to depend on. Nor will any method do the final work of interpreting what one has found; that again has to come from within. I have often suspected that some of the less fortunate uses of, say, biblical exegesis for literary interpretation have sprung partly from a tacit assumption that once one has consulted a few commentators, the interpretation will take care of itself. In reality, of course, sophisticated medieval authors employ traditional allusion in a dazzling variety of ways, so that defining its functions can be strenuous work indeed. Here as elsewhere, literary interpretation is partly a science, partly an art.

Though a 'how-to' without some demonstration is at best sterile and at worst suspect, a full bibliography of studies employing traditional material successfully or provocatively for the interpretation of medieval imagery, while eminently desirable in itself, would be well on the way to another book; and an attempt at a brief representative list – given the extraordinary variety both of the kinds of material covered and of the ways of using it – presents endless difficulties of selection. At the risk of sounding parochial, I therefore fall back on the device of illustrating by some of my own studies, which have at least the advantage of being intimately related to the methods described in the subsequent chapters.

'*Gigas* the Giant in *Piers Plowman*,' *Journal of English and Germanic Philology* 56 (1957) 177-85

'The Summoner's Garleek, Oynons, and eek Lekes,' *Modern Language Notes* 74 (1959) 481-4

'The Speech of "Book" in *Piers Plowman*,' *Anglia* 77 (1959) 117-44

'Langland's Walnut-Simile,' *Journal of English and Germanic Philology* 58 (1959) 650-4

'Two Cruxes in *Pearl:* 596 and 609-10,' *Traditio* 15 (1959) 418-28

'Eve's "Leaps" in the *Ancrene Riwle*,' *Medium Ævum* 29 (1960) 22-4

'Patristic Exegesis in the Criticism of Medieval Literature: The Defense,' in *Critical Approaches to Medieval Literature: Selected Papers from the English Institute, 1958-1959* ed. Dorothy Bethurum (New York 1960) pp 27-60 and 158-9 (abridged in *Interpretations of Piers Plowman* ed. Edward Vasta [Notre Dame 1968] pp 319-38; and in *Geoffrey Chaucer: A Critical Anthology* ed. J.A. Burrow [Penguin Books 1969] pp 233-9)

'Dante's "DXV" and "Veltro",' *Traditio* 17 (1961) 185-254 (abridged, with some important additions, as 'Dante's DXV,' in *Dante: A Collection of Critical Essays* ed. John Freccero, Twentieth Century Views [Spectrum Books 1965] pp 122-40)

'The *Canticum canticorum* in the *Miller's Tale*,' *Studies in Philology* 59 (1962) 479-500

'*Ex vi transicionis* and Its Passage in *Piers Plowman*,' *Journal of English and Germanic Philology* 62 (1963) 32-60 (repr. in *Style and Symbolism in Piers Plowman: A Modern Critical Anthology* ed. Robert J. Blanch [Knoxville, Tenn. 1969] pp 228-63)

'The Character *Figura* in *Le Mystère d'Adam*,' in *Mediaeval Studies in Honor of Urban Tigner Holmes, Jr* ed. John F. Mahoney and John Esten Keller (Chapel Hill, N.C. 1966) pp 103-10

'*Piers Plowman* and Local Iconography,' *Journal of the Warburg and Courtauld Institutes* 31 (1968) 159-69

'A Poem of the Cross in the Exeter Book: "Riddle 60" and "The Husband's Message",' *Traditio* 23 (1967) 41-71

'"Sì si conserva il seme d'ogne giusto" (*Purg.* XXXII, 48),' *Dante Studies* 89 (1971) 49-54

'Horn and Ivory in the *Summoner's Tale*,' *Neuphilologische Mitteilungen* 73 (1972) 122-6 (*Studies Presented to Tauno F. Mustanoja on the Occasion of His Sixtieth Birthday*)

'Dante's *Purgatorio* XXXII and XXXIII: A Survey of Christian History,' *University of Toronto Quarterly* 43 (1974) 193-214

'The Seven *Status ecclesiae* in *Purgatorio* XXXII and XXXIII,' in
   *Dante, Petrarch, Boccaccio: Studies in the Italian Trecento in
   Honor of Charles S. Singleton* ed. Aldo S. Bernardo and Anthony
   L. Pellegrini, Medieval & Renaissance Texts & Studies 22
   (Binghamton, N.Y. 1983) pp 89-113
'The *gifstol* Crux in *Beowulf,*' *Leeds Studies in English* N.S. 16 (1985)
   142-51 (*Sources and Relations: Studies in Honour of J.E. Cross*)
'Pandarus's "vertue of corones tweyne",' *Chaucer Review* 21 (1986)
   226-33 (*A Volume of Essays in Memory of Judson Boyce Allen,
   1932-85*)
'The Character Hunger in *Piers Plowman,*' in *Medieval English
   Studies Presented to George Kane* ed. Edward D. Kennedy, Ronald
   Waldron, and Joseph S. Wittig (Cambridge 1988) pp 187-97
'*Piers Plowman* and Local Iconography: The Font at Eardisley,
   Herefordshire,' to appear in *Journal of the Warburg and Courtauld
   Institutes.*

A brief note in explanation of the use of boldface might be helpful. Full
bibliographical details on any published work are given only once, either
in the section where the said work receives its fullest discussion [if it is
discussed], or where it is first cited [if it is not discussed]. Boldface is
used to draw attention to authors (both medieval and modern) and titles at
such points. Boldface is also used sparingly in the indices: in the index of
modern authors, in the case of multiple citations of the same work, to indicate which page carries the full bibliographic citation; and in the index
of manuscripts, to indicate where manuscripts are not discussed, but only
cited in titles.

MEDIEVAL CHRISTIAN LITERARY IMAGERY

A GUIDE TO INTERPRETATION

1
Biblical Exegesis

Introductory

Interpretation of the Bible occupied a central place in the intellectual life of the Middle Ages. Its results are preserved systematically in the abundant commentaries on the Bible itself, as well as in various collections of exegetical commonplaces; they are embodied piecemeal in many other traditional forms, such as the liturgy, hymns and sequences, sermons and homilies, and the visual arts. Within this wilderness of broadly exegetical material, the most extensive single category – and, happily, the one which lends itself most easily to organized research – is that formed by the biblical commentaries and the compendia of exegetical commonplaces, which will be the subject of the present chapter. Other more awkward bodies of material (the liturgy and the rest) will be taken up in subsequent chapters.

It is of course a commonplace that the 'Bible' for the Middle Ages at large was the collection of Latin translations which eventually came to be known as the Vulgate – partly translated, and partly revised or merely assembled from earlier versions, by Jerome during the period 383-405. Convenient brief accounts are those of **A. Tricot** in *Guide to the Bible: An Introduction to the Study of Holy Scripture*, ed. **A. Robert** and **A. Tricot**, trans. **Edward P. Arbez** and **Martin R.P. McGuire** (Paris 1960) I, 645-52; **B.M. Peebles** in *New Catholic Encyclopedia* (for which see p. 13 below) II, 439-44; and especially **E.F. Sutcliffe** in *The Cambridge History of the Bible* II, *The West from the Fathers to the Reformation*, ed. **G.W.H. Lampe** (Cambridge 1969) pp 80-101. The modern Vulgate (which, as we shall see, cannot be directly equated with the medieval Vulgate) exists in many editions and can be purchased with no great difficulty. The English translation of it is the one known as the 'Douai-Rheims' translation (the Old Testament was first published at Douai in 1609-10, the New Testament at Rheims in 1582), also available in many modern editions.

To begin with the most obvious caution, the King James Bible, literary monument though it is for later periods, differs from the Vulgate in several important respects and must never, under any circumstances, be used for any study concerning the Middle Ages. One broad difference is that the Vulgate includes a number of Old Testament books or parts of books that are found in the Septuagint (to be discussed below) but not in the Hebrew canon, and so are not included in the King James Bible: Tobias, Judith, Esther 10:4-16:24, Sapientia (Wisdom), Ecclesiasticus, Baruch, Daniel 3:24-9 and 13:1-14:42, and 1 and 2 Maccabees. These books and chapters, though their canonicity was sometimes questioned even during the Middle Ages, were generally accepted as part of the medieval canon. (The books known as the Oratio Manassae and 3 and 4 Esdras, which do not appear in the King James Bible, were included in the medieval Vulgate but were removed from the canon by the Council of Trent; they are relegated to an appendix in modern editions of the Vulgate and omitted from the Douai-Rheims translation.) It is perhaps worth mentioning also that the King James Bible occasionally differs from the modern Vulgate or Douai-Rheims in the numbering of chapters and verses – most noticeably in the Psalms, where Vulgate Ps 9 corresponds to King James 9-10, Vulgate 10-112 to King James 11-113, Vulgate 113 to King James 114-15, Vulgate 114-15 to King James 116, Vulgate 116-45 to King James 117-46, and Vulgate 146-7 to King James 147. Much more dangerous for our purposes, however, is the fact that the King James Bible often differs strikingly from the Vulgate and Douai-Rheims versions in its rendering of individual words, verses, and passages – especially in the Old Testament, where at many points the King James Bible translates the Hebrew text while the Vulgate and Douai follow the Greek of the Septuagint. For example, the widely quoted Vulgate text of Canticles 2:4, 'ordinavit in me charitatem' (Douai, 'he set in order charity in me') appears in the King James as 'His banner over me was love'; and an otherwise respectable study of the Middle English poem *The Owl and the Nightingale* includes at one point a list of biblical references to the owl drawn unfortunately from the King James Bible, a good half of which are represented in the Vulgate by *struthio*, 'ostrich.'

In dwelling at such length on the unsuitability of the King James translation for present purposes, I have of course been concerned not with the difference between Catholic and non-Catholic translations, but with the difference between those that render the Vulgate (the Bible available to medieval authors) and those that do not. An illuminating example is the admirable and Catholic translation of Ronald Knox, which, besides being an eloquent paraphrase rather than a close rendering, freely consults sources beyond the Vulgate (Cant 2:4 appears as '... shewn me the blazon of his love'), and so is as useless for our purposes as the King James.

A less obvious problem is created by the difference between the medieval and the modern texts of the Vulgate itself. The great watershed between the medieval and modern Vulgates is the so-called 'Sixto-Clementine' revision, issued under Pope Sixtus V in 1590 and, after further revision, under Pope Clement VIII in 1592; convenient accounts are given by Tricot in *Guide to the Bible* I, 656-60; Peebles in *New Catholic Encyclopedia* II, 450-1; and **F.J. Crehan** in *The Cambridge History of the Bible* III, *The West from the Reformation to the Present Day*, ed. **S.L. Greenslade** (Cambridge 1963) pp 207-13. This difference between the medieval and modern texts can of course be avoided fairly easily, by consulting a Vulgate Bible printed before 1590.

Much less tractable is the problem presented by the text of the medieval Vulgate itself; throughout the Middle Ages the Latin Bible was continually being re-edited and revised, so that there were in effect many medieval 'Vulgates,' often differing appreciably according to time and place. Though this awesomely complex history can be acknowledged here only in passing, its main lines are summarized by Tricot in *Guide to the Bible* I, 652-64 and 674-5; Peebles in *New Catholic Encyclopedia* II, 444-50; and especially **Raphael Loewe** in *Cambridge History of the Bible* II, pp 102-54, with a diagram on pp 103-5. In general, printed Bibles of the fifteenth and sixteenth centuries are worth checking for possible medieval readings, since most of them rest to varying degrees on two great medieval recensions – the 'Alcuin Bible' produced at the court of Charlemagne, and especially the so-called 'Paris text' popularized by the University of Paris in the twelfth and thirteenth centuries – neither of which had achieved anything like a critical edition of Jerome's Vulgate. A critical edition of the Vulgate itself (normally not the most useful text for a problem involving the Vulgate of the Middle Ages) is underway at the Benedictine Abbey of St Jerome in Rome, under the title *Biblia sacra iuxta Latinam Vulgatam versionem ad codicum fidem* (Rome 1926ff), 16 vols through Daniel in 1981; in the meantime, a provisional text has appeared, ed. **Bonifatius Fischer** et al., *Biblia sacra iuxta Vulgatam versionem* (2nd ed. Stuttgart 1975), 2 vols. It may be worth mentioning that the text of the Vulgate included among the works of Jerome in Migne's *Patrologia Latina* (vols 28-9) is a reprinting of the edition of **Jean Martianay** (1647-1717) et al., and is of no particular value for our purposes.

A final complication for our use of the medieval Latin Bible is the sporadic appearance of readings from pre-Vulgate Latin translations, which often retain some currency throughout the Middle Ages – particularly in quotations by the Fathers and quotations petrified by liturgical use. A famous example occurs in Ps 95:10, where the Vulgate reads 'dicite in gentibus, quia Dominus regnavit,' and the Old Latin, 'dicite in gentibus, Dominus regnavit *a ligno*' (apparently following an early Septuagint reading ἀπὸ ξύλου), thus providing an inevitable suggestion of the Cross, which is exploited by many early writers – for example by Venantius Fortunatus in the hymn 'Vexilla regis prodeunt,' line 16: 'regnavit a ligno Deus'; for further examples see Walpole, *Early Latin Hymns* (discussed on p. 75 below) pp 175-6. Convenient accounts of the Old Latin Bible are given by Tricot in *Guide to the Bible* I, 639-45 and 674, and Peebles in *New Catholic Encyclopedia* II, 436-9.

The best complete edition remains that of **Pierre Sabbathier** (Petrus Sabatier), *Bibliorum sacrorum Latinae versiones antiquae, seu Vetus Italica* (Rheims 1739-49, Paris 1751), 3 vols in 6, which includes the Old Latin text along with the Vulgate and a translation of the Hebrew; extensive citations of quotations by other authors; and at the end of vol. III, indices of quotations from the Old Testament by Christ and the Apostles, proper names and their meanings, and biblical subjects and events. This edition is being revised on a massive scale by **Bonifatius Fischer** et al., *Vetus Latina: Die Reste der altlateinischen Bibel nach Petrus Sabatier neu gesammelt und herausgegeben von der Erzabtei Beuron* (Freiburg i.B. 1949ff); the index of sigla, Genesis, and parts of Sapientia (Wisdom), the Pauline Epistles, and the Catholic Epistles have already appeared. In the meantime, the Old Latin texts of the four Gospels have been edited by **Adolf Jülicher** et al., *Itala: Das Neue Testament in altlateinischer Überlieferung* (Berlin 1938-63), 4 vols, the first three of which have appeared in a revised edition (Berlin 1970ff).

This whole complex situation with regard to medieval texts of the Latin Bible, which on the face of it may seem to preclude any reliable use of the Bible for literary interpretation, is in practice much less troublesome than it appears. If one is reading commentaries on a particular passage of Scripture, he can hardly remain unaware of any significant variations in the text, since the commentators themselves normally quote the medieval form (or forms) of the verses they are interpreting. The fact to be kept in mind is simply that such differences do exist, so that one can respond to them intelligently when they appear.

Besides the Latin Bible, there are of course Bibles in other languages which can occasionally bear upon the interpretation of medieval literature. The earliest is the Septuagint, a Greek translation of the Old Testament made by Jewish scholars between the third century B.C. and the second century A.D. Its importance for our purposes springs from the fact that it was from the beginning adopted by Christian scholars as an authentic or even divinely inspired version of the Old Testament; as such, it is frequently quoted, particularly in the patristic period. Convenient accounts of the Septuagint are presented by **G. Bardy** in *Guide to the Bible* I, 622-31, and **P.W. Skehan** in *New Catholic Encyclopedia* II, 425-9.

Among many editions of the Greek text, the handiest are probably those of **Henry Barclay Swete**, *The Old Testament in Greek according to the Septuagint* (Cambridge, many eds, 1887-94 to 1909), 3 vols, and **Alfred Rahlfs**, *Septuaginta, id est Vetus Testamentum Graece iuxta LXX interpretes* (Stuttgart [1935] and later eds), 2 vols; there is also a text with parallel translation, [**Launcelot Charles Lee Brenton**], *The Septuagint, with an English Translation* (London, n.d.), and a separate translation by **Charles Thomson**, rev. **C.A. Muses**, *The Septuagint Bible* (2nd ed. Indian Hills, Colo. 1960).

In the course of the Middle Ages, translations of the Bible or parts of it appeared in all the great medieval vernaculars, and are of course potentially important for the interpretation of medieval literature. Brief accounts of the Bible in the various vernaculars are presented by **M.J. Hunter** (Gothic), **Geoffrey Shepherd** (English before Wyclif), **Henry Hargreaves** (the Wycliffite translations), **W.B. Lockwood** (Germany and the Low Countries), **C.A. Robson** (France), **Kenelm Foster** (Italy), and **Margherita Morreale** (Spain), in *Cambridge History of the Bible* II, 338-491, with bibliographies on pp 525-35. So far as I can see, systematic research in these vernacular versions is best approached by way of the Vulgate, following methods to be outlined in this chapter.

For any research involving detailed use of the Bible, an indispensable tool is the biblical concordance; and since any concordance is of course completely dependent on the text it analyzes, one's selection of a concordance to the Bible will inevitably face the same problems already described for the text. A concordance based on the critical text of the Vulgate by Bonifatius Fischer has been edited by **Fischer**, *Novae concordantiae bibliorum sacrorum iuxta Vulgatam versionem* (Stuttgart 1977), 5 vols.

Among the many concordances to the post-Clementine Vulgate, the best are probably those of **F.P. Dutripon**, *Vulgatae editionis bibliorum sacrorum concordantiae* (Paris 1838, repr. Hildesheim 1976); and **Henri Roux de Raze, E. de Lachaud,** and **J.B. Flandrin**, *Concordantiarum ss scripturae manuale* (Lyon 1852, often re-edited; repr. Barcelona 1964). The concordance to the Douai-Rheims translation of the post-Clementine Vulgate is by **Newton Thompson** and **Raymond Stock,** *Complete Concordance to the Bible (Douay Version)* (St Louis 1942, London 1945, several later printings).

The best of the several sixteenth-century concordances to the pre-Clementine Vulgate is that of **Robert Estienne,** *Concordantiae bibliorum utriusque Testamenti Veteris et Novi ...* (Paris 1555).

The complexities of the medieval concordance are explored by **R.H. Rouse** and **M.A. Rouse, 'The Verbal Concordance to the Scriptures,'** *Archivum fratrum praedicatorum* 44 (1974) 5-30, who modify the previously accepted account in some important ways; for present purposes, it is sufficient to notice that there were basically three medieval concordances, all originating in the thirteenth century – the third of which, produced by the Dominican scholars at St Jacques, was the best known and is the ultimate ancestor of the modern concordance (Rouse, p. 25). Even this third medieval concordance, however, is not likely to be reliably reflected in any of the early printed concordances, since the fifteenth-century printers themselves tried to improve upon it (information kindly supplied to me by Richard Rouse). The many printed concordances bearing the name of Hugh of St Cher do not, of course, represent medieval concordances, but have been progressively revised by later editors.

The standard concordance to the Septuagint is by **Edwin Hatch** and **Henry A. Redpath,** *A Concordance to the Septuagint and the Other Greek Versions of the Old Testament* (Oxford 1892-7), with supplement (Oxford 1906).

Before turning to our subject proper – biblical exegesis and how it can be used for the interpretation of medieval literature – let us survey briefly the major collections in which the bulk of our exegetical texts are found. The set which (despite its many glaring inadequacies) will be central for most research of this kind is **J.-P. Migne**'s great *Patrologiae cursus completus, sive Bibliotheca universalis ... omnium ss patrum, doctorum scriptorumque ecclesiasticorum qui ab aevo apostolico ad usque Innocenti III tempora floruerunt ... Series [Latina]* (Paris 1844-64), 221 vols, popularly known as the 'Patrologia Latina' and abbreviated PL (or sometimes by earlier scholars *ML* or *MPL*). The PL covers, with many omissions, theological writings from the second century to about 1216, thus excluding most of the thirteenth century as well as the fourteenth and fifteenth. Its texts are reprinted from earlier editions of the individual writers – often including notes – and vary greatly in quality. The first 217 volumes contain texts; the last four (vols 218-21, sometimes referred to as A, B, C, and D) are a set of almost unbelievably full, complex, and sometimes inaccurate indices.

A separate unnumbered volume, compiled by an anonymous Carthusian and entitled *Elucidatio in 235 tabulas Patrologiae Latinae* (Rotterdam 1952), is in effect an index to the indices; if, for example, one is interested in the subject *Patientia,* the simplest approach will be to look it up first in the *Elucidatio,* which will in turn direct him to the relevant indices in vols 218-21.

Another addition by **P. Glorieux,** *Pour revaloriser Migne: Tables rectificatives,* Mélanges de science religieuse 9, Cahier supplémentaire (Lille 1952), though not completely reliable or up to date, is an initial attempt to correct the many misattributions in the PL, arranged by volume-numbers. If the work one is interested in is not mentioned by Glorieux, its attribution in the PL is correct so far as his information goes; if it is incorrectly attributed in the PL, the correction is given.

There is also a supplement to the PL for the patristic period (vols 1-96), ed. **Adalbert Hamman,** *Patrologiae cursus completus ... series Latina: Supplementum* (Paris 1958-74), 5 vols (abbreviated PLS), whose purpose is to add patristic texts not included in PL 1-96, correct erroneous attributions, unite works erroneously separated, and provide the results of recent scholarship on works of disputed origin. The first four volumes contain texts (vol. I covering the period of PL 1-21, II the period of PL 22-48, III the period of PL 49-65, and IV the period of PL 66-96), while vol. V adds indices of proper names, texts attributed to particular authors, incipits, and (on pp 222-307) scriptural citations; a list of relevant manuscripts; and tables relating the texts in the PLS to the PL and to the *Clavis patrum Latinorum* (for which see p. 13 below).

As has been hinted above, the PL itself is far from ideal as an edition on which to base serious research. Its texts are antiquated, and usually should not be quoted when there is a more modern edition available; many of its attributions are inaccurate or suspect, often with disastrous results if they are taken seriously (as a single example, an *Enarrationes in Psalmos* attributed to Remi of Auxerre in PL 131, cols 149-844, is now assigned to the twelfth century; Glorieux, *Tables rectificatives* p. 58); and its indices are, to put it kindly, frequently erratic. A small independent masterpiece of confusion is created by the fact that the indices of individual volumes follow sometimes the column-numbers of the volume, sometimes the squat prominent numbers which are inserted into the text at intervals and represent the page-numbers of the original edition. With all these maddening obstacles, however, the PL remains the most useful basis for the kind of research I will be describing. Its very inclusiveness sets it apart from all other collections of this kind; its voluminous indices, for all their errors and other eccentricities, offer an analytical approach to theological works of the first twelve centuries that is unique so far as I know; its partially antiquated footnotes and appendices sometimes furnish a wealth of information not found in later and 'better' editions (e.g. those accompanying Isidore's *Etymologiae* in PL 82, cols 73-1054, which provide a welcome addition to the more reliable but bare text of Lindsay [for which see p. 185 below]); and even its readings are occasionally superior to those of modern texts. In practice, one will probably find himself most often using the PL for the actual work of research, and then citing and quoting from better editions wherever they exist. As Helen Waddell once remarked of the famous first edition of the *Carmina Burana,* it 'has earned the obloquy and affection' of more than a century.

Besides countless sets of limited inclusiveness and individual editions of particular works, there are a number of large collections which, when they include works found also in the PL, can usually be counted on to provide later and better texts. One is the *Corpus scriptorum ecclesiasticorum Latinorum* (abbreviated CSEL; Vienna 1866ff), 88 vols through 1981, covering the patristic period; individual volumes contain indices of various kinds, usually including a subject index and an index of scriptural citations. A lexical supplement to the CSEL (1973ff) includes the following volumes as of 1985: vols I-III and V, *Vorarbeiten zu einem Augustinus-Lexikon,* ed. **Werner Hansellek** and **Peter Schilling** (A3, *De ordine;* A1, *Contra academicos;* A14, *De utilitate credendi;* and A13, *De vera religione,* respectively); and vol. IV, *Vorarbeiten zu einem Lexicon Ambrosianum: Wortindex zu den Schriften des hl. Ambrosius,* ed. **Otto Faller** and **Ludmilla Krestan.** A more recent series, whose texts where they exist seem generally accepted as standard, is the *Corpus Christianorum, series Latina* (abbreviated CCSL or CCL; Turnhout 1954ff), vols 1-177 through 1985 (though still with many lacunae), covering the patristic period through Bede; practically all volumes have indices of scriptural citations, most have subject indices, and some have other indices as well.

An extension of the above series, entitled *Corpus Christianorum: Continuatio mediaeualis* (abbreviated CCLCM; Turnhout 1964ff), vols 1-62 through 1985 (with many lacunae), covers the later medieval period; the indices are similar to those for the CCSL. Concordances for both series are appearing with great rapidity – some as bound volumes, some as bound volumes with microfiche supplements – under the general title *Thesaurus patrum Latinorum,* with various subtitles; for example, those for Augustine are entitled *Catalogus verborum quae in operibus Sancti Augustini inveniuntur* (Eindhoven 1976ff), those for Gregory *Thesaurus Sancti Gregorii Magni* (Turnhout 1986ff). (There is also, incidentally, a computerized concordance to the complete works of Augustine, which can be consulted by writing to Professor Adolar Zumkeller, O.S.A., Augustinus-Institut, Steinbachtal, Würzburg, West Germany.) Two separate volumes, *Initia patrum Latinorum* (Turnhout 1971) and *Initia patrum Latinorum: Series altera* (Turnhout 1979), both ed. **J.-M. Clément,** offer an index of incipits for both the CCSL and the CCLCM.

A particularly full and useful series, *Sources chrétiennes* (abbreviated SC; Paris 1940ff), over 300 vols through 1985 (with some lacunae), includes both Latin and Greek writers from the early centuries through the entire Middle Ages, with parallel French translations; nearly all the volumes include indices of scriptural citations, and most have other indices as well.

A massive and complex set which is not primarily devoted to theological works but which nevertheless includes some relevant texts, is the *Monumenta Germaniae historica* (abbreviated MGH; various places and dates), including several series each consisting of many volumes; individual volumes consistently have indices of proper names and glossaries, the latter sometimes including subject indices. The various series of the MGH and their component volumes are analyzed in the *Repertorium fontium historiae medii aevi* (Rome 1962-76) I, 466-79, with a first supplement (1977), pp 87-91.

Translations of individual works and of well-defined groups of works are increasingly plentiful. A general approach to them – as well as to translations from medieval literature at large – is provided by **Clarissa P. Farrar** and **Austin P. Evans**, *Bibliography of English Translations from Medieval Sources* (New York 1946), supplemented by **Mary Anne Heyward Ferguson**, *Bibliography of English Translations from Medieval Sources, 1943-1967* (New York and London 1974).

In addition, there are several large sets of early Christian works in English translations, though unfortunately all are confined to the patristic period. An early but particularly valuable series is *A Library of Fathers of the Holy Catholic Church, anterior to the Division of the East and West, translated by Members of the English Church* [ed. **E.B. Pusey** et al.] (Oxford 1838-85), 29 vols in 46, containing works of Ambrose, Athanasius, Augustine, Chrysostom, Cyprian, Cyril of Alexandria, Gregory the Great, Irenaeus, Justin, and Tertullian, and including, for example, the only complete translations yet available of Augustine's *Enarrationes in Psalmos* (vols 24-5, 30, 32, 37, 39) and Gregory's *Moralia in Iob* (vols 18, 21, 23, 31); all volumes have full and useful subject indices and indices of scriptural citations.

Another prominent early collection of the Fathers in translation is made up of three separate series: *The Ante-Nicene Fathers*, ed. **Alexander Roberts** and **James Donaldson**, rev. A. Cleveland Coxe (various places and dates), usually 10 vols; and *A Select Library of the*

Nicene and Post-Nicene Fathers of the Christian Church, ed. **Philip Schaff** et al., First Series (New York 1886-90), 14 vols, and Second Series (New York 1890-1900), 14 vols. Each volume has an index of subjects and a biblical index.

An excellent more recent collection is *Ancient Christian Writers: The Works of the Fathers in Translation*, ed. **Johannes Quasten** et al. (Westminster, Md 1946ff), many vols; each volume includes a scholarly introduction, full notes, a biblical index, and an index of subjects. Another is *The Fathers of the Church: A New Translation* (New York, etc. 1947ff), many vols, with a brief subject index in each volume.

Among the many encyclopedias that can help guide one through the wilderness of medieval theological writings, the best is probably the *Lexikon für Theologie und Kirche*, ed. **Josef Höfer** and **Karl Rahner** (2nd ed. Freiburg i.B. 1957-67), 10 vols plus index, arranged alphabetically; the index-volume contains an elaborate alphabetical general index, an index of authors, and 23 more specialized indices.

Other useful works of this kind are the *Dictionnaire de théologie catholique*, ed. **A. Vacant, E. Mangenot,** and **E. Amann** (Paris 1909-50), 15 vols in 30, arranged alphabetically, with an alphabetical general index ed. **Bernard Loth** and **Albert Michel** (Paris 1953-72), in 3 pts; the *Enciclopedia cattolica* (Vatican 1949-54), 12 vols, with 42 specialized indices at the end of vol. XII; and the *New Catholic Encyclopedia* (New York 1967), 16 vols, of which vol. XV is an alphabetical general index and XVI (publ. 1974) a supplement to bring it up to date.

A very convenient chronological guide to Catholic theological writers from the beginning through the sixteenth century is provided by **F. Cayré,** *Manual of Patrology and History of Theology*, trans. **H. Howitt** (Paris 1935-40), 2 vols, with an index of authors in II, 869-82, and an elaborate doctrinal index in II, 883-916.

For the patristic period (through Bede, d. 735), an indispensable reference manual is the *Clavis patrum Latinorum* by **E. Dekkers** and **A. Gaar,** Sacris erudiri 3 (2nd ed. Bruges 1961), which includes complete information (through 1961) about authors' dates, attributions of works, essential scholarship, editions, etc.; pp 525-631 contain an index of names and works, a topical index, an index of incipits, and concordances between the *Clavis* and other major research tools and editions.

Potentially the fullest account of patristic literature, unhappily still incomplete, is by **Johannes Quasten,** *Patrology* (Utrecht 1950ff), 3 vols through 1960, extending through 'The Golden Age of Greek Patristic Literature' (till 451); each section is accompanied by a bibliography, and each volume has a biblical index, an index of ancient Christian writers, an index of modern authors, an index of Greek words, and a general index. Quasten's bibliographies and indices are brought up to date, his indices each augmented by a liturgical index, and his coverage extended through the Latin Fathers till 451, in an Italian edition, *Patrologia*, ed. **Angelo di Berardino** et al., trans. **Nello Beghin** et al. ([Rome] 1978-80), 3 vols; vol. I corresponds to vols I-II of the original edition, II corresponds to III of the original edition, and III (whose only index is one of proper names) contains the continuation of the Latin Fathers.

Briefer but complete surveys of patrology are those of **Otto Bardenhewer,** *Patrologie* (3rd ed. Freiburg i.B. 1910), trans. from 2nd ed. (1901) by **Thomas J. Shahan** as *Patrology: The Lives and Works of the Fathers of the Church* (Freiburg 1908); and **Berthold Altaner,** *Patrologie: Leben, Schriften, und Lehre der Kirchenväter* (6th ed. Freiburg i.B. 1963), trans. from 5th ed. (1958) by **Hilda C. Graef** as *Patrology* (Freiburg 1960).

A convenient account of translations from Greek to Latin during the first twelve centuries A.D. is provided by **Albert Siegmund,** *Die Überlieferung der griechischen christlichen Literatur in der lateinischen Kirche bis zum zwölften Jahrhundert*, Abhandlungen der Bayerischen Benediktiner-Akademie 5 (Munich 1949), with several useful indices.

General Tools and 'Research Situations'

I turn now to the proper subject of this chapter: medieval biblical exegesis and its uses for the interpretation of medieval literature. Among many general accounts of medieval exegesis itself, there are four which for our purposes are likely to provide the best introductions:

1/ **Beryl Smalley,** *The Study of the Bible in the Middle Ages* (3rd ed. Oxford 1983), is a chronological survey from the beginning to about 1300.

2/ C. Spicq, *Esquisse d'une histoire de l'exégèse latine au moyen âge*, Bibliothèque Thomiste 26 (Paris 1944), is a chronological survey from the eighth century through the fourteenth. Both Smalley and Spicq seem to me to exaggerate somewhat the decline in allegorical interpretation after the twelfth century; in any case, their statements that there was *less* allegorical interpretation after the twelfth century have sometimes been taken by literary scholars to mean that there was in absolute terms very little, thus creating a misconception of some importance for the interpretation of late medieval literature.

3/ **Robert E. McNally**, *The Bible in the Early Middle Ages*, Woodstock Papers 4 (Westminster, Md 1959; repr. by Scholars Press, Atlanta, Ga 1986), is a brief study, organized topically, of the period from 650 to 1000.

4/ **Henri de Lubac**, *Exégèse médiévale: Les quatre sens de l'Ecriture*, Théologie: Etudes publiées sous la direction de la Faculté de théologie S.J. de Lyon-Fourvière 41, 42, 59 ([Paris] 1959-64), 2 vols in 4, following a broadly chronological organization which allows also for a good bit of topical arrangement, is the fullest and in my opinion the most rewarding study of the four; besides its treatment of biblical exegesis, it includes (II/ii) useful brief accounts of a number of related subjects: number symbolism, architectural symbolism, mythography, etc.

Typology – the interpretation of Old Testament characters and events as foreshadowing characters and events in the New Testament – is conveniently treated by **Jean Daniélou**, *Sacramentum futuri: Etudes sur les origines de la typologie biblique* (Paris 1950), trans. [by **Wulstan Hibberd**] as *From Shadows to Reality: Studies in the Biblical Typology of the Fathers* (London [1960]); and **A.C. Charity**, *Events and Their Afterlife: The Dialectics of Christian Typology in the Bible and Dante* (Cambridge 1966).

Just as in other areas of knowledge, however, the reading of secondary works on biblical exegesis rarely turns up the kind of detail that can help throw light on a specific literary text. Writers of surveys, when they are concerned with details at all, are usually concerned with those that are important for the development of the tradition, or for the essential quality of medieval biblical exegesis as such; and within so vast and complex a body of learning, it would be remarkable if those details happened very often to be the same ones that somehow caught the imagination of a medieval poet. Inevitably, the illumination of a literary text by way of biblical commentaries requires close and often extended digging in the commentaries themselves.

The great basic bibliographical tool for work on medieval biblical exegesis generally is **Friedrich Stegmüller** et al., *Repertorium biblicum medii aevi* (Madrid 1950ff), to be completed in 12 vols, of which 11 have already appeared. Vol. I presents basic bibliographical information on the Bible itself; bibliographical information on the various Old and New Testament apocrypha (Old Testament pseudepigrapha), useful, for example, in checking on translations of the apocrypha into Latin; a list of prologues to individual books of the Bible; and other information. Vols II-V, which are the most pertinent for our purposes, contain a catalogue of biblical commentaries (including various exegetical compendia such as encyclopedias, *distinctiones,* etc.), arranged alphabetically by author; entries include biographical facts, basic bibliography, incipits and explicits, and lists of editions and manuscripts. VI-VII are a catalogue of anonymous commentaries, arranged alphabetically by the cities where the manuscripts are preserved. VIII contains supplements to the apocrypha, the prologues to individual books, and the commentators with names beginning A-E. IX contains supplements to the commentators with names beginning F-Z and the anonymous commentaries; and a book-by-book analysis of the *Glossa ordinaria* (pp 465-567). X-XI are an index of incipits covering both the attributed and the anonymous commentaries. XII, I am informed, is to be an index by books of the Bible. From the preceding description, it will be evident that while Stegmüller's *Repertorium* can make many incidental contributions to the kind of research we are considering – providing, for example, the correct attributions of particular works, the locations of manuscripts for unpublished works, the number of manuscripts and probable popularity of a given work, and so on – it cannot, for the present, be used to assemble a list of commentaries on a given book of the Bible, and so cannot yet serve as one of our primary research tools. This limitation will presumably be removed by the appearance of vol. XII, which may well make it the most effective single tool of all.

Pending the appearance of Stegmüller's vol. XII, however, our basic problem remains: Assuming that a substantial amount of medieval imagery does come from the Bible as elaborated by medieval exegesis, how do we approach the given instance? If we have before us a literary work containing an image that we suspect may somehow be biblical and perhaps exegetical, what books do we pick up first to try to find out? The method as I propose to outline it will in itself seem long and complicated enough to dampen the enthusiasm of the most dedicated scholar, and it may well be asked whether, if medieval poets did pack their work with this kind of allusion, life is long enough to allow us to pursue it. The happy fact, however, is that one almost never has to exhaust the possibilities as I will outline them. For one thing, particular problems automatically impose their own limitations of scope; and in any case, common sense usually dictates that one carry his research far enough either to build up a convincing argument or to convince himself that he is following a false lead, and then stop. (I can, to be sure, conceive of a situation in which a particular image or allusion is on the one hand so important for the interpretation one is proposing and on the other so out-of-the-way, and in which one's leads are so unusually tantalizing, that he might want to carry the search to the bitter end; but that is surely the unlikely exception.) Another mitigating circumstance is that to some extent at least, the interpretations easiest for us to come by are likely to have been the ones easiest for a medieval poet to come by – those found, that is, in compilations whose 'cliché value' must have been immense, like for example the *Glossa ordinaria,* the commentary on the whole Bible by Hugh of St Cher, and the great *distinctiones* (alphabetical dictionaries of biblical symbolism). Though this principle obviously does not apply to all works (as a single important exception, many of the most useful *distinctiones* and other late medieval exegetical works remain unpublished), it may in some cases help pattern one's approach to this otherwise daunting body of material.

From the point of view of a modern scholar trying to interpret a medieval literary work, a figure or allusion can be 'biblical' or 'exegetical' in one of two ways, requiring basically different approaches. In making this statement, I do not have in mind any difference in the figures themselves, or even in the way they relate to the Bible or its exegeses; rather, I am referring to the different ways in which they come to our attention, and the differing initial problems they present to us as scholars – what might be called two different 'research situations.' The first situation is that in which one thinks he recognizes some reference to a particular verse or passage of the Bible, perhaps along with its exegesis. For example, any reference to Christ as a giant must derive either immediately or ultimately from Psalm 18:6, 'Exsultavit ut gigas ad currendam viam'; any reference to Christ leaping is derived from Canticles 2:8, 'Vox dilecti mei; ecce iste venit, saliens in montibus, transiliens colles'; and any reference to Christ as a 'figure' of the Father is derived from Hebrews 1:3, 'qui cum sit splendor gloriae et figura substantiae ejus ....' The second situation is that in which one suspects a possible biblical or exegetical image, but cannot connect it offhand with a particular place in the Bible – for example the sun as God, or a mountain as the Church. In the first case one begins with a biblical reference, in the second with simply a concept. I emphasize the difference so strongly because for the present-day scholar it dictates two sharply different ways of getting started; later, of course, either situation may turn out to be really the other kind, or the two may merge in all sorts of unpredictable ways. In either situation, it is well to begin by checking the key words or the concept in a biblical concordance, on the chance of uncovering similar or related verses, possible typological patterns, and so on.

Identifiable Biblical Echoes

BASIC CHECKLISTS

In the first of the two situations I have outlined, the problem obviously is to find out who has said what about the biblical verse or passage in question. To begin with, there are at present four valuable checklists of medieval biblical commentators arranged by books of the Bible:

1/ In PL 219 (i.e. index-vol. 2, or B), cols 101-14 contain an index of commentaries on individual books of the Bible, and cols 113-22 contain a similar index of commentaries on individual chapters, many of which are in fact sermons on individual chapters or verses. Both of these lists cover the same period as the PL itself – that is, from the beginning of the Christian era to about 1216 – and references are to the editions in the PL itself.

2/ In Dekkers and Gaar, *Clavis patrum Latinorum,* pages 549-50 of the 'Index systematicus' contain a list of exegetical works from the beginning through the seventh century, following the order of the Bible. References are to items in the *Clavis* itself, which in turn cite editions; one advantage of this list is that it often provides references to later and better editions than the PL.

3/ In McNally, *Bible in the Early Middle Ages,* pages 89-117 contain a list of commentaries from 650 to 1000, divided into general commentaries, commentaries on the Old Testament, and commentaries on the New Testament, with references to editions.

4/ In Spicq, *Esquisse d'une histoire de l'exégèse latine,* pages 395-401 contain a list of commentators from the eighth century through the fourteenth, followed by a short list of commentaries on special biblical subjects. References are to pages in the *Esquisse* itself, which in turn cite editions in the footnotes. Items preceded by asterisks exist only in manuscript. Spicq's list is particularly valuable because it covers the thirteenth and fourteenth centuries and includes unpublished commentaries, as none of the other three do; a glance at the number of asterisks in his list, incidentally, presents melancholy evidence of how many important exegetical works from the thirteenth and fourteenth centuries remain unprinted.

These four lists, which are partly overlapping, provide a fairly complete survey of the commentaries on any book of the Bible – except, of course, for commentaries published since the lists themselves appeared. (If the forthcoming vol. XII of Stegmüller's *Repertorium* does provide a usable index of commentaries by books of the Bible, it may virtually supplant all the rest.) Having found out what medieval commentaries there are on the biblical book in question, one can read systematically through their interpretations of the passage he is interested in.

COMMENTARIES ON THE WHOLE BIBLE

There are, however, many further avenues of approach. Most obviously, there are a number of great commentaries which cover the entire Bible more or less verse by verse, and so will almost certainly include any passage one happens to be working on. Of the four that have been published, one is from the twelfth century, one from the thirteenth, one from the fourteenth, and one from the fifteenth:

1/ The *Glossa ordinaria*, consisting of a marginal gloss and an interlinear gloss, is a work of many hands which took final form in the twelfth century. It is often printed along with the Vulgate Bible from the fifteenth to the seventeenth century (e.g. Venice 1495, 1588; Douai and Antwerp 1617, etc.; see Gosselin on Nicholas of Lyre, below), usually in 6 folio volumes with a full subject-index at the end of vol. VI. Though an edition of sorts is included among the works of Walafrid Strabo in PL 113-14, it omits the interlinear gloss and drastically abridges the long quotations from earlier writers, and should not be used for serious scholarship. The *Glossa* remained the standard commentary on the Bible for the rest of the Middle Ages, and its value as a repository of traditional material is obviously enormous.

2/ **Hugh of St Cher** (Hugo de Sancto C[h]aro), *Opera omnia in universum Vetus et Novum Testamentum*, is a commentary on the whole Bible dating from the second quarter of the thirteenth century, and making substantial use of the famous 'four senses' of biblical exegesis. There are many editions from the fifteenth through the eighteenth century (Stegmüller, *Repertorium* III, 114), usually in 8 folio volumes, with an extremely full subject-index occupying the whole of vol. VIII. Though it is not equally detailed for all books of the Bible (e.g. its exposition of the Psalms is unusually full, those of the Books of Kings and Paralipomenon rather jejune), it is in general a wonderfully rich and eclectic commentary, whose popularity seems to have been almost as great as that of the *Glossa ordinaria*. In my own experience it is the most valuable single exegetical work for the interpretation of late medieval literature.

3/ **Nicholas of Lyre** (Nicolaus de Lyra), *Postilla litteralis in Vetus et Novum Testamentum* and *Postilla moralis in Vetus et Novum Testamentum*, both containing substantial material that does not impress a modern reader as 'literal,' date from the early fourteenth century. They appear in many editions from the fifteenth to the seventeenth century, either separately or along with the Vulgate Bible and the *Glossa ordinaria* (see Stegmüller, *Repertorium* IV, 52, #5829-5923, and 90, #5929-74; and especially **Edward A. Gosselin, 'A Listing of the Printed Editions of Nicolaus de Lyra,'** *Traditio* 26 [1970] 406-11); the *Postilla litteralis* is regularly accompanied by the *Additiones* of Paul of Burgos (a critique) and the *Defensorium* or *Replicationes* of Matthias Döring (a defence), both from the fifteenth century. Though

Nicholas's commentaries represent a distinct step away from the intensive allegorizing of earlier centuries and toward a more severely philological interpretation, they do nevertheless include enough traditional material to be valuable for our purposes.

4/ **Denis the Carthusian** (Denis le Chartreux/van Leeuwen/de Ryckel, Dionysius Cartusianus), *Enarrationes*, in *Doctoris ecstatici D. Dionysii Cartusiani opera omnia* (Montreuil and Tournai 1896-1912), vols I-XIV, are a full and traditional commentary on the whole Bible dating from around the middle of the fifteenth century. Each volume includes a detailed subject-index, and a full general index occupies the whole of vol. XIV, pt ii. Though Denis is later than the great flowering of English literature in the second half of the fourteenth century, his commentaries – like his work generally – are traditional rather than original; and he can, I think, be used with some caution for the interpretation of fourteenth-century writers, on the assumption that he is reflecting exegeses already 'in the air.'

In addition to these four great medieval commentaries on the whole Bible, there is one similar post-medieval compilation which can be used in much the same way, though of course with the appropriate precautions: the famous early-seventeenth-century commentary of **Cornelius a Lapide** (Cornelis van den Steen, Cornelie de la Roche), which in its original form covered the entire Bible except for Job and the Psalms and consisted of 10 volumes with varying titles, each beginning with the word *Commentarius* .... There are many later editions into the nineteenth century, in varying numbers of volumes and with varying titles (see *NUC* 316, pp 46-8), often *Commentaria in sacram scripturam*; the latest edition is that of Paris 1866-74, consisting of 21 volumes plus a 3-volume supplement. Commentaries on the Psalms by **Robert Bellarmine** and on Job by **Balthasar Corder** are included in several editions – for example those of Malta 1843-6 (10 vols), Paris 1859-63 (22 vols), and Paris 1866-74 (above), where they occupy supplement-vols 1-2 and 3 respectively. A very useful alphabetical subject-index is added by **J.M. Péronne**, *Memoriale praedicatorum* (3rd ed. Paris 1872), 2 vols, accompanying the edition of Paris 1866-74.

In consulting Cornelius's great compilation, one must of course be careful to avoid using his own exegeses, which are too late to be directly relevant for medieval literature; but since most of the interpretations he offers are in fact repeated from the Fathers and later medieval exegetes, with the sources clearly identified, he can serve in various ways as a guide to medieval commentary. In particular, his explanation of a given biblical verse will often include quotations taken not from avowed commentaries on that verse but from other medieval sources – for example a comment on a passage of Matthew which appears not in medieval commentaries on Matthew but in Gregory's *Moralia in Iob*. In such cases, Cornelius provides a valuable short-cut to interpretations that might otherwise be missed entirely.

Returning to medieval works, there are also a number of compilations that, while they deal with the Bible as a whole, make no attempt to do so verse by verse – freely skipping verses, chapters, or entire books to concentrate on passages or subjects of unusual interest. The most notable are:

1/ **Richard of St Victor** (12th C), *Liber exceptionum*, ed. **Jean Chatillon** (Paris 1958). The *Allegoriae in Vetus et Novum Testamentum* incorrectly attributed to Hugh of St Victor (PL 175, cols 635-924) is for the most part identical with Richard's *Liber* (cols 635-774, 789-828), with the commentaries on John and the Pauline Epistles (cols 827-924) taken from another source; see Glorieux, *Tables rectificatives* p. 68.

2/ **Peter Comestor** (12th C), *Historia scholastica*, PL 198, cols 1053-1722, a work of tremendous popularity (Stegmüller, *Repertorium* IV, 288-90, #6543-6565).

3/ **Peter Riga**'s *Aurora* (late 12th C), revised and expanded by Aegidius of Paris (early 13th C), ed. **Paul E. Beichner**, *Aurora Petri Rigae, Biblia versificata: A Verse Commentary on the Bible*, Publications in Medieval Studies 19 (Notre Dame 1965), 2 vols, with an informative introduction (I, xi-lv). The *Aurora*, which attained immense currency in the later Middle Ages (Beichner, I, xxvii-xlvii; Stegmüller, *Repertorium* IV, 380-2, #6823-6825), is a popularized commentary on the Bible in Latin verse, covering Genesis, Exodus, Leviticus, Numbers, Deuteronomy, Josue, Judges, Ruth, 1-4 Kings, Tobias, Judith, Esther, Job, Canticles, Daniel, 1-2 Maccabees, the Gospels, and the Acts of the Apostles. Further accretions to the *Aurora* – like, for example, the *Tobias* by Matthew of Vendôme (12th C; PL 205, cols 933-80) and the *Hortus deliciarum Salomonis*, a verse commentary on Proverbs by one Hermannus Werdinensis (13th C; edited in excerpts by Pitra, *Spicilegium Solesmense* (for which see p. 33 below) II-III passim, and indexed in III, 607) – are discussed by Beichner, I, xxiv-xxvii. The *Aurora* is translated rather freely into Old French verse by Macé de la Charité (13th-14th C), *La Bible,* edited by various hands as *La Bible de Macé de la Charité,* Publications romanes de l'Université de Leyde 10 (Leyden 1964ff), 7 vols: I, Genesis and Exodus, ed. **J.R. Smeets**; II, Leviticus, Numbers, Deuteronomy, Josue, and Judges, ed. **P.E.R. Verhuyck**; III, Kings, ed. **A.M.L. Prangsma-Hajenius**; IV, Ruth, Judith, Tobias, Esther, Daniel, and Job, ed. **Hendrikus Cornelis Maria van der Krabben**; V, Canticles and Maccabees, and VI, Gospels and Acts of Apostles, both ed. **J.R. Smeets**; and VII, Apocalypse, ed. **R.L.H. Lops**. A much lesser but broadly similar work, which does not fit any classification very well, is *Le laie Bible* (early 14th C), ed. **John Alfred Clarke**, Columbia University Studies in Romance Philology and Literature (New York 1923, repr. 1966) – really a moral poem or sermon in verse, based throughout on interpretation of parts of the Bible.

4/ An *Expositio mystica in sacram scripturam* apparently found in a single manuscript (Stegmüller, *Repertorium* II, 119, #1381,1) and attributed to **Anthony of Padua** (13th C), ed. **Jean de La Haye,** *Sancti Francisci Assisiatis ... nec non S. Antonii Paduani ... opera omnia* (Paris 1641, Lyon 1653, Ratisbon 1739), pp 365-608 in the Lyon edition, with a subject-index to the entire volume following p. 744.

5/ **Peter Aureoli** (13th-14th C), *Compendium sensus litteralis totius divinae scripturae,* ed. **Philbert Seeboeck** (Quaracchi 1896), containing very little allegory or figurative interpretation of any kind, but interesting for the organizational and thematic patterns he finds in Scripture; an index to his analysis of the Bible appears on pp 557-65, and a subject-index on pp 566-75.

6/ **Pierre Bersuire** (Petrus Berchorius, 14th C), *Moralitates super bibliam* or *Reductorium morale super totam bibliam* (originally bk 16 of his *Reductorium morale,* for which see p. 46 below), in *Petri Berchorii Pictaviensis ... opera omnia* (Cologne 1730-1) vol. I, with a 10-page subject-index preceding p. 1 (for other editions see Stegmüller, *Repertorium* IV, 241, #6426).

In addition, there is at least one Renaissance compilation that covers the entire Bible in this same selective way, including extended quotations from a variety of medieval exegetes: an anonymous *Allegoriae simul et tropologiae in locos utriusque Testamenti selectiores* (Paris

1574), which follows the order of the Bible book by book, and chapter by chapter with many omissions; within chapters the degree of inclusiveness varies greatly. Following fol. 619 is a 52-page subject-index, and preceding fol. 1 a list of thirty authors used, more than half of whom are medieval; in the text, prominent headings indicate the authors quoted.

Besides these exegetes who in one way or another cover the Bible as a whole, there are at least two who comment on enough individual books, and so cover substantial enough parts of the Bible, to be worth mentioning here:

1/ **Rabanus Maurus** (8th-9th C), who comments on Genesis (PL 107, cols 443-670), Exodus (PL 108, cols 10-246), Leviticus (PL 108, cols 245-586), Numbers (PL 108, cols 587-838), Deuteronomy (PL 108, cols 839-998), Josue (PL 108, cols 1001-1108), Judges (PL 108, cols 1111-1200), Ruth (PL 108, cols 1199-1224), 1-4 Kings (PL 109, cols 11-280), 1-2 Paralipomenon (PL 109, cols 281-540), Judith (PL 109, cols 541-92), Esther (PL 109, cols 635-70), Wisdom (PL 109, cols 673-762), Ecclesiasticus (PL 109, cols 765-1126), Jeremias (PL 111, cols 797-1272), Ezechiel (PL 110, cols 497-1084), 1-2 Maccabees (PL 109, cols 1125-1256), Matthew (PL 107, cols 729-1156), and the Pauline Epistles (PL 111, cols 1277-1616, and 112, cols 9-834). The commentary on Proverbs attributed to Rabanus in the PL (111, cols 679-792) is actually by Bede (Glorieux, *Tables rectificatives* p. 56). There is a subject-index to the complete works of Rabanus, PL 112, cols 1681-1764.

2/ **Rupert of Deutz** (12th C), who comments on Genesis, *De Sancta Trinitate et operibus eius*, ed. **Hrabanus Haacke**, CCLCM 21 (Turnhout 1971) pp 129-578 (PL 167, cols 199-566); Exodus, *ibid.*, CCLCM 22 (Turnhout 1972) pp 580-802 (PL 167, cols 565-744); Leviticus, *ibid.* pp 803-914 (PL 167, cols 743-836); Numbers, *ibid.* pp 915-1013 (PL 167, cols 837-918); Deuteronomy, *ibid.* pp 1014-1118 (PL 167, cols 917-1000); Josue, *ibid.* pp 1119-46 (PL 167, cols 999-1024); Judges, *ibid.* pp 1147-92 (PL 167, cols 1023-60); 1-4 Kings, *ibid.* pp 1193-1337, 1409-52 (PL 167, cols 1059-1178, 1233-72); Job (PL 168, cols 963-1196); Psalms, *De Sancta Trinitate*, ed. Haacke, CCLCM 22, pp 1138-1408 (PL 167, cols 1179-1234); Ecclesiastes (PL 168, cols 1197-1306); Canticles, *Commentaria in Canticum canticorum*, ed. Haacke, CCLCM 26 (Turnhout 1974) (PL 168, cols 839-

962); Isaias, *De Sancta Trinitate,* ed. Haacke, CCLCM 23 (Turnhout 1972) pp 1454-1571 (PL 167, cols 1271-1362); Jeremias, *ibid.* pp 1572-1642 (PL 167, cols 1363-1420); Ezechiel, *ibid.* pp 1643-1737 (PL 167, cols 1419-98); Daniel, *ibid.* pp 1738-81 (PL 167, cols 1499-1536); the Minor Prophets (PL 168, cols 9-836); the four Gospels, *De Sancta Trinitate,* ed. Haacke, CCLCM 23, pp 1782-1822 (PL 167, cols 1535-70); Matthew, *De gloria et honore Filii Hominis super Mattheum,* ed. Haacke, CCLCM 29 (Turnhout 1979) (PL 168, cols 1307-1634); John, *Commentaria in Evangelium Sancti Iohannis,* ed. Haacke, CCLCM 9 (Turnhout 1969) (PL 169, cols 205-826); and Apocalypse (PL 169, cols 827-1214). Most of the CCL editions include indices of scriptural citations, other authors cited, proper names, and liturgical citations; in the PL, each volume of Rupert's works has a subject index.

Another kind of compilation that to some extent can be used for finding interpretations of particular biblical verses is the commentary which, though avowedly expounding only a single book, nevertheless ranges so freely through the whole Bible that it becomes in effect a commentary on a wide variety of biblical passages, organized according to the book that is its nominal subject. The use of such works as general biblical commentaries, of course, presupposes the existence of reliable indices of scriptural citations in them. A few outstanding examples:

1/ **Augustine,** *Enarrationes in Psalmos,* the most massive and influential among the many important medieval commentaries on the Psalms. It is printed in PL 36-7, with a good subject-index to all the works of Augustine in PL 46 but no index of scriptural citations; the best edition now is that of **E. Dekkers** and **J. Fraipont** in CCL 38-40, with an index of scriptural citations in CCL 40, pp 2197-2260, and a concordance in the accompanying *Catalogus verborum quae in operibus Sancti Augustini inveniuntur* (Eindhoven 1976ff), vols 38-40. The best translation of the *Enarrationes* is that by **J. Tweed** et al., *Expositions on the Book of Psalms,* Library of Fathers of the Holy Catholic Church 24-5, 30, 32, 37, 39 (Oxford 1847-57), 6 vols, with a subject-index in VI, 459-519, and an index of scriptural citations in VI, 521-48.

2/ **Gregory the Great** (6th-7th C), *Moralia in Iob (Moralium libri, sive expositio in librum B. Job),* along with his *Homiliae in*

Hiezechihelem prophetam and *Homiliae in Evangelia*. The three works are printed together in PL 75 and 76, with a good subject-index in PL 76, cols 1314-1514, but no index of scriptural citations. The *Homiliae in Hiezechihelem* is edited by M. Adriaen in CCL 142, with an index of scriptural citations on pp 435-49 and an index of citations from other writers on pp 450-61. Bks 1-22 of the 35 books of the *Moralia in Iob* are edited by Adriaen in CCL 143 and 143A, with the indices presumably to appear in a later volume; in the meantime, indices of scriptural citations in the three works can be found in some earlier editions – for example, a 4-volume *Sancti Gregorii ... opera omnia* (Paris 1705), I, following p. 1664, along with a subject-index. The *Moralia* is translated (partly by J. Bliss) as *Morals on the Book of Job by S. Gregory the Great*, Library of Fathers of the Holy Catholic Church 18, 21, 23, 31 (Oxford 1844-50), 3 vols in 4, with an index of scriptural citations in III/ii, 703-26, and a subject-index on pp 727-919. A new translation by James J. O'Donnell is underway and will appear in the series 'The Fathers of the Church.' These three works of Gregory are probably the richest single source of exegetical imagery for the Latin Middle Ages; time and again the interpretation which becomes 'standard' in medieval exegesis of a given verse will be found to have its origin not in commentaries on that verse, but in one of these works of Gregory (for a small clear example, see my survey of the commentary on the *porri et cepe et allia* of Numbers 11:5, 'The Summoner's Garleek, Oynons, and eek Lekes,' *Modern Language Notes* 74 [1959] 481-4).

In addition, there are various kinds of medieval compilations which in one way or another are extracted from the works of Gregory:

a/ Rearrangements of Gregory's comments on individual verses or passages into a form that follows the order of the Bible. A notable collection of this kind is that of **Paterius** (7th C), the *Liber testimoniorum* or *Expositio Veteris ac Novi Testamenti*, PL 79, cols 683-916, originally covering Genesis through Canticles and continued through the Apocalypse by **Alulfus of Tournai** (12th C), *Gregorialis*, PL 79, cols 917-1424 (cols 917-1136 appear here under the name of Paterius, and are sometimes ascribed to an 'anonymous of Mont-Saint-Michel').

b/ Epitomes of the *Moralia in Iob*, which follow its order. Examples are **Lathcen mac Baith Bannaig** (7th C), *Ecloga de Moralibus Iob* *quas Gregorius fecit,* ed. **M. Adriaen,** CCL 145; and **Odo of Cluny** (9th-10th C), *Epitome Moralium Sancti Gregorii in Job,* PL 133, cols 107-512.

c/ Encyclopedias organized topically. Examples are **Taio of Saragossa** (7th C), *Sententiae,* PL 80, cols 723-990); **Peter of Waltham** (12th C), *Remediarium conversorum,* ed. **Joseph Gildea,** *Remediarium conversorum: A Synthesis in Latin of Moralia in Job by Gregory the Great* (Villanova, Pa 1984), with a table of chapters on pp 7-21; and Garner of St Victor (12th C), *Gregorianum* (for which see p. 43 below), PL 193, cols 23-462, to be taken up in more detail in the following section. The whole subject is treated more fully by **René Wasselynck** in three articles: 'Les Compilations des *Moralia in Job* du VIIᵉ au XIIᵉ siècle,' 'Les *Moralia in Job* dans les ouvrages de morale du haut moyen âge latin,' and 'L'Influence de l'exégèse de S. Grégoire le Grand sur les commentaires bibliques médiévaux (VIIe-XIIe s.),' *Recherches de théologie ancienne et médiévale* 29 (1962) 5-32, 31 (1964) 5-31, and 32 (1965) 157-204 respectively.

3/ **Bernard of Clairvaux** (12th C), *Sermones super Cantica,* ed. **J. Leclercq, C.H. Talbot,** and **H.M. Rochais,** in *Opera* (Rome 1957-77), vols I-II, with a sketch of each sermon's contents in II, 321-7 (PL 183, cols 785-1198, with a subject-index to the entire volume in cols 1203-1308); of several translations, the most recent is by **Irene Edmonds,** *Sermons on the Song of Songs,* in *The Works of Bernard of Clairvaux,* Cistercian Fathers Series 4, 7, 31, 40 (Spencer, Mass. and Kalamazoo, Mich. 1970-80), vols I-IV, with a subject-index in IV, 219-28 and an index of scriptural citations in IV, 229-59. Though the *Sermones* of Bernard extend only through Canticles 3:1, they are extraordinarily full and rich in imagery, and include enough interpretations of other biblical passages to qualify as a repository of the kind we are discussing.

The sermons are continued through Canticles 5:10, though in less extensive form, by **Gilbert of Hoyland,** *Sermones in Canticum Salomonis,* PL 184, cols 11-252, trans. **Lawrence C. Braceland** as *Sermons on the Song of Songs,* in *The Works of Gilbert of Hoyland,* Cistercian Fathers Series 14, 20, 26 (Kalamazoo, Mich. 1978-9), vols I-III, with marginal notations of other biblical citations.

An apparent further continuator, whose sermons begin with Canticles 5:8, is the long-neglected **John of Ford** (12th-13th C, not included in the PL), *Super extremam partem Cantici canticorum sermones CXX*, ed. **Edmund Mikkers** and **Hilary Costello**, CCLCM 17-18 (Turnhout 1970), 2 vols, with, in vol. II, indices of scriptural citations (pp 825-71), the Fathers and other authors (872-7), places and persons (878-81), and words and expressions (882-1006); trans. **Wendy Mary Beckett** as *Sermons on the Final Verses of the Song of Songs*, Cistercian Fathers Series 29, 39, 43-7 (Kalamazoo, Mich. 1977-84), with biblical citations in the margins throughout, and an index of names, places, and persons and a subject-index in VII, 271-306.

4/ The various exegetical works of **Bonaventura** (13th C), in the magnificent *Opera omnia* edited by the College of St Bonaventura (Quaracchi 1882-1902), 10 vols: Ecclesiastes in VI, 3-99; Wisdom in VI, 107-233; Lamentations (doubtfully attributed to Bonaventura) in VII, 607-51; Luke in VII, 3-604; and John in VI, 239-532. A full index of scriptural citations from vols V-IX, found in X, 181-264, and a subject-index to vols VI-VII (the exegetical works), found in VII, 659-857, allows these and other works of Bonaventura to be used to some extent as a commentary on the Bible at large; other useful indices are a subject-index of vol. IX (the sermons) in X, 75-179, and an index of citations of the Fathers and other authors in X, 265-77.

IMPORTANT COMMENTARIES ON INDIVIDUAL BOOKS

So far, we have been discussing ways of finding interpretations of particular parts of the Bible by using works that in one way or another address themselves to the Bible as a whole or to large parts of it. One quickly comes to realize, however, that for certain biblical books there are single pre-eminent commentaries so rich and influential that if they are not somehow automatically irrelevant for the problem at hand (e.g. on grounds of chronology), they should probably be consulted first.

On Leviticus, for example, the fullest medieval commentary is that of **Raoul of Flaix** (or of Flavigny, Radulphus Flaviacensis; 12th C), *Commentatiorum in Leuiticum libri XX* (Stegmüller, *Repertorium* V, 38-9, #7093), in *Maxima bibliotheca veterum patrum* ed. **Marguerin de La Bigne** (Lyon 1677) XVII, 48-246.

On Job, by far the most prominent exposition – and, as we have seen, one of the monuments of medieval exegesis generally – is Gregory's *Moralia in Iob*.

Though there are of course many important medieval commentaries on the Psalms, the pre-eminent one remains Augustine's *Enarrationes in Psalmos*; the next-most-important is probably that of **Peter Lombard** (12th C), *Commentarius in Psalmos*, PL 191, cols 55-1296, with a brief subject-index in PL 192, cols 1351-60.

On Canticles, though again there are many important commentaries (e.g. the several found in the volumes of the PL numbered 200+), the richest and most influential of all is clearly the *Sermones* of Bernard of Clairvaux, continued by Gilbert of Hoyland and apparently also by John of Ford.

On Wisdom, the *lectiones* of **Robert Holkot** (or Holcot, 14th C) are not only the most extensive medieval commentaries on that book itself, but also a great repository of mythographic and other miscellaneous lore; among many editions (Stegmüller, *Repertorium* V, 143-5, #7416), the best is *M. Roberti Holkoth ... in librum Sapientiae regis Salomonis praelectiones CCXIII*, ed. **Jacob Ryter** ([Basle] 1586), with a 15-page subject-index preceding p. 1 (the *Moralizationum historiarum liber* included on pp 703-50 is described below in the chapter on mythography).

On Isaias, the fullest commentary is by **Hervé of Bourgdieu** (12th C), *Commentaria in Isaiam*, PL 181, cols 17-592.

On the Gospels, a particularly extensive conflated commentary, with abundant incorporations from earlier exegetes, is that of **Ludolf of Saxony** (14th C), *Vita Jesu Christi* or *Meditationes vitae Jesu Christi* (many eds; see Stegmüller, *Repertorium* III, 531-2, #5437), regularly including an index of scriptural citations and a subject-index. A useful collection of commentaries on the Gospels is assembled by **Thomas Aquinas** (13th C) in the *Catena aurea*, which proceeds through the four Gospels chapter by chapter and verse by verse, quoting substantial interpretations from the Fathers (both Greek and Latin) and later exegetes; the *Catena* appears in all editions of the complete works of Aquinas as well as in many separate editions (Stegmüller, *Repertorium* V, 333-7, #8044-7) and is translated by **M. Pattison** et al., *Commentaries on the Four Gospels Collected out of the Fathers by St Thomas Aquinas* (Oxford 1841-5 and later eds), usually 4 vols.

On Luke, the fullest medieval commentary is Bonaventura's massive *Commentarius in Evangelium S. Lucae* (see the discussion of Bonaventure's works on the previous page). And on the Acts of the Apostles, the commentaries that seem to have more or less held the field through the rest of the Middle Ages are those of **Bede**, the *Expositio Actuum apostolorum* and *Retractatio in Actus apostolorum*, both ed. **M.L.W. Laistner**, Mediaeval Academy of America Publication 35 (Cambridge, Mass. 1939), with an index of scriptural citations, a subject-index, and an index of allegorical interpretation (both works appear also in PL 92, cols 937-1032).

Though as I have emphasized earlier, research of the kind we are considering must always depend primarily on the reading of medieval exegetical texts themselves, there are of course some secondary works – especially those dealing with the interpretation of particular books of the Bible – that can contribute to this very process by helping one find his way around in a possibly bewildering body of commentary. For example, a valuable checklist of commentaries on Genesis is compiled by Zahlten, *Creatio mundi* (discussed on p. 140 below) pp 284-97.

Medieval commentary on Canticles through the twelfth century is covered with great thoroughness by **Friedrich Ohly**, *Hohelied-Studien: Grundzüge einer Geschichte der Hoheliedauslegung des Abendlandes bis um 1200* (Wiesbaden 1958).

On the Sapiential Books of the Old Testament, a useful guide is provided in two articles by **Beryl Smalley**, 'Some Thirteenth-Century Commentaries on the Sapiential Books,' *Dominican Studies* 2 (1949) 318-55 and 3 (1950) 41-77, and '**Some Commentaries on the Sapiential Books of the Late Twelfth and Early Fourteenth Centuries,**' *Archives d'histoire doctrinale et littéraire du moyen âge* 18 (1950) 102-28.

Patristic interpretation of the Parables is surveyed rather sketchily by **Jean Pirot**, *Parables et allégories évangéliques: La pensée de Jésus, les commentaires patristiques* (Paris 1949); commentary on the Parables from Irenaeus to Aquinas is sketched by **Warren S. Kissenger**, *The Parables of Jesus: A History of Interpretation and Bibliography* (Metuchen, N.J. 1979) pp 1-43, with a massive general bibliography on pp 231-415; and an '**Index exegeticus parabolarum Novi Testamenti praecipuarum**' is included in PL 219, cols 263-74.

An exhaustive alphabetical list of commentaries on the Epistle to the Romans (and so to a great extent on the Pauline Epistles as a whole, since most commentators cover them as a group), from the beginning through Nicholas of Lyre, is provided by **Werner Affeldt**,

'Verzeichnis der Römerbriefkommentare der lateinischen Kirche bis zu Nikolaus von Lyra,' *Traditio* 13 (1957) 369-406.

A list of commentators (both Greek and Latin) on the Epistle to the Hebrews is included by **C. Spicq,** *L'Epitre aux Hébreux* (Paris 1952) I, 379-83. And a brief but very informative account of commentary on the Apocalypse through the twelfth century is given by Kamlah, *Apokalypse und Geschichtstheologie* (for which see p. 152 below).

INDIVIDUAL AUTHORS

Still another kind of tool suited to the approach by way of a particular biblical verse or passage is the comprehensive index to the biblical citations of a particular author or group of authors. Such indices are, of course, often appended to editions of individual authors, and some have already been mentioned incidentally. An elaborate compilation which deserves special notice is the index to biblical citations of Augustine by **Anne-Marie La Bonnardière,** *Biblia Augustiniana* (Paris 1960 ff), in many volumes and not yet completed. In the section 'Ancien Testament,' the following volumes have appeared so far: II, *Livres historiques,* covering from Josue to Job (1960); III, *Les Douze Petits Prophètes* (1963); IV, *Le Deutéronome* (1967); V, *Le Livre de la Sagesse* (1970); VI, *Le Livre de Jérémie* (1972); and VII, *Le Livre des proverbes* (1975); vol. I will cover Genesis, Exodus, Leviticus, and Numbers. In the section 'Nouveau Testament,' only vol. I has appeared: *Les Epitres aux Thessaloniciens, à Tite, et à Philémon* (1964).

For the patristic period at large, there is a massive work just getting underway, which should be of fundamental importance for this kind of research when it has progressed further: *Biblia patristica: Index des citations et allusions bibliques dans la littérature patristique* (Paris 1975 ff), 3 vols and a supplement through 1980 (publ. 1982). Vol. I covers the period from the beginning to Clement of Alexandria and Tertullian; II, the third century except Origen; III, Origen; and the supplement, Philo of Alexandria. Each volume is a simple list of biblical citations for its period, following the order of the Bible.

A more general kind of bibliographical tool is the biennial *Bibliographia patristica: Internationale patristische Bibliographie* (Berlin 1959 [for 1956] ff), which includes as pt VII or VIII of each volume 'Patrum exegesis Veteris et Novi Testamenti'; Supplementum I, by **Hermann Josef Sieben,** *Voces: Eine Bibliographie zu Wörtern und Begriffen aus der Patristik (1918-1978)* (Berlin 1980), consists basically of two alphabetical indices of Greek and Latin patristic terms, with references to modern scholarly treatments of them.

A convenient list of exegetical works of Irish provenance is assembled by **Joseph F. Kelly** in **Martin McNamara's** *Biblical Studies: The Medieval Irish Contribution,* Proceedings of the Irish Biblical Association 1 (Dublin 1976) pp 161-2; a greatly expanded version by **Kelly,** entitled '**A Catalogue of Early Medieval Hiberno-Latin Biblical Commentaries,**' will appear in *Traditio* 44-6 (1988-90).

Echoes Not Immediately Identifiable

So far, we have been considering the first of the two 'research situations' described earlier – that in which one's initial lead is an apparent echo of a particular biblical verse or passage, and the immediate problem is to find out what the potentially relevant commentators have said about that verse or passage. Let us now turn to the other situation, in which the initial lead is a concept that for one reason or another may be suspected of carrying biblical and/or exegetical overtones. For a problem of this kind, the most useful starting tools are the various dictionaries and encyclopedias of biblical symbolism that flourished in the Middle Ages – particularly in the later Middle Ages – together with some post-medieval additions. For practical purposes works of this kind, both medieval and modern, fall into two distinct types. One is made up of compilations arranged alphabetically, known in the late Middle Ages as *distinctiones.* Convenient guides to the major *distinctiones* are presented by **André Wilmart,** '**Un Répertoire d'exégèse composé en Angleterre vers le début du** XIIIe **siècle,**' in *Mémorial Lagrange,* Cinquantenaire de l'Ecole biblique et archéologique française de Jerusalem (Paris 1940) pp 335-46; and by **Richard H. Rouse** and **Mary A. Rouse,** '**Biblical Distinctions in the Thirteenth Century,**' *Archives d'histoire doctrinale et littéraire du moyen âge* 41 (1975 for 1974) 27-37, and '**Statim invenire: Schools, Preachers, and New Attitudes to the Page,**' in *Renaissance and Renewal in the Twelfth Century* ed. **Robert L. Benson** and **Giles Constable** with **Carol D. Lanham** (Cambridge, Mass. 1982) pp 201-25, esp. 212-21.

The other type of compilation is the one arranged topically, according to logical areas of classification – for example God and the things pertaining to Him, supernal creatures, the world and its parts, man, metals, woods and flowers, birds, beasts, etc. Since these two different principles of organization bear directly on the ways of using such works, let us take up each type separately, beginning with the alphabetical ones that are available in printed editions.

COLLECTIONS ORGANIZED ALPHABETICALLY

The earliest alphabetical collections of biblical symbols seem to be those drawn from the topically organized *Formulae spiritalis intelligentiae* by Eucher of Lyon (5th C; see p. 41 below): a *Glossae spirituales iuxta Eucherium episcopum* found in manuscripts of the eighth to twelfth centuries, ed. **J.B. Pitra**, *Spicilegium Solesmense* (Paris 1852-8) III, 400-6 (Stegmüller, *Repertorium* II, 304, #2259), containing 390 items, and a somewhat longer eighth-century version ed. **Karl Wotke**, 'Glossae spiritales secundum Eucherium episcopum,' *Sitzungsberichte der philosophisch-historischen Classe der kaiserlichen Akademie der Wissenschaften* (Vienna) 115 (1888 for 1887) 425-39 (Stegmüller, *ibid.* #2260), containing 442 items – both rather jejune lists offering only one or two meanings per symbol.

An unusually full and useful *distinctiones,* containing more entries than any other, is the *Liber in distinctionibus dictionum theologicalium* by **Alain de Lille** (12th C; PL 210, cols 685-1012), organized strictly alphabetically. Biblical quotations are not footnoted in the PL edition, and normally have to be identified with the help of a concordance. An interesting feature of this *distinctiones* is that it contains a good many quotations from other authors, some of them Classical – for example Vergil, Horace, Lucan, Statius, Boethius, the hymns of Adam of St Victor, etc.

Another very full and useful *distinctiones* included in the PL is the late twelfth- or early thirteenth-century *Angelus* or *Allegoriae in universam sacram scripturam,* PL 112, cols 849-1088 (where it is erroneously attributed to Rabanus Maurus), now doubtfully ascribed to **Garner** or **Warner of Rochefort** (d. after 1225); the decisive study is by **André Wilmart**, 'Les Allégories sur l'Ecriture attribuées à Raban

Maur,' *Revue bénédictine* 32 (1920) 47-56 (and see Stegmüller, *Repertorium* II, 325, #2364). The *Angelus* is arranged alphabetically by initial letter (i.e. all the words beginning with A are grouped together, then all the words beginning with B, etc.), but within the same letter the order is not alphabetical. At the beginning of each letter is a list of the words included under that letter. These lists are also not alphabetical, nor does their order correspond to that in which the words are then taken up; and most of the lists omit words which do in fact appear in the collections of significations that follow (e.g. *Murus* and *Oriens,* which are not included in the prefatory lists for M and O, but are treated at some length in cols 1003 and 1012-13 respectively), and on the other hand include words which – in the PL edition at any rate – do not appear in the following collections (e.g. *Rhinoceros,* which is included in the prefatory list in col. 1036 but nowhere else). One evident reason for at least some of these discrepancies is the fact that the work obviously existed in different redactions. A partial edition by Pitra, *Spicilegium Solesmense* II-III passim, with a controlling index in III, 428-35 (attributed to Rabanus Maurus throughout), provides substantial additions to the text edited in the PL, and should be used to supplement it; items marked by an asterisk in Pitra's index refer to passages either faulty or missing in the PL edition (Pitra, *Spicilegium Solesmense* III, 429, beginning of first footnote column). In both the PL edition and that of Pitra, all biblical citations are identified in footnotes.

A work of unique if somewhat peculiar importance for the use of *distinctiones* in printed form is the edition of the *Clavis scripturae* (an eighth-century collection of scriptural significations, arranged topically and accordingly discussed below, on p. 42) by Pitra, *Spicilegium Solesmense* II-III. Pitra, following an old tradition, mistakenly took the *Clavis* to be a Latin translation of a lost work, Ἡ κλείς, by the second-century apologete Melito of Sardes; and to show what he thought was its continuing influence through the Middle Ages, he appended to each chapter of it (under the heading 'Veterum varius commentarius') a small collection of supposedly illustrative excerpts from *distinctiones* and other medieval works, many of which remain unprinted except for these excerpts. For present purposes, the result is a substantial anthology of commentary on a wealth of biblical images, organized topically, but drawn in large part from alphabetically arranged *distinctiones* otherwise inaccessible or only partly accessible in print: the *Summa Abel* or *Distinctiones Abel* by Peter Cantor (12th C), the anonymous *Distinctiones monasticae* (13th C), the *Alphabetum* or *Rosa alphabetica* by Peter of Capua or Peter of Mora (13th C), the *Distinctiones* by Maurice of Provins or Mauritius Hibernicus (13th C), and *distinctiones* by an 'anonymus Cisterciensis' and an 'anonymus Clarevallensis' – most of which will be treated in greater detail below. This anthology, of course, can be most effectively used by way of the topically organized *Clavis scripturae*, around which it is arranged. A topical outline of the *Clavis* is included in the *Spicilegium Solesmense* II, lxxxvi-lxxxix. A more convenient approach is by way of the alphabetical 'Index rerum sive typorum aut symbolorum' in III, 614-22, so long as one bears in mind that not all of its references are to the *Clavis* and its accompanying extracts. Valuable indices of scriptural citations appear in II, 521-44 and III, 585-600; and an index of early writers quoted or cited, in III, 602-13. Though Pitra's texts are often very poorly edited and should if possible be checked against the manuscripts from which they are taken, they do provide what is probably the richest single compendium of biblical interpretations not arranged according to the order of the Bible; as Hugh of St Cher's commentary is the one I reach for first when my lead is a biblical reference, so Pitra's strange accumulation is the one I reach for first when my lead is a simple concept.

Since the *distinctiones* are obviously of major importance for the study of medieval biblical imagery, and since the great majority of them remain unprinted or only partially printed, I list those that from my knowledge of them seem particularly rewarding; many others – often too jejune or literally oriented to be of much use – can be found by paging through vols II - VII of Stegmüller's *Repertorium.*

1/ **Peter Cantor,** *Summa Abel* or *Distinctiones Abel* (12th C). Extracts are printed by Pitra, *Spicilegium Solesmense* (accompanying the *Clavis*) II - III, passim, and indexed in III, 610. For manuscripts, see Stegmüller, *Repertorium* IV, 251-2, #6451; and for a brief description, Wilmart, 'Un Répertoire' pp 336-8. A complete edition is being prepared by Stephen A. Barney.

2/ **William de Montibus** (12th-13th C), a *distinctiones* beginning 'Abyssus multiplex est ...' (Stegmüller, *Repertorium* II, 429, #2993); and a *distinctiones* beginning 'Arcus dicitur Christus ...' (Stegmüller,

Repertorium II, 429, #2995, plus the following MSS: Oxford, Bodleian 3525, fols 55r-106v; Oxford, Caius College 138; Oxford, Corpus Christi College 43; BL Royal 6 B.x, fols 42ff; BL Royal 8 G.ii, fols 2ff; BL Royal 10 A.vii, fols 1ff; and BL Royal 11 A.iii, fols 35ff).

3/ An anonymous *Distinctiones monasticae* (early 13th C), written in England and preserved in two MSS: a/ Paris, Bibl. Mazarine 3475, fols 1-127r, containing 187 entries with the remains of an index (beginning with M) on fol. 1r. b/ Oxford, Bodl. Rawlinson C.22, item 7, pp 174-230, including 97 entries between *Altare* and *Mors*, mostly in extracts, with the addition of *Sinus* (p. 204) and three other extracts at p. 149; it is described by **Richard William Hunt, 'Notes on the Distinctiones monasticae et morales'** in *Liber floridus: Mittellateinische Studien Paul Lehmann ... gewidmet*, ed. **Bernhard Bischoff** and **Suso Brechter** (St Ottilien 1950) p. 357, with a list of the entries on pp 361-2. Extracts of the *Distinctiones* are printed (from Mazarine 3475) by Pitra, *Spicilegium Solesmense* (accompanying the *Clavis*), II-III passim. The work is also partially edited by Pitra, *ibid.* III, 453-87, with an index on pp 452-3; and by Wilmart, 'Un Répertoire' pp 312-35, with a brief description on pp 308-11. As Wilmart remarks, the *Distinctiones monasticae* is an unusually attractive example of the *distinctiones* – including, among other things, a good many Latin verses from a variety of sources – though it would appear to have had little or no direct influence.

4/ **Peter of Capua** (or of Mora), *Alphabetum, Rosa alphabetica, Ars concionandi/sermocinandi,* or *Lexicon concionatorum* (early 13th C). Extracts are printed by Pitra, *Spicilegium Solesmense* (accompanying the *Clavis*) II-III passim, with an index to them in III, 496-7, an edition of the entire section 'De rosa' on pp 489-96, and a selection from the prologue on p. 498. For manuscripts, see **P. Glorieux,** *Répertoire des maîtres en théologie de Paris au XIIIᵉ siècle*, Etudes de philosophie médiévale 17 (Paris 1933) I, 111-12, #17 (*m*), and 264, #208 (*b*); and for brief descriptions, Wilmart, 'Un Répertoire' pp 339-41, and Rouse and Rouse, 'Biblical Distinctions' pp 32-3 and '*Statim invenire*' pp 218-21. The *Alphabetum* is an extraordinarily full compilation, arranged alphabetically by first letter only, and topically under each letter.

5/ **Maurice of Provins** (formerly Mauritius Hibernicus), *Distinctiones fratris Mauricii* (13th C). Extracts are printed by Pitra, *Spicile-*

gium Solesmense (accompanying the *Clavis*) II-III passim, with no index; and the letters A through E appear in a *Dictionarium sacrae scripturae Mauritii Hybernici ordinis minorum conventualium* (Venice: Ioannes Antonius & Iacobus de Franciscis, 1603). For manuscripts, see Stegmüller, *Repertorium* III, 557-8, #5566; and for brief descriptions, Wilmart, 'Un Répertoire' pp 341-2 (including an identification of the author on 341), and Rouse and Rouse, 'Biblical Distinctions' pp 33-4. Though it seems relatively unknown among modern literary scholars, the *Distinctiones Mauricii* is in my opinion an unusually rewarding collection.

6/ **Nicholas de Gorran,** *Distinctiones* (13th C). For manuscripts, see Stegmüller, *Repertorium* IV, 28-9, #5740; and for a brief description, Wilmart, 'Un Répertoire' pp 342-3.

7/ **Nicholas de Byard,** *Distinctiones* (13th C). For manuscripts, see Stegmüller, *Repertorium* IV, 17, #5693; and for brief descriptions, Wilmart, 'Un Répertoire' pp 343-4, and Rouse and Rouse, 'Biblical Distinctions' pp 34-5. A work less certainly attributed to Nicholas is the *De abstinencia,* printed under the title *Dictionarius pauperum* – an alphabetical compendium for the use of preachers, extracted from the *Distinctiones.* For manuscripts and editions, see Stegmüller, *Repertorium* IV, 17-18, #5695; and for brief descriptions, Wilmart, 'Un Répertoire' pp 344-6, and the account in my chapter on sermons and homilies (p. 87 below). In accord with the function of the *De abstinencia* as a preacher's manual, its selection of subjects emphasizes fundamental abstract concepts (e.g. *abstinentia, patientia,* etc.) rather than the symbolic meanings of concrete biblical images.

8/ **Simon of Burneston** (Boraston), *Distinctiones* (14th C). For manuscripts, see Stegmüller, *Repertorium* V, 214, #7641, plus Oxford, Caius College 27 and Merton College 216.

9/ The *Rosarium theologiae* and its longer version known as the *Floretum* (14th C). For manuscripts, see Stegmüller, *Repertorium* VI, 498, #10080; and von Nolcken, *Middle English Translation* pp 8-13. There is a Wycliffite version in Middle English, 21 entries of which are edited by **Christina von Nolcken,** *The Middle English Translation of the Rosarium theologie,* Middle English Texts 10 (Heidelberg 1979), with a list of all 302 entries on pp 14-16; one other entry (*ieiunium*) is edited by **von Nolcken, 'Some Alphabetical Compendia and How Preachers Used Them in Fourteenth-Century England,'** *Viator* 12

(1981) 285-8. The *Rosarium/Floretum*, though very full, is really a preachers' aid and so leans heavily toward the explanation of general doctrinal concepts.

There are of course a great many other medieval alphabetized dictionaries and encyclopedias which, while they are not primarily collections of figurative biblical meanings and so cannot strictly be called *distinctiones*, nevertheless bear in a variety of possible ways on the use of the Bible for literary interpretation. To illustrate the possibilities, I mention five of the most interesting:

1/ **Guillelmus Brito** (13th C), *Summa*, ed. **Lloyd W. Daly** and **Bernadine A. Daly**, *Summa Britonis sive Guillelmi Britonis expositiones vocabulorum biblie*, Thesaurus mundi 15-16 (Padua 1975), 2 vols. Though the *Summa* is concerned primarily with explaining difficult words from the Vulgate Bible (ed., I, xxiii-xxiv), it is severely literal in its scope and to the best of my knowledge contains no figurative meanings. A related work by Guillelmus, partly incorporated into the *Summa*, is edited by **Lloyd W. Daly**, *Brito Metricus: A Mediaeval Verse Treatise on Greek and Hebrew Words* (Philadelphia 1968).

2/ **Giovanni Balbi** (Joannes Balbus, 13th C), *Catholicon* (many eds 1460-1520; repr. Westmead, Farnborough, Hants. 1971). Like Brito's *Summa*, the *Catholicon* is basically a vocabulary; but it often includes figurative or allegorical meanings, moralized etymologies, and the like. Its influence was obviously immense.

3/ **Nicholas Hanap** (13th C), *De exemplis sacrae scripturae* (editions in Stegmüller, *Repertorium* IV, 49, #5815). Nicholas's work is a dictionary of virtues illustrated in the Bible, organized alphabetically according to the virtues.

4/ **Pierre Bersuire** (Petrus Berchorius, 14th C), *Repertorium morale* in *Opera omnia* (Cologne 1730-1) vols III-VI (for other editions, see Stegmüller, *Repertorium* IV, 241-3, #6427), with indices of the concepts included at the beginnings of vols III and V, and a 98-page subject-index at the end of VI. The *Repertorium* is indeed a *distinctiones*, but along with much else; the title-page of the edition cited, for example, announces that it is 'in quatuor [sic] partes divisum, Catholicum, philosophicum, historicum, tropologicum et dogmaticum: vtpote variis rerum quarumvis definitionibus, Catholicae fidei dogmatibus, scripturarum figuris, apophthegmatibus, hieroglyphicis, nominum etymologiis, rerum proprietatibus, historiarum, & exemplorum cujusvis argumenti copia refertum ....'

5/ Two closely related works by **Antonio de Rampegolis** (14th-15th C), each of which appears under various titles: the *Compendium bibliae* (Stegmüller, *Repertorium* II, 125-6, #1419), and the *Figurae bibliorum* (*ibid.* #1420; seventeenth-century editions are abridged). Both these works are devoted almost entirely to explaining general concepts (e.g. *abstinentia, zelus*).

In surveying commentaries that follow the organization of the Bible itself, I remarked that the great seventeenth-century commentary of Cornelius a Lapide, though too late to be used directly as an aid to the interpretation of medieval literature, is nevertheless of immense value as a repository of traditional medieval exegesis. The same is true of two massive alphabetically organized compendia of biblical significations produced during the sixteenth century:

1/ The later, more influential, and more generally useful of the two is by **Jerónimo Lloret** (Hieronymus Lauretus), *Sylva allegoriarum totius sacrae scripturae*, which went through twelve editions – the earliest that of Barcelona in 1570, the latest that of Cologne in 1744; the 10th edition [ed. **S. Champier**] (Cologne 1681) was reprinted by Wilhelm Fink Verlag (Munich 1971), with a very informative introduction by Friedrich Ohly on pp 5-12 preceding the reproduction itself (the following analysis is based on this edition). The *Sylva* is an extraordinarily full *distinctiones*, with respect to both the number of entries it includes and the length at which individual words are treated. Each entry begins with a literal definition of the word in question and proceeds to its extra-literal significances, first the favourable and then the unfavourable. The inner margin of each page provides a checklist of these significances; the outer margin, the references to the authors from which they are cited. Numbers appear separately in an 'Appendix ... de allegoriis numerorum' (pp 1069-96), organized numerically instead of alphabetically. There is a 72-page subject-index following p. 1096, and a list of authors cited on a prefatory p. *5.

2/ The earlier and much less influential alphabetical compendium of the sixteenth century is the *Isagoga ad mysticos sacrae scripturae sensus* by **Santes Pagnino of Lucca**, printed in *Santis Pagnini Lucensis ... Isagogae ad sacras literas, liber unicus. Eiusdem Isagogae ad mysticos sacrae scripturae sensus, libri xviii* (Lyon 1536, Cologne 1545) pp 51-818, with citations from the Bible and from other authors (especially the Fathers) in the margins; a 4-page list of the entries it contains, along with a 22-page index of biblical citations and a 5-page subject-index both covering the entire volume, is included between the title-page and the prefatory epistles. Though the *Isagoga* contains fewer entries than Lloret's *Sylva* and reflects a less wide range of earlier interpretations, it is nevertheless an enormous compilation with respect to both number of entries and fullness of treatment, and is more exclusively concerned with the 'mystical' (i.e. extra-literal) significance of biblical words than is the *Sylva*. Pagnino's *Isagoga ad sacras literas* (printed in the same volume, pp 1-51), though full of interesting information (e.g. a discussion of figures of speech applied to God, pp 36-41), is not a work of the kind we are considering. Like the commentaries of Cornelius, Lloret's *Sylva* and Pagnino's *Isagoga ad mysticos ... sensus* are both important Renaissance tools for the study of medieval exegetical imagery; and, like Cornelius, they are particularly useful in guiding one to interpretations found elsewhere than in the avowed commentaries on the verse in question.

Finally there is at least one modern work that, for the Gospels, can be used somewhat in the manner of the medieval *distinctiones:* **Reinildis Hartmann**, *Allegorisches Wörterbuch zu Otfrieds von Weissenburg Evangeliendichtung*, Münstersche Mittelalter-Schriften 26 (Munich 1975), based on Otfrid's ninth-century poem paraphrasing and commenting on the Gospels in Old High German. The 'allegorical dictionary' itself, arranged alphabetically according to the Old High German words, is on pp 35-509, with a separate section on the numbers, arranged numerically, on 510-33. This plan, which on the face of it might seem to defeat any hope of usefulness, is redeemed by the addition of three indices: on pp 546-9, an index of Modern German words with their OHG equivalents, arranged topically; on 550-4, an index of Latin words with their OHG equivalents, arranged alphabetically; and on 555, an alphabetical index of 'significata' (the things signified in the allegories). What makes the *Wörterbuch* worth mentioning here is the fullness of its information for the concepts covered; each entry includes a detailed account of how the concept appears in the *Evangelienbuch,* relevant passages from earlier or contemporary writers, and any pertinent bibliography on the image.

COLLECTIONS ORGANIZED TOPICALLY

Let us recall at this point that we have been considering the tools available for finding the traditional figurative associations of biblical concepts which do not immediately suggest a particular verse or passage, and that we have begun with those arranged alphabetically; we now turn to those that are arranged topically, according to areas of logical classification. Inevitably, such works shade off into a different type of compilation: encyclopedias that aim to present accumulated knowledge in many fields, often including biblical significances because they are a part of it. In the course of the Middle Ages, such encyclopedic works increasingly include allegorizations not only of concepts from the Bible but also of material drawn from the natural sciences and elsewhere, thus enriching still further the fund of traditional medieval imagery. The following sketch will make no attempt to distinguish sharply among these different elements and emphases, and will in fact include some works in which the Bible receives little or no attention; its aim is to outline briefly what in my own experience have been the most fruitful medieval repositories of figurative meanings based on biblical and/or other material, arranged topically. A fuller list of encyclopedias – partially overlapping and of course still highly selective – is included below in the appendix compiled by Michael W. Twomey. It will be noticed that some of the most famous and important encyclopedias of the Middle Ages (e.g. Isidore of Seville's *Etymologiae,* Vincent of Beauvais's *Speculum maius,* and Bartholomaeus Anglicus's *De rerum proprietatibus*) are absent from the present list. Like any great compendium of colourful material, such encyclopedias can of course supply some of the raw material of imagery; but since they do not ordinarily deal in figurative significances as such, they are included in the appendix rather than here.

The earliest topically organized collection of extra-literal biblical interpretations is the ***Formulae spiritalis intelligentiae*** by **Eucher of Lyon** (5th C), the alphabetical glosses to which have already been mentioned. Like the glosses, it exists in two versions, a shorter and a longer:

1/ Forms of the shorter version (Stegmüller, *Repertorium* II, 304, #2257) are edited by **J.B. Pitra,** *Analecta sacra Spicilegio Solesmensi parata* (Paris 1884) II, 511-43, with Eucher's own list of chapters on pp 512-13, an alphabetical subject-index on 571-5, and a similar brief 'Liber secundus' under the name of Eucher on 543-56; and by **Karl Wotke**, *Sancti Eucherii Lugdunensis Formulae* ..., CSEL 31 (Vienna 1894) pp 1-62, with Eucher's list of chapters on p. 6.

2/ The longer version (Stegmüller, *Repertorium* II, 304, #2258) appears in PL 50, cols 727-72, with Eucher's list of chapters in col. 729. Though rather meagre compared with later compilations, the *Formulae* can be rewarding for the study of medieval imagery, particularly in literature of the first millennium. The alphabetical glosses described earlier can of course be used as an index of sorts to it.

Another early collection of interpretations arranged topically is the eighth-century *Clavis scripturae* (or *Clavis Melitonis*), mistakenly identified as the translation of a lost work by Melito of Sardes (see p. 34 above). The most popular form of the *Clavis* (Stegmüller, *Repertorium* III, 559-61, #5574) is edited by Pitra, *Spicilegium Solesmense* II, 1-519 and III, 1-307, accompanied, as we have seen, by sizeable extracts from *distinctiones* and other works; the text of the *Clavis* itself consists of the brief notations preceded by arabic numerals, which in each chapter stand between the large roman numeral and the heading 'Veterum varius commentarius.' This edition includes a topical outline of the *Clavis* in II, lxxxvi-lxxxix; a more convenient 'Index rerum sive typorum aut symbolorum' (covering, however, the whole of vols II-III) in III, 614-22; indices of scriptural citations in II, 521-44 and III, 585-600; and an index of early writers quoted or cited in III, 602-13.

Another version of the *Clavis*, considered by Pitra to be the earliest (Stegmüller, *Repertorium* III, 561-2, #5575), is edited by him in *Analecta sacra* II, 6-127, with a subject-index on pp 147-54.

Excerpts from the *Clavis* found in the Bible manuscripts of Theodulf of Orléans (8th-9th C; Stegmüller, *Repertorium* III, 562-3, #5576) are edited by Pitra, *Spicilegium Solesmense* II, lxvii-lxxxiii. Like the *Formulae* of Eucher, the *Clavis* appears jejune by comparison with later collections; but also like the *Formulae*, it can be a valuable aid in the interpretation of early medieval imagery.

The *De universo* of Rabanus Maurus (8th-9th C), in 22 books, is of course one of the great encyclopedias of the Middle Ages; for details of publication see p. 186 below. Besides being a mine of information generally, the *De universo* is especially rich in allegorical meanings, drawn chiefly from the Bible though with an occasional bit of allegorized scientific lore. So far as I know, allegorical interpretation forms a substantial part of every chapter.

A work of more limited design, but still of immense scope, is the *Gregorianum* compiled in the twelfth century by **Garner of St Victor** (or of Paris) – a topically organized encyclopedia made up entirely from the works of Gregory the Great. The *Gregorianum* is printed in PL 193, cols 23-462, with the sources in Gregory's works cited in footnotes. (A complication is created by the fact that Garner's editor in PL 193 uses the old chapter-designations for certain works of Gregory, whereas the edition of Gregory in PL 75-9 uses the modern ones; but since the edition of Gregory in the PL does also include the old chapter-designations in brackets, the difficulty is not insuperable.) The *Gregorianum* is accompanied in PL 193 by an alphabetical subject-index (cols 1813-40) and a topically organized table of contents (cols 1839-44), which provides a convenient key to its contents. Unlike most other encyclopedias, the *Gregorianum* can be useful in two distinct ways. First, it can serve as still another means of finding one's way around in the works of Gregory. And second, since it does not always repeat Gregory exactly, and in any case has its own identity as a twelfth-century encyclopedia, it can also be used as evidence in its own right; an example appears in my article 'Dante's *Purgatorio* XXXII and XXXIII: A Survey of Christian History,' *University of Toronto Quarterly* 43 (1974) 201 and 212-13 n.18, where the passage from Garner offers a distinctly more relevant interpretation of the fig-tree than does the corresponding one from Gregory.

The treatise *De naturis rerum* by **Alexander Neckham** (12th-13th C) and his metrical paraphrase *De laudibus divinae sapientiae* (see p. 192 below) are edited by **Thomas Wright**, Rolls Series 34 (London 1863; repr. Nendeln, Liechtenstein 1967) pp 1-354 and 357-503 respectively, with a long English preface summarizing their contents, a very brief glossarial index on pp 507-9, and a rather sparse subject-index in English on pp 513-21. The *De naturis* seems originally to have comprised the first two books of a work in five books, the last three devoted to a commentary on Genesis and Ecclesiasticus (Wright ed. p. xiv; Stegmüller, *Repertorium* II, 76-7, #1172). Both the *De naturis* and the *De laudibus* are rich collections of highly moralized scientific lore, embellished by a good bit of Classical learning and an occasional biblical reference; the *De naturis* includes many illustrative stories, most of which are omitted in the *De laudibus*. Though Alexander's two works are negligible as repositories of strictly biblical imagery, I include them here because they are full of the same kind of moralized meanings found in compendia of biblical interpretations – often applied to the same concepts – and so can be used in much the same way.

An encyclopedia of similar significance, though it includes fewer figurative interpretations, is the *De natura rerum* by Thomas of Cantimpré (13th C; see p. 196 below), ed. **H. Boese, *Thomas Cantimpratensis, Liber de natura rerum*** (Berlin 1973) vol. I, containing the text; presumably the notes and indices will appear in a second volume. The *De natura* as a whole is organized topically into 20 books; within each book, the order of chapters is alphabetical by initial letter only, and the longer books are preceded by lists of the chapters they include (pp 6-11, 101, 173-4, 231, 250, 275, 292, 312, 330, 341, and 354). Though Thomas's encyclopedia is predominantly scientific in outlook, offering only an occasional figurative interpretation or biblical reference, I have found it unusually rewarding for the pursuit of medieval imagery; a single example is its moralization of 'does' (*dammulae*), ' ... illos signant, qui animo segnes et ignavi resistere nolunt dyabolo temptatori' (4.30, p. 125), which, I suspect, underlies the significance of the female deer in *Sir Gawain and the Green Knight* (see my article '*Sir Gawain and the Green Knight*,' in *Medieval and Renaissance Studies: Proceedings of the Southeastern Institute of Medieval and Renaissance Studies, Summer, 1979* [No. 10] ed. George Mallary Masters [Chapel Hill, N.C. 1984] p. 28). The popularity of the *De naturis* during the rest of the Middle Ages is evidenced by several translations, described below on pp 197-8.

The ***Lumen animae*** ([Augsburg] 1477, [Reutlingen] 1479, [Strassburg] 1482), a major source-book for preachers in central Europe that has been attributed to Berengar of Landorra, Godfrey of Vorran, John XXII, and Matthias Farinator, is actually three somewhat interrelated works compiled by different hands after 1317 and before 1357. A convenient brief account is presented by Thorndike, *History of Magic* (for which see pp 183-4 below) III, 546-67; the best account of the textual tradition is by **Mary A. Rouse** and **Richard H. Rouse**, 'The Texts Called *Lumen anime*,' *Archivum fratrum praedicatorum* 41 (1971) 5-113, with a list of the contents of the three versions on pp 94-113.

The work consists of two parts, the first of which, though it seems completely without biblical references, contains a great deal of moralized natural science. It is made up of 76 large titles (e.g. 'De nativitate Christi,' 'De beata virgine,' 'De abstinencia,' 'De accidia,' 'De somno,' and the like), each of which is expounded partly by means of scientific material. The text is preceded by a table enumerating these large titles; an 18 to 20-page alphabetical index of subjects from natural science; and a 40-odd-page alphabetical index of moralizations. For our purposes, the most profitable approach will probably be to look up subjects in the index of natural science; if, for example, one is interested in moralizations of the dog, this index will guide him to the sections 'De alacritate,' 'De accinctione,' 'De dulcedine,' 'De aggressione,' and six others. (Pt II of the *Lumen* is a collection of quotations from earlier writers on 267 doctrinal subjects, arranged alphabetically.)

An encyclopedia devoted wholly and explicitly to moralized scientific lore – chiefly from the *De rerum proprietatibus* of Bartholomaeus Anglicus – is the anonymous *Liber de moralitatibus* (or *Proprietates rerum naturalium moralisatae,* or *Tractatus septiformis de moralitatibus rerum*), apparently composed in the late thirteenth or early fourteenth century and variously attributed to Aegidius (Gilles) of Rome, Thomas Walleys, Marco of Urvieto, and an anonymous Franciscan. This important work, cited as a belated partial source by Bersuire in the prologue to his *Reductorium* (see below; the citation is in *Opera* II, 2, 2nd col.), remains mostly unprinted. Bks 3 and 4, 'De avibus' and 'De arboribus sive plantis,' appear more or less completely in the form of excerpts in Pitra's *Spicilegium Solesmense* II, 347-467 and 470-519 passim (based on Paris, Bibl. nationale, MS. lat. 3332), under the designation 'Moralitatum lib.'; and an index of the chapters in bk 6 is printed by **Léopold Delisle**, 'Traités divers sur les propriétés des choses,' *Histoire littéraire de la France* 30 (1888) 347-51.

A total of twelve manuscripts of the work are cited in the partly complementary lists of **J. Engels**, 'Berchoriana, I (suite): Notice bibliographique sur Pierre Bersuire, supplément au *Repertorium biblicum medii aevi*,' *Vivarium* 2 (1964) 117, and **Morton W.**

Bloomfield et al., *Incipits of Latin Works on the Virtues and Vices, 1100-1500 A.D.*, Mediaeval Academy of America, Publication No. 88 (Cambridge, Mass. 1979) p. 430, #5027. In my own experience, the most easily legible MSS are those of Assisi, Bibl. comunale 243, with prefatory table of books and chapters on fols 1r-3v and alphabetical subject-index on fols 4r-6r; Padua, Bibl. Antoniana 388, with table on fols 1r-5r and subject-index on fols 5r-8r; and Bibl. Vaticana lat. 5935, with table on fols 1r-4v and subject-index on fols 4v-7v.

The *De moralitatibus* is divided into seven books: 1, 'De corporibus celestibus'; 2, 'De elementis singulis'; 3, 'De avibus'; 4, 'De piscibus'; 5, 'De animalibus'; 6, 'De arboribus sive plantis'; and 7, 'De lapidibus preciosis et aliis mineralibus.' Within each book, the arrangement of chapters is generally alphabetical. Each chapter is divided into paragraphs, each of which presents in order 1/ a 'property' of the subject being discussed in the chapter, 2/ a moralization of that property, and 3/ texts supporting the moralization. Though the overall plan of the *De moralitatibus* is as a compendium not of biblical interpretations but of moralized science, the texts cited to support its moralizations include an abundance of biblical quotations. In the range of the subjects it covers, it is generally much less inclusive than the *Reductorium* of Bersuire; but when it does include a subject one is interested in, the interpretations it offers are apt to be unusually rewarding. Brief general accounts are presented by Delisle, 'Traités divers' pp 334-53; and more recently by Samaran, 'Pierre Bersuire' (see below) pp 317-19.

The most elaborate medieval compendium of moralized science is **Pierre Bersuire's** fourteenth-century *Reductorium morale*, bks 1-14, the latest and best edition of which is in *Opera omnia* (Cologne 1730-1) vol. II (for other editions, see Stegmüller, *Repertorium* IV, 236-8, #6425; and especially Samaran, 'Pierre Besuire' p. 444); preceding p. 1 are a list of the books which make up the *Reductorium* and a 3-page table of the chapters in each book. In some books the chapters are arranged alphabetically, in others not. Like the *Liber de moralitatibus,* Bersuire's *Reductorium* depends for its scientific lore chiefly upon the *De rerum proprietatibus* of Bartholomaeus Anglicus; a valuable account of it and his other sources is provided by Bersuire himself in his prologue (pp 1-3). The method of treating a subject in the *Reductorium* is essentially like that described above for the *De moralitatibus:* literal property, moralization, and supporting texts; and here again, the supporting texts are frequently biblical. The richness and variety of the moralizations to be found in the *Reductorium* can hardly be overstated – though it should also be pointed out that since many of them seem to originate with Bersuire himself, its value as a repository of previous tradition cannot be taken for granted. The best overall account of Bersuire and his works is by **Charles Samaran** [and **C. Monfrin**], 'Pierre Bersuire,' *Histoire littéraire de la France* 39 (1962) 259-450.

Another great fourteenth-century encyclopedia of moralized scientific lore is the *Summa de exemplis et rerum similitudinibus* by **John of San Gimignano** (Joannes a S. Geminiano/Gorini/de Goro), printed in many editions from the fifteenth to the seventeenth century (Stegmüller, *Repertorium* III, 420-1, #4932), regularly with an alphabetical subject-index of 20-odd pages preceding p. 1 or fol. 1. The *Summa* consists of a prologue and 10 books: 1, 'De celo et elementis'; 2, 'De metallis et lapidibus'; 3, 'De vegetabilibus et plantis'; 4, 'De natatilibus et volatilibus'; 5, 'De animalibus terrestribus'; 6, 'De homine et membris eius'; 7, 'De visionibus et somniis'; 8, 'De canonibus et legibus'; 9, 'De artificibus et rebus artificialibus'; and 10, 'De actibus et moribus hominis.' Within each book, the chapters are arranged alphabetically; but just as in the *Lumen animae,* the organization into chapters is based not on the concepts to be interpreted (e.g. *canis, bubo, manus*), but on the truths or qualities signified by them (*abstinentia, prosperitas hominum peccatorum, opera humana*) – a structure that makes the collection difficult to use for our purposes except by way of the prefatory index. Though the material of the *Summa* is drawn primarily from the natural sciences, its moralizations are liberally supported by biblical quotations, clearly noted in the margins of most editions.

These topically arranged medieval compendia of biblical and other symbolism may be supplemented by at least two modern compilations. One is **Dorothea Forstner**'s *Die Welt der Symbole* (2nd ed. Innsbruck 1967) – which, though not confined to the medieval period, inevitably includes a preponderance of medieval symbolism. It is divided most broadly into eleven large subjects – I, 'Zeichen und Schrift'; II, 'Zahlen und Figuren'; III, 'Kosmische Erscheinungen'; IV, 'Farben'; V, 'Steine und Metalle'; VI, 'Pflanzen'; VII, 'Tiere'; VIII, 'Biblische

Gestalten und Personifikationen'; IX, 'Mythologische Gestalten und Mischgestalten'; X, 'Körperteile und Körpersubstanzen'; XI, 'Verschiedene Symbole' – each of which is more or less elaborately subdivided, either topically or alphabetically. Entries are very full and detailed, and there are 32 illustrations. An index of symbols (pp 495-504) allows the work to be used alphabetically.

A second modern tool of this general kind – though dealing specifically with Christian biblical symbolism, and restricted to the first millennium – is **Hans-Jörg Spitz's** *Die Metaphorik des geistigen Schriftsinns: Ein Beitrag zur allegorischen Bibelauslegung des ersten christlichen Jahrtausends*, Münstersche Mittelalter-Schriften 12 (Munich 1972). Its longest part, entitled 'Metaphorische Grundvorstellungen' (pp 14-233), is a list of figurative interpretations of biblical concepts, organized topically on the basis of the literal concepts. The broadest division is into six large areas: I, 'Ganzheitliche Metaphorik: Körper der Wahrheit'; II, 'Deckmetaphorik'; III, 'Verwandlungsmetaphorik'; IV, 'Stufungsmetaphorik'; V, 'Strukturmetaphorik'; and VI, 'Übereinstimmung: Instrumentale Metaphern.' Each of these is then topically divided and subdivided, with very full accounts of the figurative interpretation of each individual concept; sources of the particular interpretations appear in the footnotes. There are indices of biblical citations (pp 257-9), authors and works (260-2), and subjects and important words (263-77).

Let me close this sketch of our second kind of 'research situation' – that involving the interpretation of concepts possibly biblical, but not obviously attached to particular biblical contexts – by mentioning a few miscellaneous possibilities. Most obviously, any alphabetical index to a volume or volumes containing biblical exegesis is in effect a tool for this kind of problem. Outstanding examples are the index at the end of vol. VI in most editions of the *Glossa ordinaria;* the general index to the *Enarrationes* of Denis the Carthusian in vol. XIV/ii of his *Opera omnia*, along with the indices in each of the preceding volumes; and especially the great index that occupies the whole of vol. VIII in most editions of the commentary on the whole Bible by Hugh of St Cher (all treated in detail above).

The PL of course includes a variety of indices, both to single volumes and to the works of individual authors – for example the indices in PL 46 to the complete works of Augustine and pseudo-Augustinian works, and the index at the end of PL 76 to the *Moralia in Iob* and other important works of Gregory (see pp 25-6 above). These indices in the PL differ greatly in usefulness, according to the competence of the individual editor and the apparatus available to him in earlier editions; overall handicaps are a plethora of misprints, frequent persistent errors of a column or two, and the confusion often caused by the two systems of numbering used in the indices (see p. 10 above).

For the PL as a whole, there is a rather erratic '**Index de allegoriis**' in vol. 219, cols 123-242, divided broadly into Old Testament and New Testament and then elaborately subdivided by topic; though this index is apt to be much less useful than its title seems to promise (e.g. it depends to a disappointing degree on the two elaborate *distinctiones* in PL 112 and 210, discussed on pp 33-4 above), it is by no means worthless. It is followed in cols 241-64 by a more useful '**Index figurarum**' – that is, an index of biblical typology – similarly organized; and cols 263-74 contain an '**Index exegeticus parabolum**,' arranged topically by parable. It may be worth adding that this same volume, PL 219, includes a number of other exegetical indices that can be related in various ways to our present subject – for example an '**Index tum virorum tum mulierum**' for both the Old and New Testaments (cols 273-316), an '**Index de prophetiis**' (323-32), an '**Index de miraculis**' (331-62), an '**Index de Christo**' (449-76), an '**Index nominum omnium quibus ss patres Christum designarunt**' (475-84), an '**Index de nomine Jesu**' (483-8), an '**Index de Spiritu Sancto**' (487-94), and an '**Index Marianus**' (493-528).

Finally, it is worth mentioning that if the problem is important enough, and if the concept one is interested in does not occur too often in the Bible, the second of our 'research situations' can easily be transformed into one of the first kind, by the simple procedure of translating the concept into as many Latin terms as possible and checking them in a biblical concordance; the result will be a list of biblical references, the medieval commentaries on which can then be systematically consulted by the method I have outlined. This approach of course quickly collapses of its own weight if the concept being checked appears with any frequency in the Bible itself; an example, if one were needed, could be supplied from an attempt I once saw made to use it for a study of the exegetical overtones of 'treasure' (*thesaurus*), with predictably disastrous results.

Appendix: The Apocrypha

Though the apocrypha of the Old and New Testaments contribute to medieval literature in various ways, they produced no body of exegesis like that surrounding the canonical books of the Bible, and the study of them for our purposes cannot be systematized to anything like the same extent. I include here a few basic references.

A factual guide to the apocrypha (including, e.g., the languages in which they appear and editions in which they are available) is provided in Stegmüller's *Repertorium:* for the Old Testament apocrypha, I, 25-101, with general bibliography on p. 25, and the supplement in VIII, 3-70, with general bibliography on p. 3; and for the New Testament apocrypha, I, 105-250, with general bibliography on pp 105-6, and the supplement in VIII, 73-219, with general bibliography on p. 73. With regard to the apocrypha of the Old Testament, it must be remembered that the tradition surrounding the King James Bible consistently applies the term 'apocrypha' to books that are canonical in the Vulgate (Tobias, Judith, Ecclesiasticus, Wisdom, etc., as discussed earlier), and refers to most of those outside the Vulgate canon – from our point of view, the 'real apocrypha' – as 'pseudepigrapha.' Very often, of course, such works survive only in languages unfamiliar to most Western medievalists: Hebrew, Ethiopic, Coptic, Armenian, Syriac, and the like.

The most recent translations of these apocryphal works, by various scholars, are edited by **James H. Charlesworth,** *The Old Testament Pseudepigrapha* (New York 1983-5), 2 vols; vol. I contains 'Apocalyptic Literature and Testaments,' II 'Expansions of the "Old Testament" and Other Legends, Wisdom and Philosophical Literature, Prayers, Psalms, and Odes, Fragments of Lost Judeo-Hellenistic Works.' An earlier collection of translations is by **R.H. Charles** et al., *The Apocrypha and Pseudepigrapha of the Old Testament in English* (Oxford 1913) II, 'Pseudepigrapha,' with full introductions and notes and an elaborate subject-index on pp 835-71. A much earlier collection with Latin translations, still occasionally useful, is that of **Johann Albert Fabricius,** *Codex pseudepigraphus Veteris Testamenti* (Hamburg 1713-23), 2 vols, with an index of biblical citations and a 21-page subject-index following I, 1174.

There is also a new English edition of the most important Old Testament pseudepigraphon, *The Book of Enoch or I Enoch*, by **Matthew Black** in consultation with **James C. Vanderleam**, Studia in Veteris Testamenti pseudepigrapha 7 (Leiden 1985). A useful new guide to the pseudepigrapha is provided by **James H. Charlesworth**, *The Pseudepigrapha and Modern Research, with a Supplement*, Society of Biblical Literature, Septuagint and Cognate Studies Series 7S (rev. ed. Chico, Calif. 1981).

The best assembly of studies and translations of the New Testament apocrypha is by **Edgar Hennecke**, *New Testament Apocrypha*, ed. **Wilhelm Schneemelcher**, trans. ed. **R. McL. Wilson** (Philadelphia 1963-5), 2 vols, including scholarly accounts of the various apocrypha by many hands; complete translations of important texts and extracts from others; and in II, 811-52, an index of biblical citations and a subject-index. Also of value is *The Apocryphal New Testament, being the Apocryphal Gospels, Acts, Epistles, and Apocalypses, with Other Narratives and Fragments*, trans. **Montague Rhodes James** (Oxford 1924 and later eds), with indices of apocryphal writings mentioned, writers cited, proper names, and subjects. An earlier collection with Latin translations of the Greek texts, still occasionally useful, is **Fabricius**'s *Codex apocryphus Novi Testamenti* (Hamburg 1719), 3 vols in 2, with an index of biblical citations and a subject-index following III, 1036.

Important editions of the major types of New Testament apocrypha, in the original Greek or Latin texts, are *Apocalypses apocryphae Mosis, Esdrae, Pauli, Iohannis, item Mariae dormitio, additis Evangeliorum et Actuum apocryphorum supplementis*, ed. **Konstantin von Tischendorf** (Leipzig 1866); *Evangelia apocrypha*, ed. **von Tischendorf** (2nd ed. Leipzig 1876); and *Acta apostolorum apocrypha*, ed. **Richard Adelbert Lipsius** and **Max Bonnet** (Leipzig 1891-1903, repr. Darmstadt 1959), 2 vols in 3, with indices of proper names, Greek words, and Latin words in vol. I, and indices of biblical citations, Greek words, and Latin words in vol. II (ii, 303-91). The most famous and influential of the New Testament apocrypha, *Evangelium Nicodemi* or the *Gospel of Nicodemus*, is edited by **von Tischendorf** in his *Evangelia apocrypha* pp 333-432, and more recently, from a single manuscript, by **H.C. Kim**, *The Gospel of Nicodemus*, Toronto

Medieval Latin Texts 2 (Toronto 1973); it is translated in Hennecke's *New Testament Apocrypha* I, 444-81, and in James's *Apocryphal New Testament* pp 94-146.

Another enormous and related field which contributes sporadically to the imagery of medieval literature is that of Jewish legend. Though it is of course impossible to do it justice here, the most useful guide for our purposes that I know of is **Louis Ginzberg**, *The Legends of the Jews*, trans. **Henrietta Szold** (Philadelphia 1909-38, many later impressions), 7 vols. Vols I-IV contain the text, which follows the chronology of Jewish history; V-VI contain voluminous notes; and VII is an elaborate subject-index, compiled by Boaz Cohen, which makes the entire set an extraordinarily valuable tool for the kind of research I have been describing.

2
The Liturgy

Introductory

Although the direct currency of exegetical works themselves in the Middle Ages is often underestimated by modern scholars, it is obvious that the liturgy must, at the very least, have provided a more popular channel for the dissemination of biblical, exegetical, and other imagery through the medieval world; as a single example, the *lectiones* from the Fathers which make up part of the service of matins in the breviary abound in images and motifs that frequently find their way into literature. Unfortunately, the use of the liturgy for the interpretation of medieval imagery cannot be systematized to anything like the degree that I have described for exegetical works. For one thing, liturgical works by their very nature have little or none of the logical organization (by verses of Scripture, alphabetical, by areas of classification, etc.) that we have found in biblical commentaries and compendia, so that they hold out few handles for systematic coverage. Again, there are of course profound differences between the medieval and post-medieval liturgies; and most of the apparatus that exists (concordances, indices, and the like) is either geared specifically to the modern Roman liturgy or is at least not oriented particularly toward the medieval ones. And finally, the medieval liturgical books themselves are to a very great extent the products of their own particular times and places, and so present a bewildering variety of texts – a situation well summarized by Cyrille Vogel, *Introduction* (see p. 55 below) pp 5-6:

> Aucune uniformité ne règne à l'intérieur de chaque catégorie de livres: chacune d'elles recouvre des types et des familles différents.

Cette diversité tient à deux causes principales: *a*) Le moyen âge n'a pas connu d'uniformité liturgique, même pas à l'intérieur d'une même province; diverses variétés cultuelles divergeant notablement entre elles ont coexisté à l'intérieur d'une même famille liturgique, sans parler des familles liturgiques différentes qui furent en usage dans un même pays ou une même région. Avant le XIIIᵉ siècle, et même avant les premières éditions imprimées de la fin du XVᵉ siècle, ont regné dans l'Eglise latine, après des périodes fort longues de chaos et d'anarchie cultuelle, une diversité dont il est difficile de se faire une idée exacte et que ne venait contrarier aucune législation liturgique efficace. *b*) Le moyen âge ignore le principe de la répartition moderne des livres cultuels: à savoir *un* livre pour chaque fonction ou *actio* cultuelle (Missel pour l'Eucharistie, Rituel pour les sacrements et les bénédictions, Bréviaire et Psautier pour l'Office divin); il s'en tient au système d'un livre pour chaque ministre (célébrant prêtre ou évêque, diacre et ministres inférieurs, choeur) et souvent chaque ministre dispose d'un livre spécial pour chaque fonction. En aucun cas la répartition n'est opérée d'une manière systématique.

Even in the face of such obstacles, however, a given image can often be profitably pursued in the liturgy. What follows is a selective list of books that may be useful, and some suggestions about possible approaches.

By far the most useful bibliographical guide to the complexities of the medieval liturgy is that of **Richard W. Pfaff**, *Medieval Latin Liturgy: A Select Bibliography*, Toronto Medieval Bibliographies 9 (Toronto 1982), hereafter *MLL*, which can profitably be used to augment the present account – particularly by its references to further liturgical texts of different kinds, times, and places. A brief general bibliography by **Thomas A. Vismans** and **Lucas Brinkhoff**, *Critical Bibliography of Liturgical Literature*, trans. **Raymund W. Fitzpatrick** and **Clifford Howell**, Bibliographia ad usum seminariorum E1 (Nijmegen 1961), can be of help, though it is oriented toward the seminary student interested primarily in the modern Roman liturgy.

Herman A.P. Schmidt, *Introductio in liturgiam occidentalem* (Rome 1960), includes an elaborately organized 'Selecta bibliographia generalis' on pp 742-85, and substantial 'Bibliographiae selectae' at the ends of individual chapters. In addition, a number of major liturgical journals include bibliographies or bibliographical surveys: *Ephemerides liturgicae* (1887ff); *Questions liturgiques* (1910ff); *Jahrbuch für Liturgiewissenschaft* (1921-35), continued as *Archiv für Liturgie-*

wissenschaft (1950ff); *Jahrbuch für Liturgik und Hymnologie* (1955ff); and *Yearbook of Liturgical Studies* (1960ff). Other bibliographies and liturgical periodicals are listed by Pfaff, *MLL* pp 3 and 8-9; Vismans and Brinkhoff, *Critical Bibliography* pp 10-12; and Schmidt, *Introductio* pp 749-52.

A packed survey of liturgical scholarship during the past twenty-odd years is presented by **Réginald Grégoire**, 'Tradizione liturgica nell'alto medioevo,' in *La cultura in Italia fra tardo antico e alto medioevo: Atti del convegno tenuto a Roma, Consiglio nazionale delle ricerche, dal 12 al 16 novembre 1979* (Rome 1981) II, 679-99.

The standard encyclopedia for matters liturgical is the *Dictionnaire d'archéologie chrétienne et de liturgie (DACL)*, ed. **F. Cabrol** and **H. Leclercq** (Paris 1907-53), 15 vols in 30; many of its volumes, however, are now quite antiquated. A one-volume encyclopedia – organized topically, though with an alphabetical index – is edited by **R. Aigrain**, *Liturgia: Encyclopédie populaire des connaisances liturgiques* (Paris 1930). For present purposes, the best dictionaries are by **Joseph Braun**, *Liturgisches Handlexikon* (2nd ed. Regensburg 1924); **Ludwig Eisenhofer**, *Handbuch der katholischen Liturgik* (Freiburg i.B. 1932-3), 2 vols; and **Gerhard Podhradsky**, *Lexikon der Liturgie: Ein Überblick für die Praxis* (Innsbruck 1962).

Two especially useful guides through the medieval liturgy are those of **Leonhard Fendt**, *Einführung in die Liturgiewissenschaft*, Sammlung Töpelmann 2/5 (Berlin 1958), organized chronologically, with a particularly valuable 'Quellen-Schlüssel' on pp 258-67; and **Cyrille Vogel**, *Introduction aux sources de l'histoire du culte chrétien au moyen âge*, Biblioteca degli 'Studi medievali' 1 (Spoleto [1966], 2nd ed. 1975), organized broadly chronologically with a good deal of attention to locality and types of liturgical books, though it 'unfortunately omits virtually everything pertaining to the divine office' (Pfaff, *MLL* p. 10). Schmidt's *Introductio* is a detailed summary, based though it is on the modern Roman liturgy; besides the bibliographies already mentioned, it contains, as we shall see, a number of useful tables and indices – including on pp 840-9 an 'Index analyticus,' or detailed analysis of its own contents.

The best general treatment of the Roman liturgy is that of **Joseph Lechner** and **Ludwig Eisenhofer**, *The Liturgy of the Roman Rite*, trans. **A.J.** and **E.F. Peeler**, ed. **H.E. Winstone** (Freiburg i.B. 1961), with bibliographies at the ends of sections and chapters. Non-Roman liturgies are covered in three books by **Archdale A. King**, all with excellent bibliographies: *Liturgies of the Religious Orders* (London 1955), *Liturgies of the Primatial Sees* (London 1957), and *Liturgies of the Past* (London 1959). The difficult subject of early English liturgy is treated by **G.G. Willis**, '**Early English Liturgy from Augustine to Alcuin**,' in his *Further Essays in Early Roman Liturgy*, Alcuin Club Collections 50 (London 1968), pp 189-243, with a full bibliography on pp 247-58.

The liturgical year is of course a vast and complex subject, which can receive no more than passing notice here. Though studies of the liturgical year in the modern church abound, the best four general historical accounts are probably those of 1/ **Karl Adam Heinrich Kellner**, *Heortologie, oder Die geschichtliche Entwicklung des Kirchenjahres und der Heiligenfeste von den ältesten Zeiten bis zur Gegenwart* (3rd ed. Freiburg i.B. 1911), trans. from the second German edition (1906) by a priest of the Diocese of Westminster as *Heortology: A History of the Christian Festivals from their Origin to the Present Day* (London 1908), with a convenient chronological table on pp 449-56; 2/ **John Dowden**, *The Church Year and Kalendar*, Cambridge Handbooks of Liturgical Study [2] (Cambridge 1910); 3/ **A. Allen McArthur**, *The Evolution of the Christian Year* (London 1953), with a list of biblical references on pp 191-2; and 4/ best of all, **Josef Pascher**, *Das liturgische Jahr* (Munich 1963), with valuable indices of biblical citations (pp 732-48), liturgical texts (748-65), persons (765-71), and subjects (771-81). More specialized studies are assembled by Pfaff, *MLL* pp 45-59.

    Anton Baumstark, *Missale Romanum: Seine Entwicklung, ihre wichtigsten Urkunden, und Probleme* (Eindhoven 1929), pp 205-38 'Uebersicht über die Entwicklung des unbeweglichen Festjahres vom 6. bis 16. Jahrhundert,' presents a calendar of the liturgical year, day by day, drawing on a total of 46 prominent medieval manuscripts and early printed missals, sacramentaries, capitularies, and antiphonaries, and showing the liturgical designation of each day.

An exhaustive study of the modern liturgical year is that of **Polycarp Radó,** *Enchiridion liturgicum, complectens theologiae sacramentalis et dogmata et leges iuxta novum codicem rubricarum* (Rome 1961) II, 1077-1398, 'De ecclesia sanctificante tempora seu heortologia,' with detailed bibliographies on pp 1087-8, 1101-2, 1217-18, 1272-3, 1316-17, 1362-3, and 1397-8; a brief account is the section 'L'année liturgique' in Aigrain's *Liturgia* pp 611-93.

The kinds of service-books embraced by the medieval liturgy present a bewildering variety. Vogel, *Introduction* pp 4-5, having enumerated seven 'livres fondamenteaux' of the Latin liturgy – *missale, breviarium* (with *psalterium*), *graduale, antiphonale, martyrologium, pontificale,* and *rituale* – adds (p. 5),

> Au moyen âge, les livres nécéssaires à l'accomplissement du culte etaient beaucoup plus nombreux et plus complexes. A s'en tenir aux termes techniques, l'on en dénombrerait plus d'une centaine. Compte tenu des doublets et des synonymes, ce chiffre doit être réduit de moitié environ; il en reste donc au moins une cinquantaine. Encore au xve siècle, parmi les livres liturgiques incunables, 27 variétés différentes se laissent déceler. Citons le *Sacramentarium,* les *Lectionaria* (Epistolier et Evangéliaire), l'*Antiphonarium missae* (différent de l'*Antiphonarium officii*) ou *Graduale* ou *Antiphonale* avec le *Responsale,* le *Troparium,* le *Liber sequentialis,* le *Psalterium,* le *Passionarium,* l'*Hymnarium,* les *Ordines,* le *Pontificale,* le *Benedictionale* et le *Martyrologium,* entre autres.

A more concrete idea of the variety of medieval liturgical books can be obtained by paging through the table of contents or the text of Pfaff's *MLL.* The subject is analyzed in detail by **Francesco Antonio Zaccaria,** *Bibliotheca ritualis* bk I, ch. iii, art. 4-9; ch. iv, art. 3-7; ch. v, art. 3-5; ch. vi, art. 2; ch. vii, art. 1-2 (Rome 1776, repr. New York [1964] vol. I, 29-79, 96-136, 144-60, 164-80; and for the English (Sarum) rite by **William Maskell,** *Monumenta ritualia ecclesiae Anglicanae: The Occasional Offices of the Church of England according to the Old Use of Salisbury ...* (2nd ed. Oxford 1882) I, iii-ccxxxiii, with a 'List of the Titles of Service Books' on pp ccxxx-ccxxxiii.

A brief general account is presented by **Fernand Cabrol,** *Les Livres de la liturgie latine* ([Paris 1930]), trans. by the Benedictines of Stanbrook as *The Books of the Latin Liturgy,* Catholic Library of Religious Knowledge 22 (London [1932]); and for England by

Christopher Wordsworth and Henry Littlehales, *The Old Service-Books of the English Church* (London 1904), and Henry B. Swete, *Church Services and Service-Books before the Reformation* (3rd ed. London 1914).

A convenient list of detailed scholarly studies of specific kinds of medieval liturgical books (e.g. sacramentary, missal, ordinal, etc.) is given by Vogel, *Introduction* p. 6, nn 8-14; a similar list of detailed studies according to country or district appears on the same page, n. 7.

The most important single anthology of medieval liturgical texts, covering primarily French liturgies but including much else, is by **Edmond Martène, *De antiquis ecclesiae ritibus libri tres* ...** (many eds; see *DACL* x, 2305-6, n. 3), 4 vols, with elaborate indices in IV, 363-451, including an 'Index generalis rerum, nominum, et verborum' on pp 365-413. A slim but interesting anthology, including also excerpts from medieval liturgists (discussed below), is compiled by **Willibrord Lampen, *Florilegium liturgicum medii aevi*** (Fulda 1923), with an 'Index nominum et rerum' on pp 100-4.

Early liturgical texts are edited by **Fernand Cabrol** and **Henri Leclercq, *Reliquiae liturgicae vetustissimae ex ss patrum necnon scriptorum ecclesiasticorum monumentis selectae***, Monumenta ecclesiae liturgica 1 (Paris 1900-13), 2 vols, with a general index in II, 243-72; and by **Johannes Quasten, *Monumenta eucharistica et liturgica vetustissima***, Florilegium patristicum 7 (Bonn 1935-6), 7 fascs, with indices in fasc. 7: 'Index sacrae scripturae' (pp 359-62), 'Index auctorum' (363-9), 'Index nominum et rerum' (370-6), and a conspectus of the entire collection (377). Further collections are listed by Pfaff, *MLL* pp 12-13.

Important series containing liturgical texts are the **Henry Bradshaw Society Publications** (London and Chichester 1891ff), 99 vols (texts); the **Bibliothèque liturgique**, ed. **Ulysse Chevalier** (Paris 1893-1923), 22 vols (texts and studies); the **Alcuin Club Collections** (London et al. 1899ff), 55 vols (texts and studies); **Texte und Arbeiten I: Beiträge zur Ergründung des älteren lateinischen christlichen Schrifttums und Gottesdienstes** (Beuron, Hohenzollern 1917ff), 54 vols (texts and studies); and **Liturgiewissenschaftliche Quellen und Forschungen** [earlier titles *Liturgiegeschichtliche Quellen* and *Liturgiegeschichtliche Forschungen*] (Münster i.W. 1918ff), 60 vols (texts and studies).

Missal and Breviary

Out of this liturgical wilderness, the two books that presumably had the greatest popular currency, and therefore hold the greatest promise for the study of medieval literary imagery, are the missal and the breviary along with their predecessors. Let us turn first to the missal, a convenient general account of which is given by Cabrol, *Books of the Latin Liturgy* pp 2-5, 28-36, and passim. The best study of the Roman missal is that of **Josef Andreas Jungmann, *The Mass of the Roman Rite: Its Origins and Development*,** trans. **F.A. Brunner** (New York 1951), 2 vols. Missals of other rites are treated in the books of Archdale A. King (see p. 56 above), and those of the English church will be taken up below.

For the early Middle Ages (roughly pre-twelfth-century) individual texts and studies must be consulted. An early text of particular importance is the famous Gregorian sacramentary (an ancestor of the missal, containing also prayers used by the bishop or priest at other services), the oldest manuscripts of which date from the early ninth century, edited with its various supplements and additions by **Jean Deshusses,** *Le Sacramentaire grégorien: Ses principales formes d'après les plus anciens manuscrits*, Spicilegium Friburgense 16, 24 (2nd ed. Fribourg 1979), 2 vols, each including indices of proper names, principal subjects, and incipits.

ROMAN RITE

Within the Roman rite, the great watershed between late medieval and modern missals is the revised missal of 1570, issued by Pius V as a result of the Council of Trent. Printed Roman missals from before this date are not difficult to find; the earliest edition is the famous *Missale Romanum* of Milan, 1474, ed. **Robert Lippe**, Henry Bradshaw Society 17, 33 (London 1899-1907), 2 vols.

The basic tool for finding printed editions of medieval missals, Roman and other, is **W.H. Jacob Weale,** *Bibliographia liturgica: Catalogus missalium ritus Latini ab anno MCCCCLXXIV impressorum*, ed. **H. Bohatta** (London 1928), which is divided broadly into 'Missalia ecclesiarum' (i.e. dioceses, or for practical purposes geographical localities) and 'Missalia ordinum' (i.e. religious orders); included in the apparatus are a 'Bibliographia liturgica' on pp xvi-xxxii, and an

'Index chronologicus' on pp 333-45. Because of the differences between medieval and later missals, however, it must be used with some caution.

As a general rule, missals printed before 1570 (the date of the Tridentine revision) are likely to represent more or less accurately medieval texts. With specific regard to the missals of dioceses and religious orders, the revised missal of 1570 was accompanied by a papal bull stipulating that dioceses and orders having rites over two hundred years old (including, e.g., the ancient dioceses of Braga, Lyon, Milan, and Toledo, and the great orders of Carthusians, Cistercians, Premonstratensians, Carmelites, and Dominicans) could continue using their ancient liturgies. In a general way, what this implies is that for non-Roman missals belonging to rites that originated before 1370, the editions found in Weale and Bohatta's *Bibliographia* can be used with some confidence. It must be remembered, however, that the liturgy everywhere was to some extent in a continuous state of change, and that in any case a general rule does not always govern the particular instance – so that, for an important image or motif, one must try to determine on what manuscript sources a printed missal is based. Convenient guides are Vogel, *Introduction* pp 223-34; the *Lexikon für Theologie und Kirche* ed. Höfer and Karl Rahner (see p. 13 above), VI, 1092-5; and the books by Archdale A. King already cited.

The breviary, because of its greater figurative richness, variety, and openness to change, generally offers more possibilities for the creation or transmission of medieval literary imagery than does the missal. The standard history of the breviary at large is by **Suitbert Bäumer**, *Histoire du bréviaire*, trans. **Réginald Biron** (Paris 1905, repr. Rome 1967), 2 vols.

The Roman breviary is treated by **Jules Baudot**, *Le Bréviaire romain: Ses origines, son histoire* (Paris 1907), trans. anon. as *The Roman Breviary: Its Sources and History* (London 1909); and by **Pierre Batiffol**, *Histoire du bréviaire romain* (3rd ed. Paris 1911), trans. **Atwell M.Y. Baylay** as *History of the Roman Breviary* (London 1912). Breviaries of other rites are treated in the books of Archdale A. King (see p. 56 above); those of the English church will be taken up below.

Here again, individual texts and studies must be consulted for the predecessors of the breviary during the early Middle Ages; and once again the great watershed between the late medieval and the modern breviary is the revised Tridentine breviary of 1568. Fifteenth-century printed breviaries are listed (along with other liturgical works except missals and books of hours) by **Hanns Bohatta**, *Liturgische Bibliographie des XV. Jahrhunderts* (Vienna 1911, repr. Hildesheim [1960?]), pp 3-24. Breviaries printed after 1500 are listed by **Bohatta** in *Bibliographie der Breviere 1501-1850* (Leipzig 1937, 2nd unalt. ed. Stuttgart 1963), which is divided broadly into 'Breviarium Romanum,' 'Orden' (subdivided into 'Canonici regulares,' 'Ordines monastici,' 'Ordines mendicantium,' and 'Ordines militares'), and 'Diözesen' (for practical purposes geographical localities); the apparatus includes a 'Titelverzeichnis' (places) on pp 281-4, and a 'Chronologisches Verzeichnis' on pp 285-314. What has been said above about the need for caution in using Weale and Bohatta on the missal applies here also, in approximately the same way.

ENGLISH RITES

In England, the most important late medieval rite is of course not the Roman but the Salisbury, or Sarum. General accounts of the Sarum and other English missals can be found in Maskell, *Monumenta ritualia* I, lvi-lxxxvii; Wordsworth and Littlehales, *Old Service Books* pp 170-94; and Swete, *Church Services* pp 74-121. The Sarum Missal appears in two editions: **J. Wickham Legg**, *The Sarum Missal* (Oxford 1916), with an index of 'Masses and Other Services' on pp 549-56 and a 'Liturgical' index (an index of liturgical forms) on pp 557-612; and **Francis Henry Dickinson**, *Missale ad usum insignis et praeclarae ecclesiae Sarum* (Burntisland 1861-83, repr. Farnborough 1969), with indices following p. 934*: 'Passages from Holy Scripture' (pp 1-11), 'Introits' (12-14), 'Collects &c.' (15-28), 'Sequences &c.' (29-30), 'Secrets' (31-40), 'Prefaces' (41-2), 'Post-commons' (43-52). Some related texts are edited by **Legg** in *Tracts on the Mass*, Henry Bradshaw Society 27 (London 1904), with a list of manuscript Sarum missals on pp xiv-xv (supplemented by a few additions in his *Sarum Missal* p. vii).

The Sarum Missal is translated by **A. Harford Pearson**, *The Sarum Missal* (2nd ed. London 1884), with a very useful 'Comparative Table of the Epistles, Sequences and Gospels in the Proper of Seasons ... in the Sarum, York, and Hereford Missals' on pp 605-10, and the calendars of York and Hereford on pp 611-12 (for comparison with that of Sarum on pp lxxiii-lxxxiv); and by **Frederick E. Warren**, *The Sarum Missal in English* (London 1911), 2 vols, with a valuable 'Scriptural Index' in II, 589-613, an 'Index of Proper Names' on pp 615-23, and a 'General Index and Glossary' on pp 625-40.

The two other important late medieval rites in England are those of York and Hereford. The York Missal is edited by **W.G. Henderson**, *Missale ad usum insignis ecclesiae Eboracensis*, Surtees Society 59-60 (Durham 1874), 2 vols, with an elaborate appendix in II, 239-360, including a list and collections of Kyries (pp 241-52), a comparative calendar of feasts through the year in the Sarum, York, and Hereford uses (257-72), a 'General Index of Fixed Feasts' (273-80), a collection of proses [sequences] (281-318), and an 'Index sequentiarum' (349-53).

The Hereford Missal is edited by **W.G. Henderson**, *Missale ad usum percelebris ecclesiae Herfordensis* (Leeds 1874, repr. Farnborough 1969), with an 'Index sequentiarum' (p. viii), a table of 'Feasts according to the Use of Hereford' (ix-xii), a 'Calendarium' (xiii), and an 'Index of Fixed Feasts, Octaves, and Commemorations according to the Use of Hereford' (xiv-xvii).

The Sarum, Bangor, York, Hereford, and Roman versions of the ordinary and canon of the Mass are printed in parallel columns by **William Maskell**, *The Ancient Liturgy of the Church of England* (3rd ed. Oxford 1882; reissued New York 1973) pp 1-206. The fullest and most important English monastic missal is edited by **John Wickham Legg**, *Missale ad usum ecclesie Westmonasteriensis*, Henry Bradshaw Society 1, 5, 12 (London 1891-7), 3 vols, with an 'Index sanctorale' in III, 1632-5 and an 'Index of Liturgical Forms' on pp 1637-1729.

General accounts of the Sarum and other English breviaries can be found in Maskell, *Monumenta ritualia* I, xcvi-cii and III, i-xxxiv; Wordsworth and Littlehales, *Old Service Books* pp 69-100; and Swete, *Church Services* pp 26-73.

The best edition of the Sarum Breviary is by **Francis Procter** and **Christopher Wordsworth**, *Breviarium ad usum insignis ecclesiae Sarum* (Cambridge 1879-86, repr. Farnborough 1970), 3 vols (I,

'Kalendarium' and 'Ordo temporalis'; II, 'Psalterium'; III, 'Proprium sanctorum'), with a 'conspectus' of the entire breviary in I, 6-23, and elaborate indices: to vol. I, a 'Tabula hystoriarum' (cols cclxxvii-ccccii), an 'Index hymnorum et prosarum' (mccccxcv-mccccxcviii), and an 'Index generalis' (mccccxcix-mdxxxvi); to vol. II, a 'Tabula psalterii' (cols 261-8), a 'Canticorum index' (267-8), a 'Hymnorum index' (269-70), a 'Tabula de festorum divisione' (462-76), and an 'Index hymnorum et sequentiarum' (561-4); to vol. III, an 'Index generalis' on pp xlv-xlviii; and to all three volumes, many indices in III, xxvii-cxvi, including an 'Index indicum' (p. xxvii), an 'Index festorum, sanctorum, &c.' (xxix-xxxvii), an extremely valuable 'Index biblicus' (lii-lxi), an 'Index antiphonarum' (lxii-lxxxi), a 'Hymnorum index' (lxxxviii-xci), and an 'Index responsoriorum' (xcvi-cvii).

A much less full version of the Sarum Breviary is translated as *The Breviary of the Renowned Church of Salisbury, Rendered into English according to the Use of the Society of the Holy Trinity, Devonport* (London 1889), 2 vols (I, 'Winter Season,' II, 'Summer Season,' each volume containing ordinary, psalter, and proper of saints for that season; the calendar is at the beginning of I). In my own experience the Sarum Breviary, particularly in the Procter-Wordsworth edition, is the most rewarding single work in the English liturgy for the interpretation of literary imagery.

The York Breviary is edited by **Stephen W. Lawley**, *Breviarium ad usum insignis ecclesie Eboracensis*, Surtees Society 71, 75 (Durham 1880-3), 2 vols with, in vol. II, an 'Index antiphonarum' (cols 821-52), an 'Index capitulorum' (cols 853-8), an 'Index hymnorum et sequentiarum' (859-62), an 'Index invitatoriorum' (863-4), an 'Index prosarum' (865-6), an 'Index responsoriorum' (867-82), and an 'Index versiculorum' (883-6).

The Hereford Breviary is edited by **Walter Howard Frere** and **Langton E. G. Brown**, *The Hereford Breviary*, Henry Bradshaw Society 26, 40, 46 (London 1904-15), 3 vols, with indices of antiphons, benedictions, Bible lessons, collects, liturgical Gospels, homilies, hymns and proses, invitatories, processions, responds, rubrics, and saints, and a table of feasts and psalms, in III, 93-268.

Medieval Liturgists

So far, we have been concerned with the liturgy as an important repository of traditional imagery, and a likely means of its dissemination in
medieval civilization; in addition, however, the liturgy itself is given
highly symbolic interpretations by medieval liturgists, who thus
become a further major repository of such imagery. By far the greatest
single liturgical work of the Middle Ages is the *Rationale divinorum
officiorum* written between 1285 and 1291 by **William Duranti
(Guilielmus Durandus)**, the importance of which for the study of traditional Christian imagery can hardly be overstated. It consists of eight
books: 1, 'De ecclesia et partibus ejus'; 2, 'De ministris et ordinibus';
3, 'De indumentis'; 4, 'De missa'; 5, 'De divinis officiis in genere'; 6,
'De officiis dominicarum'; 7, 'De sanctorum festivitate'; 8, 'De com-
puto et calendario.' Though there is no critical edition, it has been
printed ninety-four times, with varying indices; the most recent edition
is that of Naples, 1859, with a detailed table of contents by book and
chapter and an 'Index rerum ac verborum' on pp 847-82.

During the Middle Ages the *Rationale* was translated into Spanish,
French, and German. The fourteenth-century German translation is
edited by **G.H. Buijssen**, *Durandus' Rationale in spätmittelhoch-
deutscher Übersetzung*, Studia Theodisca 6, 13, 15-16 (Assen 1966-
1983), 4 vols; the French translation of 1372 by Jean Golein is printed
as *Le Racional des divins offices, translaté de latin en françois ... par
frère Jehan Goulain ...* (Paris: Anthoine Vérard, 1503). A modern
French translation by **Charles Barthélemy**, *Rational, ou Manuel des
divins offices* (Paris 1854), 5 vols, is accompanied by useful notes.

There are two partial translations into English: of bk 1 by **John
Mason Neale** and **Benjamin Webb**, *The Symbolism of Churches and
Church Ornaments* (3rd ed. London 1906); and of bk 3 by **T.H.
Passmore**, *The Sacred Vestments* (London 1899).

Among countless other medieval liturgists, the following are the most
promising for our purposes:

1/ **Isidore of Seville** (7th C), *De ecclesiasticis officiis*, PL 83, cols
737-826.

2/ **Rabanus Maurus** (8th-9th C), *De clericorum institutione*, PL
107, cols 293-420.

3/ **Amalarius of Metz** (9th C), *Liber officialis*, ed. Jean-Michel Hanssens, *Amalarii episcopi opera liturgica omnia*, Studi e testi 138-40 (Vatican 1948-50) vol. II (PL 105, cols 985-1242, title *De ecclesiasticis officiis*), with lesser liturgical works in vols I and III; in III, 323-480 are an 'Index documentorum' (including indices 'E sacra scriptura,' 'Ex ecclesiasticorum aliorumque virorum scriptis,' and 'E libris liturgicis'), an 'Index formularum seu initiorum,' an 'Index verborum philologicus,' and an 'Index rerum liturgicus.'

4/ **Pseudo-Alcuin**, *De divinis officiis* (11th C?), PL 101, cols 1173-1286.

5/ **Berno of Reichenau** (11th C), *Libellus de quibusdam rebus ad missae officium pertinentibus*, PL 142, cols 1055-80; followed by three treatises on times in the liturgical year, cols 1080-98.

6/ **John of Avranches** (11th C), *De officiis ecclesiasticis*, PL 147, cols 27-116; followed by miscellaneous other works by various authors, cols 117-262, with an index in cols 1311-24.

7/ **Bernold of Constance** (11th C), *Micrologus*, PL 151, cols 973-1022; preceded by a liturgical miscellany entitled 'Monumenta liturgica,' cols 807-974.

8/ **Rupert of Deutz** (12th C), *Liber de divinis officiis*, ed. **Hrabanus Haacke**, CCLCM 7 (Turnhout 1967), with an 'Index locorum sacrae scripturae,' an 'Index auctorum,' an 'Index liturgicus,' an 'Initia locorum liturgiae,' and an 'Ordo rerum' (pp 421-77). Appears also in PL 170, cols 11-332.

9/ **Honorius Augustodunensis** (12th C), *Gemma animae*, PL 172, cols 542-738; *Sacramentarium*, ibid. cols 737-806; *Speculum ecclesiae*, ibid. cols 807-1108.

10/ **Pseudo-Hugh of St Victor**, *Speculum de mysteriis ecclesiae* (12th C), PL 177, cols 335-80; **Robert Paululus** (?), *De caeremoniis, sacramentis, officiis, et observationibus ecclesiasticis* (12th C), ibid. cols 381-456; and **Richard of Wedinghauser** (12th C), *Libellus de canone mystici libaminis*, ibid. cols 455-70.

11/ **John Beleth** (12th C), *Summa de ecclesiasticis officiis*, ed. **Heribert Douteil**, CCLCM 41-41A (Turnhout 1976), 2 vols. Vol. 41A contains the text along with an 'Index locorum sacrae scripturae,' an 'Index scriptorum,' an 'Index formularum seu initiorum,' and an 'Index personarum et rerum' (pp 325-433); vol. 41 contains various catalogues and an important appendix of later additions to the *Summa* (pp 1-181). Appears also under the title *Rationale divinorum officiorum* in PL 202, cols 13-166; and with the *Rationale* of Durandus (Naples 1859) pp 753-845.

12/ **Prepositinus** (Praepositinus) **of Cremona** (12th C), *Tractatus de officiis*, ed. **James A. Corbett**, Publications in Mediaeval Studies, the Mediaeval Institute, University of Notre Dame 21 (Notre Dame 1969).

13/ **Sicard of Cremona**, *Mitrale* (1200), PL 213, cols 13-436.

14/ **Innocent III** (12th-13th C), *De sacro altaris mysterio*, PL 217, cols 763-916.

15/ **Radulf de Rivo** (14th C), *Liber de officiis ecclesiae* and lesser works *De canonum observantia liber* and *Tractatus de psalterio observando,* ed. **Cunibert Mohlberg**, *Radulf de Rivo: Der letzte Vertreter der altrömischen Liturgie*, Université de Louvain, Recueil de travaux ... des Conférences d'histoire et de philologie 29, 42 (Louvain and Münster 1911-15) vol. II, with an index of biblical references (pp 282-5), an index of quotations from other authors (286-91), an index of proper names (292-7), and a liturgical index (298-309).

Further titles and additional information about medieval liturgical writers can be found in **Adolph Franz**, *Die Messe im deutschen Mittelalter* (Freiburg i.B. 1902) pp 333-740; Vogel, *Introduction* pp 10-15; a 'Lexique des principaux liturgistes' by René Aigrain, appended to his *Liturgia* pp 1033-88; and *Lexikon für Theologie und Kirche* VI, 1096.

The liturgical writers who appear in the PL are analyzed in various indices: an **'Index liturgicus,'** arranged alphabetically by subject, in PL 219, cols 1031-42; an **'Index de festis,'** arranged topically as a whole and chronologically within each section, in PL 220, cols 465-536; lists of **'Opera liturgica,'** PL 218, cols 957-60, and **'Scripta liturgica,'** ibid. cols 1037-40; and a guide to further liturgical indices in *Elucidatio in 235 tabulas Patrologiae Latinae* (Rotterdam 1952) pp 50-1.

Finally, there is a large anthology of medieval liturgical works compiled by **Melchior Hittorp**, *De divinis catholicae ecclesiae officiis et mysteriis, varii vetustorum aliquot ecclesiae patrum ac scriptorum ecclesiasticorum libri* ... (Paris 1610, repr. Farnborough 1970), including selections from many of the writers mentioned above, with a 52-page index of subjects and words following col. 1452.

A liturgical commentary of a somewhat different kind is the *Ecclesiale*, a poem of 2002 lines expounding the liturgical year and full of miscellaneous lore, written around 1200 by **Alexander of Villedieu**, and edited and translated by **L.R. Lind**, *Ecclesiale by Alexander of Villa Dei* (Lawrence, Kansas 1958).

A programme of symbolism closely related to the liturgy is that of the church building itself, developed particularly by Honorius, Sicard, and Durandus; its fullest medieval treatment is by Durandus, *Rationale* I (trans. Neale and Webb, *Symbolism of Churches*). The fullest modern study is by **Joseph Sauer**, *Symbolik des Kirchengebäudes und seiner Ausstattung in der Auffassung des Mittelalters, mit Berücksichtigung von Honorius Augustodunensis, Sicardus, und Durandus* (2nd ed. Freiburg i.B. 1924; repr. Münster i.W. 1964), with a useful 'Ortsregister' and 'Personen- und Sachregister.' Concise surveys are included by de Lubac, *Exégèse médiévale* (for which see p. 15 above) II/ii, 41-60; and by **Hennig Brinkmann**, *Mittelalterliche Hermeneutik* (Tübingen 1980) pp 123-32.

Possible Approaches

The ultimate question, of course, is whether this whole terrifying accumulation can be searched in any systematic way so as to contribute to our understanding of medieval literary imagery. Though, as I have emphasized, it is by its very nature much less tractable than biblical commentaries, compendia, and the like, some approaches can be contrived. Most obviously, concordances and indices, where they exist, will provide a method broadly analogous to that which I suggested for the 'floating' scriptural or exegetical image in chapter 1.

A particularly useful general tool is provided by **Albert Blaise**, *Le Vocabulaire latin des principaux thèmes liturgiques* (Turnhout [1966]), consisting basically of two parts: an elaborate, topically organized catalogue of liturgical themes and their sources (pp 113-632), with a detailed table of its contents (633-9); and an alphabetical index of words found in these themes, with numbers referring to paragraphs in the catalogue (pp 23-112).

For the early period, a catalogue compiled by **Georg Manz**, *Ausdrucksformen der lateinischen Liturgiesprache bis ins elfte Jahrhundert*, Texte und Arbeiten, 1. Abt.: Beiträge zur Ergründung des älteren lateinischen christlichen Schrifttums und Gottesdienstes, Suppl. 1 ([Beuron] 1941), offers an alphabetical list of prominent expressions in the liturgy till the eleventh century, each accompanied by quotations from the places it occurs.

An elaborate set of concordances by **Jean Deshusses** and **Benoit Darragon**, *Concordances et tableaux pour l'étude des grands sacramentaires*, Spicilegii Friburgensis subsidia 9 (Fribourg 1982-3), 3 vols in 6 pts, covering the great early sacramentaries, contains in vol. I an alphabetical index of liturgical formulas ('pièces'), with a supplement (pp 262-303) correlating the item-numbers of the concordance with the location of the formulas in each of the individual sacramentaries; in vol. II, synoptic tables showing correspondences and differences among the various sacramentaries; and in the four parts of vol. III, a massive verbal concordance.

A proposed liturgical concordance in many volumes is represented so far only by a concordance to the post-Tridentine Roman missal: **André Pflieger**, *Liturgicae orationis concordantia verbalia: Prima pars, Missale Romanum* (Rome 1964). A slender and not very inclusive (or rewarding) index to the modern Roman breviary is the anonymous *Index breviarii Romani* (London 1939).

There are, however, further possibilities. My preceding outline of prominent liturgical texts has mentioned many specialized indices of various kinds; and the list can of course be expanded greatly by the many such indices found in other individual liturgical works. For the use of the Bible in the modern Roman liturgy, there is in addition an extremely valuable general catalogue, following the order of Scripture and identifying each appearance of it in the liturgy: **Karl Marbach**, *Carmina scripturarum, scilicet antiphonas et responsoria ex sacro scripturae fonte in libros liturgicos sanctae ecclesiae Romanae* (Strassburg 1907, repr. Hildesheim 1963), with an informative introduction, an 'Appendix carminum ex ss ecclesiae patribus' (pp 538-40 and index p. 591), an 'Index librorum sacrae scripturae' (549), various indices 'Psalmorum et canticorum' (550-3), an 'Index alphabeticus omnium s. scripturae carminum' (554-90), and an 'Index alphabeticus festorum proprii sanctorum' (592-5). If one's initial lead is a biblical verse or passage, Marbach's volume or some of the biblical indices to individual liturgical texts cited above – like, for example, those to Warren's translation of the Sarum Missal and to the Procter-Wordsworth edition of the Sarum Breviary – will be potentially useful.

Another promising handle is provided by the fact that books and passages of the Bible, as well as other images, are traditionally connected in various ways with particular seasons, days, or feasts in the liturgical calendar, and often to specific parts of the liturgy for these times or dates. Once an image or theme has been found attached to a particular time or liturgical context, it can of course be checked for more or less systematically in missals, breviaries, commentaries on the liturgy, and other liturgical books. Though I know of no dependable method for discovering such connections in the first place, there are some large fundamental patterns worth bearing in mind. For example, by a scheme known as *lectio continua,* certain books and parts of Scripture are traditionally read at particular times in the liturgical year; this plan, as found in the Epistles and Gospels of various times and rites, is fully treated by **G. Godu** in his articles **'Epitres'** and **'Evangiles,'** *DACL* v/i, 245-344 and 852-923 respectively, with an elaborate table for the Epistles in cols 335-42.

Commentary on the Epistles of the Roman Mass for the entire liturgical year, in the period covered by the PL, is analyzed in an **'Index concionatorius in epistolas quae inter missarum solemnia leguntur per anni circulum, juxta ritum Romanum,'** PL 221, cols 49-60; and on the Gospels, in an **'Index concionatorius in evangelia ...,'** ibid. cols 59-70.

A type of compilation common in the early sixteenth century contains the Epistles and Gospels for either the entire liturgical year or some significant part of it, accompanied by the commentary of one of the major exegetes. Examples are a collection of Epistles and Gospels for the entire year with the comment of Hugh of St Cher, *Hugonis de Sancto Charo ... Postilla super epistolas et evangelia de tempore quam de sanctis, per totum anni circulum* (Paris: Iohan Petit, 1506), 3 vols; and a collection of Epistles and Gospels for the quadragesimal season with the comment of Nicholas of Lyre and others, *Postilla seu expositio litteralis & moralis Nicolai de Lyra ordinis minorum super epistolas & evangelia quadragesimalia, cum questionibus fratris Antonii Betontini eiusdem ordinis, necnon Alexandri de ales ...* (Venice: Alexander de Bindonis, 1519). A somewhat similar modern work is *The Sunday Sermons of the Great Fathers,* trans. and ed. **M.F. Toal** (Chicago 1957; first publ. as *Patristic Homilies on the Gospels,* Chicago 1955), 4 vols, which assembles in translation the homilies of the Fathers and Doctors on the Sunday Gospels, along with translations of the relevant commentaries from Aquinas's *Catena aurea.*

In the *lectiones* of the Roman, Sarum, Hereford, and York missals, Isaias is prominent during Advent; Isaias and Romans at the Epiphany; the Pauline Epistles on Sundays and passages from the Old Testament on weekdays during the septuagesimal season; the Catholic Epistles on Sundays and the Pauline Epistles on weekdays during the Easter season; the Acts of the Apostles during the week of Pentecost; the Catholic Epistles on Sundays and the Pauline Epistles on weekdays during the time from Pentecost to the third Sunday after Pentecost; and the Pauline Epistles on both Sundays and weekdays between the fourth and twenty-fifth Sundays after Pentecost. In the office of matins in the Roman, Sarum, York, and Hereford breviaries, Isaias is used from the beginning of Advent to the Epiphany; the Pauline Epistles from the first Sunday after the Octave of the Epiphany to Septuagesima Sunday; Genesis from Septuagesima Sunday to the third week of the quadragesimal season; Exodus during the fourth week of the quadragesimal season; Jeremias and Lamentations during Passiontide; Acts (Roman) and the Apocalypse (Sarum, York, Hereford) during the first week after Easter; the Apocalypse, the Epistle of James, I John (in Hereford, I Peter), and Acts from the second week after Easter to Trinity Sunday; the Books of Kings (I-IV Roman, I Sarum, I-II York and Hereford) from Trinity Sunday to the beginning of August; Proverbs, Ecclesiastes, Wisdom, and Ecclesiasticus during August; Job, Tobias, Esther, and Judith during September; Maccabees (I-II Roman, I Sarum, York, Hereford) during October; and Ezechiel, Daniel, and the minor prophets during November. (Within matins, this pattern is particularly apt to be violated on Sundays; and hours other than matins vary so greatly in their uses of Scripture that a meaningful pattern is difficult to establish.)

Finally, if one's problem is in a literary work whose date and provenance are fairly well established, it may be possible simply to survey the surviving liturgy of that time and place, making judicious use of Pfaff's *MLL* along with bibliographies like those of Weale and Bohatta on the missal and breviary. Particular problems will, it is hoped, combine with ingenuity to suggest other approaches.

3

Hymns

Another great repository of traditional imagery, intimately related to the liturgy and in some ways inseparable from it, is formed by the medieval hymns and sequences (the latter often known as 'proses'). The difference between the hymn and the sequence, though interesting and important in other contexts, is of no real significance for our present purpose. Very briefly, hymns are simply the songs which from the earliest time of the Church were attached to its public worship; sequences or proses originated in the ninth century, as texts written to accompany what had hitherto been a wordless musical extension of the final -*a* of the *Alleluia* at the end of the gradual or antiphon sung between the Epistle and Gospel in festal seasons (e.g. see below the article 'Latin Hymnody' in Julian, *Dictionary of Hymnology* pp 640-9). Though by the late Middle Ages hymns and sequences were sometimes indistinguishable, the general characteristics of the sequence are its precise attachment to the Mass and to specific times in the liturgical year, and the characteristic parallelism of its structure and music. Throughout this chapter I will use 'hymn' as the generic term, embracing also the sequence or prose.

Like the liturgy at large, hymns must have been an extremely popular channel for the dissemination of traditional imagery. Much of what I have said about the difficulties of using the liturgy for interpreting literary imagery will of course apply to them as well. Their total bulk and complexity, however, is much less than that of the liturgy as a whole; and apart from their liturgical contexts they are in effect collections of poems, and so are at least subject to the kinds of indexing and systematic research that such collections allow. As a result, the problems they present are a bit less formidable.

An exhaustive bibliography of the medieval hymn through the nineteenth century (including the early commentaries and great collected editions preceding the *Analecta hymnica*) is assembled by **H. Leclercq** in his article '**Hymnes**,' *DACL* VI/ii, 2922-8.

The *Jahrbuch für Liturgik und Hymnologie* (1955ff) includes, along with its annual 'Literaturbericht zur Liturgik,' a 'Literaturbericht zur Hymnologie'; the hymns are also included, passim, in the annual bibliographies of the journals mentioned above in my chapter on the liturgy. A recent 'Hauptbibliographie' of around 5500 titles (to be greatly expanded) appears in Szövérffy's new *Repertorium* (see below), I, 63-293.

A useful selected bibliography is included in what is probably the best comprehensive account of the medieval hymn: **Josef Szövérffy**, *Die Annalen der lateinischen Hymnendichtung: Ein Handbuch*, Die lyrische Dichtung des Mittelalters (Berlin 1964-5), 2 vols (bibliography is in I, 35-41), to which may be added a useful collection of Szövérffy's articles, *Religious Lyrics of the Middle Ages: Hymnological Studies and Collected Essays*, Medieval Classics, Texts and Studies 15, 'Psallat chorus caelestium' (Berlin 1983).

An excellent fundamental bibliography, now partly outdated, accompanies **Ruth Ellis Messenger**'s brief sketch, *The Medieval Latin Hymn* (Washington, D.C. 1953) pp 123-34.

The medieval hymn in England, including the Anglo-Saxon period, is brilliantly covered by **Helmut Gneuss**, *Hymnar und Hymnen im englischen Mittelalter: Studien zur Überlieferung, Glossierung, und Übersetzung lateinischer Hymnen in England*, Buchreihe der *Anglia* 12 (Tübingen 1968), with various indices including an index of Latin hymns (pp 425-30) and an index of persons and subjects (434-9).

The standard dictionary or encyclopedia on hymns is by **John Julian**, *A Dictionary of Hymnology* (2nd ed. London 1907; repr. London 1915 and New York 1957, in 2 vols), with indices of first lines (pp 1307-1504 and 1730-60) and of authors, etc. (1505-21 and 1761-8).

The definitive catalogue of medieval Latin hymns down to 1550, now just underway, will be **Josef Szövérffy**'s *Repertorium hymnologicum novum*, Medieval Classics, Texts and Studies 16 (Berlin 1983ff), in 8 pts. The first volume of pt I, which has already appeared, contains an introduction (pp 3-23), the bibliography mentioned above

(63-293), and an essay 'Religiöse Dichtung als Kulturphänomen und Kulturleistung' (24-62); the full bibliography will appear in the third volume of pt I. Pt II will contain indices of authors and categories of hymns; III, an index of accompanying melodies; IV, an index of the contents and definitions of individual texts; V and VI, indices of manuscripts and proper names; VII, a catalogue of the most important themes, motifs, metaphors, images, and legends in the hymns (presumably of special importance for our purposes); and VIII, an index of meters and rhythms and a catalogue of forms.

For the time being, the standard inclusive catalogue of medieval hymns is **Ulysse Chevalier**'s antiquated *Repertorium hymnologicum: Catalogue des chants, hymnes, proses, séquences, tropes en usage dans l'église latine, depuis les origines jusqu'à nos jours* (Louvain and Paris 1892-1919), 6 vols. Vols I and II are an alphabetical catalogue of hymns by first lines. Vols III and IV are two independent supplements to this catalogue, and V contains its 'Addenda et corrigenda,' so that for a complete check vols I-II, III, IV, and V must all be separately consulted. Vol. VI is a series of indices: 'Festorum, sanctorum, etc.'; 'Auctorum, editorum, etc.'; 'Librorum liturgicum'; and 'Fontium bibliographicus.' Corrections and further information on a large scale are provided by **Clemens Blume**, *Repertorium repertorii: Kritischer Wegweiser durch U. Chevalier's Repertorium hymnologicum. Alphabetisches Register falscher, mangelhafter, oder irreleitender Hymnenanfänge und Nachweise ...*, Hymnologische Beiträge, Quellen und Forschungen zur Geschichte der lateinischen Hymnendichtung 2 (Leipzig 1901, repr. Hildesheim 1971).

Hymns found in early hymnaries generally and in English hymnaries through the sixteenth century are catalogued alphabetically by **James Mearns**, *Early Latin Hymnaries: An Index of Hymns in Hymnaries before 1100, with an Appendix from Later Sources* (Cambridge 1913).

There are also two mutually supplementary alphabetical catalogues of Latin poetry generally, which, though they include hymns as a matter of course, give them no particular emphasis and so are of marginal importance here: 1/ for the first three centuries B.C. and the first Christian millennium, **Dieter Schaller** and **Ewald Könsgen**, *Initia carminum Latinorum saeculo undecimo antiquiorum: Bibliographisches Repertorium für die lateinische Dichtung der Antike und des früh-*

eren Mittelalters (Göttingen 1977); and 2/ for the period 1000-1500, **Hans Walther,** *Initia carminum ac versuum medii aevi posterioris Latinorum: Alphabetisches Verzeichnis der Versanfänge mittellateinischer Dichtungen* (2nd ed. Göttingen 1969), with an index of names and subjects on pp 1151-86, and addenda by **Dieter Schaller** and **Jürgen Stohlmann** in *Mittellateinisches Jahrbuch* 7 (1972) 293-314, 8 (1973) 288-304, 9 (1974) 320-44, 12 (1977) 297-315, 15 (1980) 259-86, and 16 (1981) 409-41. A fuller and more recent tool of the same kind is **Otto Schumann's** *Lateinisches Hexameter-Lexikon: Dichterisches Formelgut von Ennius bis zum Archipoeta*, MGH Hilfsmittel 4 (Munich 1979-83), 6 pts, the last of which is an alphabetical 'Register' of initial and other significant words in their uninflected forms, supplementing the basic alphabetical listing by first lines.

The standard collected edition of medieval Latin hymns is the *Analecta hymnica medii aevi* (AH), ed. **Guido Maria Dreves** and **Clemens Blume** (Leipzig 1886-1922), 55 vols, which includes some 10,000 texts dating from 1060 to 1220, with full textual and other factual notes accompanying each hymn. Each volume has an index of first lines, and many have indices of authors and subjects of the hymns. In addition, there is now an *Analecta hymnica medii aevi: Register*, ed. **Max Lütolf** (Bern 1978), 2 vols in 3 – vol. I of which contains a comprehensive index of first lines, and II indices of 'Gattungen' (e.g. 'Abcdarius,' 'Alleluja,' 'Antiphona,' etc.; pp 9-56) and of 'Liturgische Bestimmungen' (in effect, subjects, e.g. 'Crux,' 'Gaudia BMV,' etc.; pp 59-224).

An extremely useful anthology of hymns from AH is *Ein Jahrtausend lateinischer Hymnendichtung: Eine Blütenlese aus den Analecta hymnica*, ed. **Dreves** and **Blume** (Leipzig 1909, repr. Bologna 1969), 2 vols, with informative introductions to the individual authors and hymns, and at the end of vol. II indices of hymns by author and by times in the liturgical year, an index of first lines, and a general index of persons, places, and subjects.

Earlier inclusive editions, as well as collections of more limited scope, are of course so numerous as to defy listing. Among the larger editions, those most worthy of mention are perhaps the *Thesaurus hymnologicus*, ed. **Hermann Adalbert Daniel** (2nd ed. Leipzig 1855-6), 5 vols, with 'Indices rerum' (in effect indices of images) in I,

357-61 and II, 394-403, and general indices of times in the liturgical year and first lines in V, 351-411; the *Lateinische Sequenzen des Mittelalters aus Handschriften und Drucken*, ed. **Joseph Kehrein** (Mainz 1873, reissued Hildesheim 1969), arranged topically, with a table of contents on pp X-XII; and the *Thesauris hymnologicis hactenus editis supplementum amplissimum*, ed. **E. Misset** and **W.H.J. Weale**, Analecta liturgica 2/1-2 (Lille and Bruges 1888-92), 2 vols, each with a 'Registrum festorum' to identify the hymns for a given feast.

Various more limited collections are valuable particularly for their annotation. Perhaps the best example is **A.S. Walpole**, *Early Latin Hymns*, Cambridge Patristic Texts (Cambridge 1922), which contains unusually detailed footnotes and an 'Index of Words' that includes words used figuratively; another is **Richard Chenevix Trench**, *Sacred Latin Poetry, Chiefly Lyrical* (3rd ed. London 1886), whose footnotes are often useful.

Among collections defined by a particular provenance or author, some particularly interesting examples are the Latin hymns of the Anglo-Saxon church, ed. Gneuss, *Hymnar und Hymnen* pp 265-413; the hymns of Notker, ed. **Wolfram von den Steinen**, *Notker der Dichter und seine geistige Welt* (Bern 1948), 2 vols, with an index 'Personen-Termini-Stichwörter' (including some images) in I, 626-40, and various tables and indices of times and first lines at the end of II; and *The Irish Liber hymnorum*, ed. and trans. **J.H. Bernard** and **R. Atkinson**, Henry Bradshaw Society 13-14 (London 1898), 2 vols.

A special word should be said about the sequences attributed to Adam of St Victor (12th C), which are by far the most intensely figurative produced during the Middle Ages and so constitute a particularly rich treasury of traditional imagery. The prolonged dispute about which of these sequences are really by Adam will probably never be completely resolved, and in any case is not relevant for our purposes; the problem is conveniently summarized by Szövérffy, *Annalen* II, 106ff, with a table (pp 107-8) of 48 sequences probably to be ascribed to Adam.

The first modern edition of sequences supposedly by Adam is by **Léon Gautier**, *Œuvres poétiques d'Adam de S.-Victor* (Paris 1858-9), 2 vols; though it is textually inadequate and includes many sequences no longer considered authentic, its notes are sometimes useful for an understanding of the biblical and exegetical imagery. Gautier's third edition, *Œuvres poétiques d'Adam de Saint-Victor: Texte critique* (Paris 1894), is textually sound, but includes no notes except textual ones.

Another useful edition, including the music, is that of **E. Misset** and **Pierre Aubry**, *Les Proses d'Adam de Saint-Victor: Texte et musique*, Mélanges de musicologie critique (Paris 1900), with an excellent chapter (pp 56-110) on 'Symbolisme des proses d'Adam de Saint-Victor.'

The best edition textually, though it includes other sequences as well, is by **Clemens Blume** and **H.M. Bannister**, *Liturgische Prosen des Übergangsstiles und der zweiten Epoche, insbesondere die dem Adam von Sanct Victor zugeschriebenen ...*, AH 54-5 (Leipzig 1915), with indices of subjects and first lines; further editions are cited by Szövérffy, *Annalen* II, 106, n. 257.

The sequences of Adam are translated by **Digby S. Wrangham**, *The Liturgical Poetry of Adam of St Victor* (London 1881), 3 vols, accompanied by the Latin texts of Gautier's first edition (which, as we have seen, include many sequences no longer thought to be by Adam); translations of some of Gautier's notes appear at the end of each volume.

Among many other highly figurative hymns of the twelfth and thirteenth centuries, we may notice for example those of Peter Abelard, ed. **Guido Maria Dreves**, *Hymnographi Latini: Lateinische Hymnendichter des Mittelalters*, vol. I, AH 48 (Leipzig 1905) pp 141-232 (conveniently listed by Szövérffy, *Annalen* II, 168-71); and more recently by **Joseph Szövérffy**, *Peter Abelard's Hymnarius Paraclitensis: An Annotated Edition with Introduction*, Medieval Classics, Texts and Studies 2-3 (Albany, N.Y. 1975), 2 vols, including an 'Index biblicus' (II, 279-82), along with valuable annotation and other apparatus.

The hymns of course play a prominent part in the liturgy, particularly in the missal and breviary, and so frequently acquire a traditional attachment to particular services or times in the liturgical year. The hymns of the medieval Roman missal and breviary, following the course of the liturgical year, are assembled in an antiquated collection by **Ulysse Chevalier**, *Poésie liturgique traditionelle de l'Eglise catholique en Occident, ou Recueil d'hymnes et de proses usitées au moyen âge et distribuées suivant l'ordre du bréviaire et du missel,*

Bibliothèque liturgique 2 (Tournai 1894), with an introduction (pp i-lxiv), a 'Calendrier du moyen âge' (lxv-lxviij), and indices of first lines and authors.

The hymns of the modern Roman missal and breviary are edited, with translations and a running commentary, by **Matthew Britt**, *The Hymns of the Breviary and Missal* (rev. ed. New York 1955); a simpler compilation is that by **Joseph Connelly**, *Hymns of the Roman Liturgy* (London 1957).

The hymns of the monastic breviary are analyzed in detail by **Aemeliana Löhr**, *Abend und Morgen ein Tag: Die Hymnen der Herrentage und Wochentage im Stundengebet* (Regensburg [1955]), with texts and translations of the hymns on pp 657-707.

An English version of the collection known as the 'New Hymnal' is edited from a single tenth-century manuscript by **Gernot R. Wieland**, *The Canterbury Hymnal, Edited from British Library MS. Additional 37517*, Toronto Medieval Latin Texts 12 (Toronto 1982), with a convenient brief sketch of the development from 'Old Hymnal' to 'New Hymnal' on pp 3-7 (a much fuller account is presented by Gneuss, *Hymnar und Hymnen* pp 10-83).

The Sarum Hymnal appears, along with the hymns included in the York and Hereford liturgies but not in the Sarum, in a useful but rare volume entitled *Hymnale secundum usum insignis ac praeclarae ecclesiae Sarisburiensis. Accedunt hymni quidam secundum usum matris ecclesiae Eboracensis et insignis ecclesiae Herford* [ed. **A.C. Wilson** and **Dr Stubbs**] (Littlemore 1850; copy at the Union Theological Seminary, New York), with a table showing the hymns used for each service in the Sarum rite (pp vii-xviii); a table 'Hymni secundum usum Ebor. qui non sunt secundum usum Sarum,' showing the services at which such hymns were used (xviii-xix); a table 'Hymni secundum usum Herford. qui non sunt secundum alios usus,' showing the services at which such hymns were used (xix-xx); and an index of all the hymns by first lines (xxi-xxvi). The hymns of the Sarum Breviary, along with other liturgical material, are translated as *The Hymner* (London 1905).

Two collections of hymns drawn from a variety of liturgical sources are edited by **John M. Neale**, *Hymni ecclesiae e breviariis quibusdam et missalibus Gallicanis, Germanis, Hispanis, Lusitanis desumpti* (Oxford 1851), and *Sequentiae ex missalibus Germanis, Anglicis, Gallicis, aliisque medii aevi, collectae* (London 1852).

Julian's *Dictionary* contains full lists of hymns appearing in various breviaries and the times in the liturgical year when they were used (pp 170-80); full lists of hymns with their sources in various *hymnaria* and the times in the liturgical year at which they were used (546-54); and full lists of sequences with their sources in the liturgy (1042-52). The hymns of the missal and breviary can, of course, be approached also by way of the various indices to editions of the missal and breviary themselves, mentioned in my preceding chapter.

The Middle Ages produced also a complex tradition of commentaries on the hymns of the liturgy, which can sometimes establish a traditional context for an image that may be of help in interpreting it elsewhere. The most popular such commentary is the schoolbook known as the *Expositio hymnorum,* a cumulative work apparently given its distinctive form in the twelfth century, which appears in a great number of early printed editions, sometimes accompanied by an *Expositio sequentiarum;* a version oriented to the hymns of the Sarum rite is the *Expositio hymnorum secundum usum Sarum*, ed. **Badius Ascensius** (Paris: André Bocard, 1502).

The best account of the *Expositio hymnorum,* its development, and its variants is by Gneuss, *Hymnar und Hymnen* pp 194-206; a shorter discussion is presented by **Judson B. Allen, 'Commentary as Criticism: Formal Cause, Discursive Form, and the Late Medieval Accessus,'** in *Acta Conventus Neo-Latini Lovaniensis: Proceedings of the First International Congress of Neo-Latin Studies, Louvain, 23-28 August 1971*, ed. **J. Ijsewijn** and **E. Kessler**, Humanistische Bibliothek I, Abhandlungen 20 (Munich 1973) pp 31-3. Fifteenth-century editions are listed by Bohatta, *Liturgische Bibliographie* ch. III, pp 40-3, and a few early sixteenth-century editions by Daniel, *Thesaurus hymnologicus* I, xvii-xviii.

A rather jejune 'Expositio hymnorum' finds its way into **John Marchesini**'s *Mammotrectus super bibliam* II, 15 (many eds; Stegmüller, *Repertorium* III, 378-80, #4777), a popular compendium of around 1300.

A particularly full fifteenth-century commentary is that of **Denis the Carthusian**, *Expositio hymnorum aliquot ecclesiasticorum* in *Opera omnia* XXXV, 17-131 – comprising expositions of 27 hymns, each running to several pages, with an outline of the *Expositio* itself (p. 673), and for the entire volume an index 'Loca s. scripturae praecipua' (pp 577-86) and an 'Index analyticus' (587-672).

The sixteenth century produced a number of further commentaries on the hymns, the best-known of which is by **Josse van Clichtove** (Iodocus Clichtoveus) in his *Elucidatorium ecclesiasticum ad officium ecclesiae pertinentia planius exponens, et quatuor libros complectens* (1st ed. Paris 1513, and others), bk I of which is a commentary on 140 liturgical hymns, II and III an explanation of various elements of the liturgy, and IV a commentary on 91 proses; the indices preceding the text include alphabetical indices of the hymns and proses by first lines along with lists according to the order of their appearance, and biblical citations are noted in the margins throughout. Clichtoveus's commentaries on the hymns and proses (bks I and IV) are expanded in his *Hymni et prosae, quae per totum annum in ecclesia leguntur* (Venice 1555).

An interesting collection of commentary on 63 sequences is a *Sequentiarum luculenta interpretatio ... per Joannem Adelphum physicum Argentinum collecta* (Strassburg 1513), with an alphabetical index by first lines on fol. 2v, and important subjects noted in the margins throughout. Other sixteenth-century commentaries are listed by Daniel, *Thesaurus* I, xviii-xxii; and Julian, *Dictionary* p. 652.

Just as with the liturgy, we are finally faced with the question of how substantial bodies of medieval hymns can be effectively searched for particular images; and once again the answer is much less satisfactory than for biblical commentaries and compendia. Indices of subjects and words (e.g. like the 'Indices rerum' in Daniel's *Thesaurus* and the 'Index of Words' in Walpole's *Early Latin Hymns*) can sometimes be used to find individual figures. Larger motifs can often be found through vol. II of the *Register* to AH and other subject indices. If the figure or motif in question is known to be attached to a particular service or time in the liturgical year, the hymns connected with that service or time can be identified fairly easily by way of the various indices and lists already described. Finally, we should not overlook the fact that the hymns, unlike the liturgy at large, are themselves brief compositions and normally present an unusually 'open' format on the page – so that, if the figure or motif one is looking for is important enough, it is quite possible to skim whole volumes of them without growing old in the process.

4
Sermons

Introductory

Medieval sermons and homilies constitute an almost inexhaustible repository of medieval tradition, as yet imperfectly explored and edited. Like the hymns and sequences they are of course related to the liturgy, and frequently exist as parts of 'sermon cycles' covering the entire liturgical year. Here for the first time, however, we encounter a body of material of which sizeable parts appear not in Latin but in the vernaculars. With regard to the difference between sermons and homilies, 'sermon' is generally taken to be the generic term, including broadly any address delivered to the audience of an ecclesiastical function. The homily is originally characterized by a much more intimate dependence on the liturgy, being essentially an exhortation based on some liturgical element, usually a passage of Scripture. In actual practice, however, the two terms seem often to have been employed more or less interchangeably; and the distinction between them is of course irrelevant for present purposes. In the following discussion I will use 'sermon' freely for both, except where there is some reason for employing the term 'homily.'

The most convenient general accounts of medieval sermons and preaching at large are probably those by **Johann Baptist Schneyer**, *Geschichte der katholischen Predigt* (Freiburg i.B. 1969) pp 17-230, with a bibliography and indices of manuscripts and preachers on pp 359-82; and especially **Jean Longère**, *La Prédication médiévale* (Paris 1983), with indices of scriptural citations (pp 267-8), treatises and sermons on Scripture (268-9), proper names (273-85), places (286-8), and manuscripts (289-90).

For the immense corpus of Latin sermons, the majority of which remain unedited, the basic research tool is **Schneyer's** *Repertorium der lateinischen Sermones des Mittelalters für die Zeit von 1150-1350*, Beiträge zur Geschichte der Philosophie und Theologie des Mittelalters 43/1-9 (Münster i.W. 1969ff), 9 pts to date. Pts I-V are a catalogue of sermons arranged alphabetically by author. Pts VI-VII catalogue sermons of councils, sermons of the great universities, sermons of various religious orders, sermons on the Scriptures (VII, 529-50), pastoral sermons, sermon-series known by title, and collections of 'prothemes' for sermons. Pts VIII-IX are a catalogue of anonymous sermons, arranged alphabetically according to the cities where the manuscripts are preserved. Individual sermons are identified throughout by their *incipits* (beginnings), which in most cases are 'themes' (usually scriptural quotations) – thus providing a massive, though for the time being rather unwieldy, list of biblical references. Pt X, not yet published, will be an 'Index initiorum,' or alphabetical index of these scriptural incipits, and so should increase immeasurably the value of the entire set for our purposes. ('Theme' and 'protheme' in sermons are fully described by Charland, *Artes praedicandi* [see p. 86 below] pp 111-35.) An informative introduction (I, 1-32) explains the use of the *Repertorium*, and includes a list of sigla (pp 17-21) which relate individual sermons to times of the liturgical year, particularly saints, etc.

A valuable adjunct to the *Repertorium* is **Schneyer's** earlier *Wegweiser zu lateinischen Predigtreihen des Mittelalters*, Bayerische Akademie der Wissenschaften, Veröffentlichungen der Kommission für die Herausgabe ungedruckter Texte aus der mittelalterlichen Geisteswelt 1 (Munich 1965), covering the period from the twelfth century to the beginning of the sixteenth. By contrast with the *Repertorium*, the *Wegweiser* is an alphabetical list of biblical 'themes' and text-incipits for the opening sermons of the four great groups within the liturgical year: Sunday sermons (*de tempore*); sermons concerning particular saints (*de sanctis*); sermons concerning the saints in general and special occasions (*de communi sanctorum*); and Lenten sermons (*de quadragesima*). There are an index to lists of incipits of the Latin sermons of scholastic preachers, arranged alphabetically by author (pp 547-55); a list of opening and closing formulas for sermons, arranged alphabetically by author (556-76); and an alphabetical index of authors (577-87), permitting the *Wegweiser* to be approached by way of author as well as *incipit*.

For the period preceding the twelfth century, a less elaborate though usable index of incipits is that of **Marco Vattasso**, *Initia patrum aliorumque scriptorum ecclesiasticorum Latinorum ex Mignei Patrologia et ex compluribus aliis libris* ..., Studi e testi 16-17 (Rome 1906-8, repr. 1959), 2 vols, which includes all works printed in the PL, including sermons, along with indices of authors and anonymous works.

The index volumes of the PL also contain a number of useful indices to sermons and homilies:

1/ Indices by books, chapters, and verses of the Bible: '**Index sermonum omnium de scripturis**,' PL 221, cols 19-28; and '**Index homiliarum omnium de scripturis**,' ibid. cols 39-42. Many sermons on chapters or passages of Scripture are included also in '**Index sacrae scripturae capitum ... quae commentariis et explanationibus ss patres elucidarunt**,' PL 219, cols 113-22.

2/ Indices by times in the liturgical year: '**Index omnium sermonum de tempore**,' PL 221, cols 27-32; and '**Index omnium homiliarum de tempore**,' ibid. cols 41-6.

3/ Indices by saints: '**Index sermonum omnium de sanctis**,' PL 221, cols 31-6; and '**Index homiliarum omnium de sanctis**,' ibid. cols 45-8.

4/ Indices by miscellaneous subjects: '**Index sermonum omnium de diversis**,' PL 221, cols 35-40; and '**Index homiliarum omnium de diversis**,' ibid. cols 49-50.

A list of the published medieval sermons in German, including editions but not secondary scholarship, is compiled by **Karin Morvay** and **Dagmar Grube**, *Bibliographie der deutschen Predigt des Mittelalters: Veröffentliche Predigten*, Münchener Texte und Untersuchungen zur deutschen Literatur des Mittelalters 47 (Munich 1974), with indices of Latin incipits (i.e. biblical and liturgical themes, along with their identifications), German incipits, biblical quotations arranged by book, chapter, and verse, and proper names (pp 221-363).

Old but still useful general studies (including both Latin and German preaching in Germany) are those of **R. Cruel**, *Geschichte der deutschen Predigt im Mittelalter* (Detmold 1879, repr. Darmstadt

1966), and **Anton Linsenmayer, *Geschichte der Predigt in Deutsch-land von Karl dem Grossen bis zum Ausgange des vierzehnten Jahr-hunderts*** (Munich 1886, repr. Frankfurt 1969); a more recent brief survey is presented by **Wolfgang Stammler, *Deutsche Philologie im Aufriss*** (2nd ed. Berlin 1957-62; repr. 1966-7) II, 980-1004, with a bibliography in cols 1096-8.

An outstanding edition of medieval German sermons is that by **Anton E. Schönbach, *Altdeutsche Predigten*** (Graz 1886-91, repr. Darmstadt 1964), 3 vols; the end of each volume contains extensive and valuable notes, a word index (vol. I only), a full and detailed subject index, an index of biblical citations, an index of patristic citations, and indices of times in the liturgical year.

Bibliography on medieval French sermons can be found in **Robert Bossuat, *Manuel bibliographique de la littérature française du moyen âge***, Bibliothèque Elzevirienne n.s., Etudes et documents (Melun 1951) pp 328-33 and 475-6, along with its *Supplément (1949-1953)* pp 75-6 and 101, and *Second supplément (1954-1960)* [with **Jacques Monfrin**] pp 79-80 and 99-101; and **D.C. Cabeen,** gen. ed., *A Critical Bibliography of French Literature*, vol. I: *The Mediaeval Period* by **Urban T. Holmes, Jr** (2nd ed. Syracuse, N.Y. 1952) pp 25-6.

Useful general studies are **L. Bourgain, *La Chaire française au XIIe siècle d'après les manuscrits*** (Paris 1879), with indices of preachers and manuscripts (pp 389-95); **A. Lecoy de la Marche, *La Chaire française au moyen âge, spécialement au XIIIe siècle*** (2nd ed. Paris 1886), with indices of sermons arranged alphabetically by author (pp 495-531), and by libraries and manuscripts (531-42); and especially **Michel Zink, *La Prédication en langue romane avant 1300*,** Nouvelle bibliothèque du moyen âge 4 (Paris 1976), with an alphabetical inventory of 688 sermons used (pp 481-524), an index of the sources of these sermons in manuscript sermon-collections (531-2), an index of sermons on times and saints (533-4), an index of exempla (535-7), and an up-to-date bibliography (539-60). Some notable editions of medieval French sermons that have appeared since the bibliographies of Bossuat and Holmes are **Robert de Gretham**'s versified cycle *Miroir, ou Les Evangiles des domnées*, ed. **Saverio Panunzio** (Bari 1967); *L'Œuvre oratoire française de Jean Courtecuisse*, ed. **Giuseppe di Stefano**, Università di Torino, Facoltà di lettere e filosofia, Filologia moderna 3 (Turin 1969); and **Jean Gerson,** *L'Œuvre française: Sermons et discours*, vol. VII/ii of *Œuvres complètes* ed. **P. Glorieux** (Paris 1960-71).

A complete list of Old English homilies, published and unpublished, is included in *A Plan for the Dictionary of Old English*, ed. **Roberta Frank** and **Angus Cameron** (Toronto 1973) pp 44-114. The outstanding collections are the homilies of Ælfric, those of Wulfstan, the Blickling Homilies, and the Vercelli Homilies; editions, plus some additional bibliography, are cited by **Fred C. Robinson,** *Old English Literature: A Select Bibliography*, Toronto Medieval Bibliographies 2 (Toronto 1970) pp 41-50 passim.

For the Middle English sermons, the best guide and bibliography is *A Manual of the Writings in Middle English, 1050-1400*, ed. **John Edwin Wells** (New Haven 1916) pp 271-303 and 803-7, along with Supplements I-IX (New Haven 1919-51), ch. V; and for the Wycliffite sermons, the revised edition by **J. Burke Severs** et al., *A Manual of the Writings in Middle English, 1050-1500* (New Haven 1967ff) II, 360-2 and 522-3.

The best comprehensive studies are those of **G.R. Owst,** *Preaching in Medieval England: An Introduction to Sermon Manuscripts of the Period c. 1350-1450* (Cambridge 1926), and *Literature and Pulpit in Medieval England* (2nd ed. Oxford 1961), the latter particularly full of interesting quotations from unpublished sermons.

A useful brief supplement on the preaching of the friars is added by **Homer G. Pfander,** *The Popular Sermon of the Friars in England* (New York University diss. 1937). An especially interesting collection of sermons in Middle English is edited by **Woodburn O. Ross,** *Middle English Sermons, Edited from British Museum MS. Royal 18 B.xxiii*, EETS 209 (London 1940).

Homiliaries

A discussion of the sermon leads naturally to a word about the homiliary – a collection of homilies for the entire liturgical year, made up of homilies drawn from various sources and conceived of as standard. Though no two completely identical manuscript homiliaries have ever been found, the two principal types are best represented by a homiliary attributed to Alanus of Farfa, and particularly the homiliary composed by Paul the Deacon at the command of Charlemagne.

The most comprehensive and useful guides to the various medieval homiliaries (including the two just mentioned) are two partly overlapping studies by **Réginald Grégoire**, *Les Homéliaires du moyen âge: Inventaire et analyse des manuscrits*, Rerum ecclesiasticarum documenta, Series maior, Fontes 6 (Rome 1966), with an informative introduction, full analyses of the contents of each homiliary, references to the printed editions of the individual homilies, a comparative table of the contents of the homiliaries (pp 231-6), and an alphabetical index of homilies by incipit (237-57); and *Homéliaires liturgiques médiévaux: Analyse de manuscrits*, Biblioteca degli 'Studi medievali' 12 (Spoleto 1980) – basically an analysis of the contents of many homiliaries, with an alphabetical index of individual homilies (pp 489-517), an index of biblical citations (518-20), indices of the names of people and places (521-32, 533-5), and an index of manuscripts (536-41).

A study of less inclusive scope is **Henri Barré's** *Les Homéliaires carolingiens de l'école d'Auxerre*, Studi e testi 225 (Vatican 1962), with an inventory of the manuscripts and the contents of each of the four great Auxerrian homiliaries (pp 143-208); comparative tables of times in the liturgical year, biblical verses, and incipits of various important homiliaries (209-35); an index of incipits (usually biblical 'themes,' pp 237-344); and a table of manuscripts (345-8). A very brief general account is given in the *Lexikon für Theologie und Kirche*, art. **'Homiliar,'** v, 465-6.

The contents of the two most important homiliaries, those of Alanus of Farfa and Paul the Deacon, are detailed by **J. Leclercq, 'Tables pour l'inventaire des homiliaires manuscrits,'** *Scriptorium* 2 (1948) 197-214, and by Grégoire, *Homéliaires* pp 17-108. The contents of the homiliary of Paul the Deacon are also listed by **Cyril L. Smetana, 'Aelfric and the Early Medieval Homiliary,'** *Traditio* 15 (1959) 165-80; and a later version appears in PL 95, cols 1159-1566, with some homilies printed in full and others represented by incipits. Another study by **Smetana, 'Paul the Deacon's Patristic Anthology,'** in *The Old English Homily and Its Backgrounds* ed. **Paul E. Szarmach** and **Bernard F. Huppé** (Albany, N.Y. 1978) pp 75-97, includes on pp 89-90 an index of the pericopes (biblical passages read according to a determined order in the liturgy) in the homilies of Paul's homiliary.

Artes praedicandi

Beginning with the thirteenth century, an important adjunct to the medieval sermon is the body of writings known as *artes praedicandi,* whose purpose is to help preachers in composing sermons. The term *artes praedicandi* is sometimes restricted to works whose purpose is basically rhetorical, and which are concerned primarily with the technique and composition of sermons. On the other hand, it can be thought of as embracing also a great range of works connected in various ways with the genesis of sermons – for example, collections of biblical 'themes,' collections of exempla, *distinctiones,* concordances, and the like, which often become identical with the compilations discussed above in chapter 1. Obviously, it is this latter miscellaneous category that will be more relevant for present purposes.

The standard introduction to the *artes praedicandi* is by **Th. M. Charland,** *Artes praedicandi: Contribution à l'histoire de la rhétorique au moyen âge,* Publications de l'Institut d'études médiévales d'Ottawa 7 (Paris 1936) – including a catalogue of authors and manuscripts and a detailed discussion of the makeup of a sermon, along with indices of proper names, incipits, and manuscripts. As the title hints, however, it is severely restricted to works concerning the technique and composition of sermons, so that its usefulness for our purposes is quite limited.

A more inclusive catalogue of works composed for the help of preachers is offered by **Harry Caplan,** *Mediaeval Artes praedicandi: A Hand-List* and *Mediaeval Artes praedicandi: A Supplementary Hand-List,* Cornell Studies in Classical Philology 24-5 (Ithaca, N.Y. 1934 and 1936), both with indices of authors and inventories of manuscripts.

The major alphabetical preachers' aids are enumerated by **H.G. Pfander** in his *Popular Sermon* and in **'The Mediaeval Friars and Some Alphabetical Reference-Books for Sermons,'** *Medium Ævum* 3 (1934) 19-29; and by **Christina von Nolcken, 'Some Alphabetical Compendia and How Preachers Used Them in Fourteenth-Century England,'** *Viator* 12 (1981) 271-88, with an outline of a sermon constructed by *distinctiones* (pp 280-1) and a list of alphabetical preachers' compendia (283-5). (The compendium known as the *Rosarium theologiae* or *Floretum* has been included among the *distinc-*

tiones discussed in chapter 1.) Though the diversity of such works is difficult to represent adequately, I cite four particularly interesting examples:

1/ **John Bromyard** (14th C), *Summa predicantium*, an extremely popular encyclopedia for preachers, arranged alphabetically. The earliest edition ([Basel: Johann Amerbach, not after 1484], 2 vols) includes at the beginning of vol. I a long 'Tabula realis,' (a list of chapters with a brief analysis of each) and a shorter 'Tabula vocalis' (an alphabetical index of words, including a great many plants, birds, and animals). The latest edition (Antwerp 1614, 2 pts) includes summaries of the beginnings of individual chapters; at the beginning of pt 1 a table of chapters and a list of the Gospels for Sundays of the liturgical year, drawn from the *Summa* itself; and at the end of pt 2 a full index.

2/ **Thomas of Ireland** (13th-14th C), *Manipulus florum* (for editions, see Rouse and Rouse [below] pp 243-5), an alphabetical collection of extracts for the use of preachers. It is treated in great detail – along with its two major thirteenth-century sources, the *Flores paradysi* and the *Liber exceptionum*, and many minor sources – by **Richard H. Rouse** and **Mary A. Rouse**, *Preachers, Florilegia, and Sermons: Studies on the Manipulus florum of Thomas of Ireland*, Studies and Texts 47 (Toronto 1979), with an annotated edition of the list of authors and works found appended to the *Manipulus florum* itself (pp 251-301), an index of the incipits in this list (301-10), and an index of the authors and works quoted in the *Manipulus florum* (408-36).

3/ **Nicholas de Byard** (13th C), printed under the title *Dictionarius pauperum, omnibus predicatoribus verbi pernecessarius, in quo multum succincte continentur materie seu sermones singulis festiuitatibus totius anni, tam de tempore quam de sanctis accomodande, vt in tabula huius operis facile et lucide cognoscetur* (Cologne: Retro Minores [Martin von Werden?], 1501; for other eds see Stegmüller, *Repertorium* IV, 18, #5695). This popular work, which is extracted from Nicholas's still unprinted *Distinctiones* for the use of preachers, consists of two parts: the 'Summula aurea,' a dictionary arranged alphabetically; and the *tabula* mentioned in the title, explaining which chapters are appropriate for times in the liturgical year.

4/ **John of Wales** (13th C), *Summa collationum* or *Communiloquium* ([Ulm: Johann Zainer], 1[4]81; for other eds, and eds of John's other works, see **Andrew G. Little**, *The Grey Friars in Oxford* [Oxford

1892] pp 144-51, and *Studies in English Franciscan History* [Manchester 1917] pp 174-92), intended as a fund of edifying material for either preaching or informal conversation. It is arranged topically, but in most editions is prefaced by a sizeable alphabetical index; the *Communiloquium siue Summa collationum Johannis Gallensis* reprinted in Phoenix Series 1 (Wakefield 1964) is from an abbreviated version (Strassburg: Johannis de Quedlinburg, 1489) and has no index.

Exempla

In sermons from the twelfth century onward, an element of special interest for our purposes is the *exemplum* – a brief narrative or description used within the sermon to illustrate or support a doctrinal or moral point. The fullest study of medieval exempla is by **J.-Th. Welter**, *L'Exemplum dans la littérature religieuse et didactique du moyen âge*, Bibliothèque d'histoire ecclésiastique de la France (Paris and Toulouse 1927), with a list of manuscripts containing collections of exempla (pp 477-502) and a bibliography of printed collections and related medieval works (503-14); **Welter**'s earlier work *La Tabula exemplorum secundum ordinem alphabeti: Recueil d'exempla compilé en France à la fin du XIIIe siècle*, Thesaurus exemplorum 3 (Paris 1926) provides an alphabetical index of exemplum-subjects, though more restricted in time and place.

An alphabetical catalogue of 5400 medieval exempla, based on 37 major collections available in print, is compiled by **Frederic C. Tubach**, *Index exemplorum: A Handbook of Medieval Religious Tales*, FF Communications vol. 86, no. 204 (Helsinki 1969), with a 'Cross-Reference Index' of subjects on pp 409-515.

Claude Bremond, **Jacques Le Goff**, and **Jean-Claude Schmitt**, *L''Exemplum,'* Typologie des sources du moyen âge occidental 40, A-VI, C.9 (Turnhout 1982), present a brief comprehensive treatment of the exemplum in all its aspects, including a valuable bibliography (pp 17-26); particularly relevant for our purposes is the bibliography of 'Editions et répertoires' (17-20).

Medieval exempla in England are surveyed by **Joseph Albert Mosher**, *The Exemplum in the Early Religious and Didactic Literature of England* (New York 1911).

Among the many collections of exempla produced during the thirteenth and fourteenth centuries (treated by Welter, *L'Exemplum* pp 211-375), the largest and most important is **Etienne de Bourbon's** *Tractatus de diversis materiis praedicabilibus* (13th C), partially edited by **A. Lecoy de la Marche,** *Anecdotes historiques: Légendes et apologues tirés du recueil inédit d'Etienne de Bourbon* (Paris 1877), with a French summary on pp xxviii-xlviii.

Of particular interest also are the exempla drawn from the sermons of Jacques de Vitry (13th C), ed. **Goswin Frenken,** *Die Exempla des Jacob von Vitry,* Quellen und Untersuchungen zur lateinischen Philologie des Mittelalters 5/i (Munich 1914), and in more inclusive and less critical form, with translations, by **Thomas Frederick Crane,** *The Exempla or Illustrative Stories from the Sermones vulgares of Jacques de Vitry* (London 1890), both with alphabetical indices of exempla; and a *Liber exemplorum ad usum praedicantium, saeculo XIII compositus a quodam fratre minore Anglico de provincia Hiberniae,* ed. **A.G. Little,** British Society of Franciscan Studies 1 (Aberdeen 1908), with indices of persons and places, and of authors and books cited.

The exemplum shades off inevitably into other types of story, particularly the fable. The fullest collection of medieval fables is by **Léopold Hervieux,** *Les Fabulistes latins depuis le siècle d'Auguste jusqu'à la fin du moyen âge* (Paris 1884-99), 5 vols, all with useful tables of contents.

A favourite source for exempla is the beast-fable; for our purposes, the two most pertinent works on it are probably **Klaus Grubmüller,** *Meister Esopus: Untersuchungen zu Geschichte und Funktion der Fabel im Mittelalter,* Münchener Texte und Untersuchungen zur deutsche Literatur des Mittelalters 56 (Zurich 1977), with extensive bibliography and indices, and **Fritz Peter Knapp,** *Das lateinische Tierepos,* Erträge der Forschung 121 (Darmstadt 1979). A new *Lexikon der Erzählforschung,* reportedly underway, was not yet available at the time of writing.

Possible Approaches

Here again, just as with the liturgy and the hymns and sequences, we are faced with the problem of how a large and unwieldy repository, for which there are no general analytical indices, can be systematically used toward the interpretation of particular images and motifs; and the possibilities that suggest themselves will be similarly unsatisfactory. Except for an occasional individual edition, the approach by way of subject-indices is not very rewarding – though compilations like Bromyard's *Summa predicantium* and Nicholas's *Dictionarius pauperum* do at least offer what are in effect indices of preaching material. A partial access to the exegesis of biblical passages in sermons is provided by the indices to the PL; less conveniently, by the biblical 'themes' which form part of the incipits listed in Schneyer's *Repertorium* and *Wegweiser;* and by the indices of individual editions like Schönbach's *Altdeutsche Predigten*. If an image or motif can be related to a time in the liturgical year, the countless sermon cycles and homiliaries will of course offer rich ground for exploration; a convenient guide to the homilies of the Fathers and Doctors on the Sunday Gospels is Toal's *Sunday Sermons* (discussed above on p. 69). If a motif has narrative elements, it may be worth checking on in the various indices to the exempla. Finally, when dealing with a work of established date and provenance, judicious reading in the known sermons of that time and place may be fruitful. Other methods will, as always, be suggested by the nature of individual problems.

5
Visual Arts

Introductory

A particularly attractive repository of traditional imagery is the iconography of the visual arts – sculpture, wood- and ivory-carving, manuscript illumination, wall-painting, tapestries, and the like. In itself, this body of material would seem to present greater difficulties than any of those we have considered so far, made up as it is of single unique objects scattered throughout Europe and America; a number of useful research-tools, however, make it considerably easier to wield than either the liturgy, the hymns, or the sermons.

A general bibliography of sorts for the past fifty-odd years appears in the *Répertoire d'art et d'archéologie* (1910ff) – which, beginning with vol. 32 (1927) and occasionally before that, includes a section indexing works on iconography. A sporadic attempt at a bibliography till 1968 (not confined to the medieval period or to Christian art) can be found in **Manfred Lurker**'s *Bibliographie zur Symbolkunde*, Bibliotheca bibliographica Aureliana 12, 18, 24 (Baden-Baden 1964-1968) I, 143-70, and III, 481-90, 'Kunstgeschichte-Archäologie-Prähistorie'; and for the time since 1968 in his annual *Bibliographie zur Symbolik, Ikonographie, und Mythologie: Internationales Referateorgan* (Baden-Baden 1968ff), 16 vols through 1983, which present brief summaries of books and articles (again, not exclusively medieval or Christian), with indices of authors and subjects at the end of each volume.

The most immediately useful guides to medieval Christian iconography are, however, works on Christian iconography at large, which usually give major emphasis to the motifs found in medieval art. Such works can be divided broadly into two kinds – those arranged topically, and those arranged alphabetically – which in turn offer themselves more or less naturally to the two 'research situations' discussed in chapter 1. If one starts with, say, a particular biblical incident (e.g. the Baptism of Christ), his most profitable initial approach will probably be through a work organized topically; if he has before him a concept or image lacking any particular context (e.g. a star) he will do better to begin with an alphabetical work.

Guides Organized Topically

Among the iconographic guides arranged topically, the most generally useful is **Gertrud Schiller**'s *Ikonographie der christlichen Kunst* (Gütersloh 1966-76, 2nd ed. rev. 1969ff, 3rd ed. rev. 1981ff), originally announced as 5 vols, of which four have appeared as of mid-1985. Vols I-II have been translated from the second edition by **Janet Seligman**, *Iconography of Christian Art* (New York 1971-2), but no further volumes of this translation are planned. Vol. I contains the Incarnation, Childhood, Baptism, Temptation, Transfiguration, and Works and Miracles of Christ; II, the Passion; III, the Resurrection and Ascension; IV/i, the Church; and IV/ii, Mary. Vol. V, which was to cover the Last Judgment and the Old Testament, has not appeared. The iconography of saints is not included. Primary emphasis is on medieval art, with some attention to Mannerist and Baroque art and none at all to the nineteenth and twentieth centuries. Treatment of the motifs takes the form of a continuous exposition, with useful footnotes; each volume includes between 400 and 800 excellent illustrations. In both German and English editions, each volume contains a select bibliography and an 'Index of Biblical Texts [vol. I, Biblical and Legendary Texts] Cited.' In addition, each volume of the German edition has an 'Ikonographisches Stichwortverzeichnis'; vol. II of the English edition introduces a 'Thematic Index to Volumes 1 and 2,' and vol. III of the German edition adds an 'Orts- und Namenverzeichnis.' The second and third German editions include only the early volumes; the revisions appear negligible for practical purposes, and the apparatus remains unchanged so far as I can see. A separate *Registerbeiheft zu den Bänden 1 bis 4,2* by **Rupert Schreiner** (Gütersloh 1980), evidently based on the second edition, offers an index of 'Ausserbiblische Quellen,' a 'Personenverzeichnis,' and a 'Topographisches Verzeichnis.'

An older work of the same general kind, now somewhat out of date, is that of **Karl Künstle**, *Ikonographie der christlichen Kunst* (Freiburg i.B. 1926-8), 2 vols, divided into 4 bks: I, 'Ikonographische Prinzipienlehre'; II, 'Ikonographie der didaktischen Hilfsmotive,' including things like beast-symbolism, motifs from calendar illustration, the Seven Liberal Arts, the Virtues and Vices, etc.; III, 'Ikonographie der Offenbarungstatsachen des Neuen und Alten Testaments'; and IV, 'Ikonographie der Heiligen,' arranged alphabetically. There are 672 illustrations; vol. I has an index of subjects, II indices of 'Heiligenattribute' and 'Patronate der Heiligen.'

An excellent shorter survey is presented by **J.J.M. Timmers**, *Christlijke Symboliek en Iconografie* (2nd ed. Bussum, Netherlands 1974), including 200 illustrations and an index of subjects and proper names.

A work comparable in scope to that of Schiller, but in my experience quite disappointing, is **Louis Réau**'s *Iconographie de l'art chrétien* (Paris 1955-9), 3 vols in 6: I, 'Introduction générale'; II, 'Iconographie de la Bible'; and III, 'Iconographie des saints,' arranged alphabetically. Illustrations are comparatively few and tend to be post-medieval. Vol. I includes several extended lists of symbols on pp 59-244, like, for example, the significances of beasts, flowers, and stones (pp 79-138) and the table of typological correspondences (201-7); II/i (Old Testament) has an index of persons, and II/ii (New Testament), indices of persons, places, and subjects; III/iii, 1385-1527, contains various indices, the most useful of which are an alphabetical index of saints with their attributes (pp 1483-98) and an alphabetical index of attributes along with the saints to whom they are attached (1499-1527). In general, however, this work is very weak in specific documentation, and must be used with caution – for example, it should probably not be cited alone as evidence for a particular iconographic significance. There are also a number of brief topically organized popular handbooks to which this same warning obviously applies, but which can nevertheless be helpful in providing an initial general hint of an iconographic significance; a single example is **Klementine**

Lipffert's *Symbol-Fibel: Eine Hilfe zum Betrachten und Deuten mittelalterlicher Bildwerke* (6th ed. Kassel 1976).

A word should be said about the great pioneering studies of **Emile Mâle**: *L'Art religieux du XIIe siècle en France: Etude sur les origines de l'iconographie du moyen âge* (Paris, many eds; 7th ed. 1966); *L'Art religieux du XIIIe siècle en France: Etude sur l'iconographie du moyen âge et sur ses sources d'inspiration* (Paris, many eds; 9th ed. 1958), trans. **Dora Nussey** (from the 3rd ed. 1910) as *Religious Art in France, XIII Century: A Study in Mediaeval Iconography and Its Sources of Inspiration* (London 1913), reprinted as *The Gothic Image: Religious Art in France of the Thirteenth Century* (London and New York, various eds); and *L'Art religieux de la fin du moyen âge en France: Etude sur l'iconographie du moyen âge et sur ses sources d'inspiration* (Paris, many eds; 6th ed. 1969). All of these volumes have some illustrations, include indices of works of art arranged alphabetically by location, and are kept somewhat up to date by appendices of additions and corrections by Mâle himself in the successive reprintings. They have now been republished in an English translation by **Marthiel Mathews**, with the general title 'Studies in Religious Iconography' (Bollingen Series 90), under the general editorship of **Harry Bober**. Mâle's own additions and corrections, along with other new material, are incorporated in the footnotes; there are new and expanded subject-indices; and many of the older illustrations are replaced by modern photographs, along with some new illustrations. The first volume appears as *Religious Art in France, The Twelfth Century: A Study of the Origins of Medieval Iconography*, Bollingen Series 90/1 (Princeton 1978); the second as *Religious Art in France, the Thirteenth Century: A Study of Medieval Iconography and Its Sources*, Bollingen Series 90/2 (Princeton 1984); and the third as *Religious Art in France, The Late Middle Ages: A Study of Medieval Iconography and Its Sources*, Bollingen Series 90/3 (Princeton 1986). Though Mâle's works are restricted to French art and are not organized rigorously as iconographic guides, they are particularly valuable in showing the traditional relations of particular motifs, and can still be profitably used; the footnotes in the thirteenth-century volume are especially informative.

Guides Organized Alphabetically

Of the iconographic works organized alphabetically, the most generally useful at present is by **Engelbert Kirschbaum** et al., *Lexikon der christlichen Ikonographie* (Rome 1968-76), 8 vols, with many illustrations throughout. Vols I-IV are devoted to 'Allgemeine Ikonographie,' arranged alphabetically by motif. Each entry includes i, sources; ii, description, development, occurrences, etc.; and iii, bibliography. Vol. IV includes a few 'Nachträge' (pp 594-622), and lists of the English and French equivalents of the motifs listed in German in the lexicon proper (630-74). Vols V-VIII contain 'Ikonographie der Heiligen'; each entry covers sources, occurrences, iconography, and bibliography, and a 'Register der Heiligenfeste' and 'Register der Attribute' appear at the end of VIII. A preface (I, 6*) promises other general indices.

A more elaborate lexicon, though geographically more restricted and much further from completion, is that of **Otto Schmitt** et al., *Reallexikon zur deutschen Kunstgeschichte* (Stuttgart 1937ff), 7 vols to date, extending alphabetically through 'Fensterladen.' It includes particularly full lists of examples, many illustrations, and a brief bibliographical notice at the end of each entry. The apparent limitation implied by its title is considerably modified in a foreword: 'Das RDK beschränkt sich geographisch auf die Denkmäler des deutschen Sprach- und Kulturgebietes, behandelt also gegebenenfalls auch Denkmäler ausserhalb der Reichsgrenzen (Österreich, Böhmen, Schweiz, Elsass, Niederlande, Polen, Baltikum). Darüber hinaus wird jedoch auch das west- und südeuropäische Ausland und der Orient herangezogen, sobald sie in irgendwelcher Weise Vorstufen zur deutschen Entwicklung bieten.'

What would probably have been the most detailed iconographic lexicon of all was begun by **Hans Aurenhammer**, *Lexikon der christlichen Ikonographie* (Vienna 1959-67) I, 'Alpha und Omega – Christus und die vierundzwanzig Ältesten,' arranged alphabetically, with large subjects broken down into particular motifs (e.g. 9 entries for 'Abel,' 24 for 'Adam und Eva'). Each entry includes an indication of the source of the motif, biblical or otherwise; an account of where and in what forms it appears; and a bibliography. The citation of examples is massive, though there are no illustrations or indices. It was discontinued after the completion of 'Christus.' Finally, there are here again a number of brief popular lexica, whose value as evidence is slight but which can be helpful in furnishing initial hints; an example is **Gerd Heinz-Mohr's** *Lexikon der Symbole: Bilder und Zeichen der christlichen Kunst* (4th ed. Düsseldorf 1976).

Princeton and Warburg Indices

By far the most comprehensive tool for the study of medieval Christian iconography, however, is the Index of Christian Art, housed in McCormick Hall at Princeton University. This index, which covers the period from the beginning of Christian art to 1400 and includes over 170,000 photographs and approximately 700,000 subject file cards, is remarkable above all for the variety of approaches it offers. The Index proper, which includes reproductions, essential data, descriptions of iconography, and bibliography for all objects indexed, is organized most broadly according to seventeen different media: enamel, fresco and other wall painting, windows and objects of glass, gold glass, glyptic (precious and semi-precious stones or imitations, and steatite), illuminated and illustrated manuscripts, ivory, leather, metal, miscellaneous (drawings, beadwork, etc.), mosaic, painting, sculpture, terra cotta, textile, undetermined material, and wax. Within each medium it is organized alphabetically by the cities where the objects are preserved, within each city by churches, museums, libraries, etc., and within each such location by individual objects or manuscripts. It thus makes possible a survey not only of all the indexed objects in a particular medium, a particular city, or a particular church, museum, or library, but also of all the indexed objects in a particular medium within a given city (e.g. the mosaics in Ravenna) or within a given church, museum, or library (e.g. the stained glass in Canterbury Cathedral, the ivories in the Bargello in Florence, or the manuscript illustrations in the Bibliothèque municipale in Tours). The extensive file of subject cards, arranged alphabetically, allows research by way of particular motifs (e.g. Abraham holding the souls of the just in a napkin), or, in combination with the makeup of the Index itself, by way of particular iconographic motifs in given media and/or locations (e.g. the Flagellation in frescoes at Siena). Another card-catalogue of biblical references corresponding to iconographic subjects makes it possible to survey the illustration of a particular biblical book or episode (e.g.

illustration of the Apocalypse, or of Amnon ravishing Thamar in II Kings 13:10-14), or of such illustrations in a given medium and/or locale. The Index can also be used to answer other kinds of questions – for example, the popularity and range of a given subject, and the manner in which a particular scene is represented. One must not, of course, slip into the habit of thinking of the Index as all-inclusive (e.g. it is less systematic in its coverage of unpublished objects than of published ones, and a complete coverage of even published material would be manifestly impossible); but as it stands, its usefulness can hardly be overstated.

An 83-page description of the Index and its uses was published forty-odd years ago by **Helen Woodruff**, *The Index of Christian Art at Princeton University: A Handbook* (Princeton 1942); though out of date in many respects, it can still be used for a general picture. A briefer but more up-to-date account is presented in an 11-page pamphlet, '**Index of Christian Art, Princeton University**,' which can be obtained from the Director of the Index for 25¢. I quote briefly from p. 3 for certain essential facts, with the inclusion of such changes in opening hours as have been made since publication of the pamphlet:

> The Princeton Index is open throughout the year. During the academic months, hours are 9 A.M. to 5 P.M. Monday through Friday. From mid-June to mid-September, hours are 9 A.M. to 4 P.M. Monday through Friday. The Index is closed on weekends, major holidays, and for two weeks at the Christmas recess. Visitors are welcome at all open hours, and notice of an impending visit is not essential. Information from the files of the Index can sometimes be supplied by mail. If more than routine research is required, a fee is charged; but the right is reserved to refuse to undertake extended compilations. Consultation by the scholar in person is always recommended. [Reproductions of the photographs in the files of the Index are no longer available.] Requests for information should be addressed to the Director, Index of Christian Art, Department of Art and Archaeology, Princeton University, Princeton, New Jersey, 08544.

Photographic duplicates of the Index, kept up to date and each attended by a trained custodian, are located in the Dumbarton Oaks Research Library and Collection of Harvard University in Washington, D.C.; in the Biblioteca Vaticana; in the Kunsthistorisch Instituut of the Rijksuniversiteit, Utrecht; and in the Art Library, University of California at Los Angeles.

A less comprehensive and systematic photograph collection, covering medieval and later periods and embracing both Christian and secular motifs, is maintained at the Warburg Institute in London. Unlike the Princeton Index, this collection cannot be used as an immense iconographic lexicon, since it makes no effort to be complete, but is fullest in areas of interest to those working at the Warburg and relevant to its primary concern with the survival of classical antiquity. There is, for example, an excellent section of many files on 'Gods and Myths,' arranged alphabetically by gods, which includes a good deal of medieval mythography; interesting files on 'Herbals,' 'Animals,' and 'Symbolic Trees'; a very full section on 'Virtues and Vices'; and a substantial section on 'Astrology.' The section on religious iconography includes, among many other headings, 'Old Testament' in the order of the Bible, 'Life of Christ including legends,' 'Teaching of Christ,' 'Parables,' 'Miracles,' 'Passion of Christ,' 'Virgin and Child,' 'Holy Family,' 'Tree of Jesse,' 'Life of the Virgin,' 'Acts of the Apostles,' 'Apostles,' 'Evangelists,' 'Church Fathers,' 'Saints,' 'Angels and Archangels,' 'Devils,' 'Hell,' 'Purgatory,' 'Heaven,' 'Typology,' 'Ecclesiastical Objects' (including 'Altarpieces'), and 'Ecclesia-Synagogue.' Photographs of manuscripts are grouped in the first instance under libraries, though there are many duplicates under the relevant subjects, and a few architectural sculpture cycles are arranged topographically. A card-catalogue provides an index to these by motifs, as well as cross-references. A '**Summary Guide to the Photographic Collection of the Warburg Institute**' is available (£2.50, including postage by surface mail) from The Photographic Collection, The Warburg Institute, Woburn Square, London, WC1H 0AB.

An ambitious system of general iconographical classification, including extensive bibliography and accompanied by a set of illustrations on separate cards, was devised by **H. van de Waal** and has been completed and edited by **L.D. Couprie** et al. as *Iconclass: An Iconographic Classification System*, Koninklijke Nederlandse Akademie van Wetenschappen (Amsterdam 1973-85), 17 vols including 3 of indices. Since its centre of concentration is on Dutch painting, it is predominantly post-medieval in emphasis and so can be of only marginal value for our purposes.

The Bible

Within the field of medieval iconography, an important large area is illustration of the Bible itself. Though the iconography of biblical illustration is of course covered by the various comprehensive works mentioned so far, it is worth adding that the most elaborate single example, dating from the thirteenth century, is edited by **A. de Laborde**, *La Bible moralisée illustrée, conservée à Oxford, Paris, et Londres* (Paris 1911-27), 5 vols. Vols I-III and part of IV reproduce the three basic manuscripts from the Bodleian Library, the Bibliothèque Nationale, and the British Library; the rest of vol. IV contains parallels from other manuscripts, and V is an introduction, including a brief selection of figurative motifs (pp 156-65) and an 'Index alphabétique des personnages et des objets représentés' (190-206).

The typologically organized *Biblia pauperum* or *Biblia picta*, a popular kind of illustrated Bible in the late Middle Ages, is surveyed most elaborately by **Henrik Cornell**, *Biblia pauperum* (Stockholm 1925), containing 72 plates at the end, plates A-H in the text, and 37 sketches in the text; sections 'Die Tituli: Übersicht der Tituli der Biblia pauperum' (pp 16-53), and 'Deutsche Tituli' (61-6), listing the titles conventionally employed in the *Biblia pauperum;* a chapter 'Die einzelnen Darstellungen' (242-313), cataloguing prominent motifs; and various indices, including 'Handschriften der Biblia pauperum' (357-8), 'Verschiedene Handschriften' (358-9), 'Historisches Namenregister' (360-1), and most important, 'Ikonographisches Register' (361-3).

Shorter studies are by **J. Engelhardt**, *Der theologische Gehalt der Biblia pauperum*, Studien zur deutschen Kunstgeschichte 243 (Strassburg 1927), with a variety of useful analytic tables on pp 103-50; **Hildegard Zimmerman**, '**Armenbibel**' in *Reallexikon zur deutschen Kunstgeschichte* I, 1072-84, with 6 illustrations and lists of typological correspondences in cols 1079-82; and **Gerhard Schmidt**, *Die Armenbibeln des XIV. Jahrhunderts*, Veröffentlichungen des Instituts für österreichische Geschichtsforschung 19 (Graz 1959), with 76 illustrations, analytic tables (pp 139-47), and an index of manuscript *Bibliae pauperum* (148-9).

The Saints

Another immense subject is the iconography of the saints, covered in a general way in several of the comprehensive works cited above. In addition, an elaborate study of the medieval iconography of the saints in Italy is being done by **George Kaftal** in his *Saints in Italian Art*, 4 vols, of which three have already appeared: *Iconography of the Saints in Tuscan Painting* (Florence 1952); *Iconography of the Saints in Central and South Italian Schools of Painting* (Florence 1965); and *Iconography of the Saints in the Painting of North East Italy* (Florence 1978). The fourth volume will cover Lombardy, Liguria, and Piedmont. Each volume is essentially an alphabetical list of saints and blessed, with an added section on unidentified saints and blessed; entries begin with the essential data about the saint, then analyze his/her iconography according to a plan that includes (where relevant) the headings 'Relics,' 'Type,' 'Inscriptions,' 'Images,' 'Cycles,' 'Literary Sources of Scenes,' 'Art Bibliography,' and 'Hagiographical Bibliography.' The three volumes include a total of 4006 illustrations. Each concludes with an alphabetical 'Index of Attributes, Distinctive Signs, and Scenes,' an 'Index of Painters,' a 'Topographical Index of Paintings,' a 'Bibliographical Index of Works Mentioned in the Text,' an 'Index of Saints and Blessed,' and (first volume only) a 'Calendar of Saints and Blessed.'

A less elaborate but quite useful guide to the apparel and attributes of the saints in German art, not confined to the Middle Ages, is **Joseph Braun**'s *Tracht und Attribute der Heiligen in der deutschen Kunst* (Stuttgart 1943). Pt I (cols 18-775) is a catalogue arranged alphabetically by names of saints, with 428 illustrations. Pt II includes an alphabetically arranged explanation of relevant items of apparel (cols 776-84); an analysis of the apparel of various classes of saints (apostles and evangelists, saints holding ecclesiastical positions, saints belonging to religious orders, and lay saints; cols 783-804); an alphabetically arranged analysis of attributes (811-28); an alphabetical index of attributes, with the saints to whom they pertain (833-42); and an alphabetical index of saints, with references to the illustrations in pt I (843-52).

A brief handbook of saints, including the most prominent features of their iconography, is **Otto Wimmer**'s *Handbuch der Namen und Heiligen, mit einer Geschichte des christlichen Kalendars* (2nd ed.

Innsbruck 1959) – essentially an alphabetical catalogue of saints and blessed, with several indices, including (pp 549-74) a 'Verzeichnis der Attribute der Heiligen.'

Specialized Studies

Another possible approach to medieval iconographic motifs is by way of inclusive editions of the art in particular media and/or regions, with the indices that usually accompany them. One notable example is **Raimond van Marle's** *The Development of the Italian Schools of Painting* (The Hague 1923-38), 19 vols, each with hundreds of illustrations; VI is a topically organized index to vols I-V – which, happily, are the volumes covering the period from the beginning through the fourteenth century.

Much less useful for our purposes is **Richard Offner** et al., *A Critical and Historical Corpus of Florentine Painting* (New York 1930ff), sections III and IV, 'The Fourteenth Century,' 15 vols in 16; though valuable as a collection of plates, it contains indices only of artists and places (along with a small appendix of 'iconographic notes' on the Coronation of the Virgin, the Last Judgment, and the Meeting of the Quick and the Dead in sec. III, vol. V, 243-63) and so does not lend itself easily to the study of particular motifs.

An elaborate alphabetical index of subjects found in the marginal illustrations of 226 North European manuscripts from the late thirteenth and early fourteenth centuries (without figurative significances) is compiled by **Lilian M.C. Randall**, *Images in the Margins of Gothic Manuscripts* (Berkeley 1966) pp 45-235, along with a bibliography (pp 21-6) and 158 plates containing 739 representative illustrations.

Medieval ivory-carving from the eighth century through the thirteenth is covered by **Adolph Goldschmidt** et al., *Die Elfenbeinskulpturen aus der Zeit der karolingischen und sächsischen Kaiser: VIII.-XI. Jahrhundert*, and *Die Elfenbeinskulpturen aus der romanischen Zeit: XI.-XIII. Jahrhundert*, Denkmäler der deutschen Kunst 2/4 (Berlin 1914-26, repr. 1969-75), 4 vols, with a total of 269 pages of illustrations, plus 152 illustrations in the texts; each volume has several full indices, including an index of iconographic motifs (I, 103-4; II, 75-6;

III, 59; IV, 69-70). A useful addition to Goldschmidt is **John Beckwith**'s *Ivory Carvings in Early Medieval England* (London 1972), with 270 illustrations and an index that includes subjects (pp 163-6).

A potentially valuable collection, now well underway, is the edition of medieval stained glass, *Corpus vitrearum medii aevi* (various places, 1956ff), 23 vols through 1985, consisting of many series by country, all incomplete so far; all volumes are richly illustrated, and most include indices of subjects or iconographic motifs.

Still another example is medieval English wall-painting, which for practical purposes is covered in three works by **E.W. Tristram**: *English Medieval Wall Painting: The Twelfth Century* (Oxford 1944), *English Medieval Wall Painting: The Thirteenth Century* (Oxford 1950), 2 vols, and *English Wall Painting of the Fourteenth Century* (London 1955) – all of which include many illustrations, catalogues of paintings, and indices of iconographic subjects. A useful supplement is **A. Caiger-Smith**'s *English Medieval Mural Paintings* (Oxford 1963), with 25 illustrations and a valuable 'Selective Catalogue' on pp 129-82. Other inclusive editions of medieval art, as well as those limited to particular times, places, subjects, and the like, can of course be used as the problem demands and their indices permit.

Secular Iconography

So far, we have been concerned almost entirely with Christian iconography, which does, to be sure, constitute by far the greatest body of extant iconography from the Middle Ages. There is, however, also a substantial body of secular iconography, the best general guide to which is provided by **Raimond van Marle**, *Iconographie de l'art profane au moyen-âge et à la Renaissance, et la décoration des demeures* (The Hague 1931-2), 2 vols. Vol. I is devoted to 'La Vie quotidienne'; II, to 'Allégories et symboles' ('L'Allégorie éthique,' 'Les Allégories philosophiques,' 'Les Sciences et les arts,' 'Allégories diverses,' 'La Mort,' 'L'Amour'). Both volumes are arranged topically, by chapter and within individual chapters; there are a total of 1047 illustrations.

An alphabetical catalogue of secular motifs, centred on the Renaissance but indirectly useful also for medieval secular iconography, is compiled by **Guy de Tervarent**, *Attributs et symboles dans l'art profane, 1450-1600: Dictionnaire d'un langage perdu*, Travaux d'humanisme et renaissance 29 (Geneva 1958-9), 2 vols, with 85 illustrations and a 'Table des entités immatérielles' (II, cols 421-30), and a *Supplément et Index* (Geneva 1964); most entries are divided into 'Sources' and 'Art,' the former of which can often be profitably consulted for medieval references.

A sizeable body of mythographical and astrological iconography is collected by **Fritz Saxl** et al., *Verzeichnis astrologischer und mythologischer illustrierter Handschriften des lateinischen Mittelalters / Catalogue of Astrological and Mythological Illuminated Manuscripts of the Latin Middle Ages* (Heidelberg/London 1915-66, vols I-II repr. Nendeln/Liechtenstein 1978), 4 vols in 5. Vol. I covers manuscripts in Roman libraries; II, manuscripts in the National-Bibliothek in Vienna; III (2 pts, by **Saxl** and **Hans Meier**, ed. **Harry Bober**), manuscripts in English libraries; and IV (by **Patrick McGurk**), manuscripts in Italian libraries other than Rome. All volumes include many illustrations, and indices of persons and subjects. Other mythographical illustrations can be found by way of the file on 'Gods and Myths' at the Warburg Institute, and in the mythographical works cited in the following chapter, passim.

6

Mythography

Introductory

Medieval interpretation of the Classics is in a broad way a parallel to medieval interpretation of the Bible, and like it is frequently allegorical. Here again we can distinguish the two basic 'research situations' introduced in chapter 1: one in which we have before us an echo from a particular Classical text (e.g. the gates of horn and ivory at the end of *Aeneid* bk 6), the other in which we have a recognizably Classical figure or motif which seems not necessarily attached to any particular literary context (e.g. Venus or Hercules). For the first of these situations, the obvious initial approach is to consult commentaries on the Classical passage in question. For the second, there are at least two major possibilities. One is to consult general mythographic works, especially those organized around prominent Classical figures; the other is to search encyclopedias and indices of major Classical works to find specific instances of the figure or motif one is interested in, and then consult commentators on the works that include them. The following sketch should provide abundant material for employing both these methods.

Medieval mythography is of course rooted firmly in Classical mythography, and any survey of it must inevitably begin there. The great comprehensive encyclopedia for things Classical, which can often be profitably consulted for the location of particular subjects, was originally compiled by **August Friedrich von Pauly** and is edited by **Georg Wissowa** et al. as *Paulys Realencyclopädie der classischen Altertumswissenschaft* (Stuttgart 1894ff), first series (A-Q) 24 vols, second series (R-Z) 10 vols through 'Zythos,' with 15 suppls (Stuttgart and Munich 1903-78); it is abridged by **Konrat Ziegler** et al. as *Der kleine Pauly: Lexikon der Antike* (Stuttgart 1964-75), 5 vols. More directly relevant for our purposes is the encyclopedia of **W.H. Roscher** et al., *Ausführliches Lexikon der griechischen und römischen Mythologie* (Leipzig 1884-1937), 6 vols with 4 suppls. Suppl. 3, ed. **Jesse Benedict Carter,** *Epitheta deorum quae apud poetas Latinos leguntur* (Leipzig 1902), is a catalogue arranged alphabetically by gods, with an index arranged alphabetically by epithets; and the first chapter of Suppl. 4, **Otto Gruppe,** *Geschichte der klassischen Mythologie und Religionsgeschichte während des Mittelalters im Abendland und während der Neuzeit* (Leipzig 1921) pp 1-26, briefly sketches the Middle Ages.

An encyclopedia of the amalgamation of Christianity and antiquity is being edited by **Theodor Klauser** et al., *Reallexikon für Antike und Christentum: Sachwörterbuch zur Auseinandersetzung des Christentums mit der antiken Welt* (Stuttgart 1950ff), 13 vols plus 3 fascs (no. 106, down to 'Hekate') and 4 supplementary fascs (no. 4, down to 'Athen I') to 1987.

A particularly useful analysis of Classical imagery is offered by **Viktor Pöschl, Helga Gärtner,** and **Waltraut Heyke,** *Bibliographie zur antiken Bildersprache,* Heidelberger Akademie der Wissenschaften, N.F. 1 (Heidelberg 1964). The first large section, *Literatur* (bibliography), is divided into two major parts: first, 'Allgemeine Literatur,' which is in turn subdivided into 'Linguistik,' 'Literaturgeschichte,' 'Literaturwissenschaft,' 'Mythologie,' 'Philosophie,' and 'Religion,' with items arranged alphabetically by author within each section, and brief notes indicating their relation to *Bildersprache;* and second, 'Literatur zu den griechischen und lateinischen Autoren,' arranged alphabetically by Classical authors. The second large section, *Bilder* (pp 447-594), is an extremely valuable list of images, arranged alphabetically and including references back to items in the bibliography; three appendices, 'Gestalten und Personifikationen' (595-6), 'Lateinische Ausdrücke' (607-11), and 'Griechische Ausdrücke' (612-19) follow the same plan. There is an index of modern authors on pp 623-53.

The annual bibliography *L'Année philologique* (1924ff), beginning with vol. 2 (1928 [covering 1927]), includes a section on 'Mythographie' (in 'Deuxième partie,' under 'I. Histoire littéraire').

Though studies of medieval mythography and its particular aspects are of course legion, four especially valuable ones may be mentioned by way of introduction.

1/ **Jean Seznec's** *The Survival of the Pagan Gods: The Mythological Tradition and Its Place in Renaissance Humanism and Art*, trans. **Barbara F. Sessions**, Bollingen Series 38 (New York 1953, repr. 1961), though oriented toward the Renaissance, includes much valuable information on medieval mythography at large – particularly in bk I, along with 91 illustrations and a useful bibliography and index.

2/ **Hugo Rahner's** *Griechische Mythen in christlicher Deutung* (Zurich 1957), trans. **Brian Battershaw** as *Greek Myths and Christian Mystery* (London 1963), surveys the great patristic symbols drawn from Hellenistic images (e.g. Odysseus at the mast).

3/ **Peter Dronke's** *Fabula: Explorations into the Uses of Myth in Medieval Platonism*, Mittellateinische Studien und Texte 9 (Leyden 1974) examines the role of myth in the Platonic tradition, including a valuable list of Latin and vernacular allusions to the 'cosmic egg' (pp 154-66) and an excellent bibliography (184-95).

4/ **Beryl Smalley's** *English Friars and Antiquity in the Early Fourteenth Century* (Oxford 1960) is a guide to the English 'classicizing friars' Thomas Walleys, John Ridevall, Robert Holkot, William D'Eyncourt, Thomas Hopeman, Thomas Ringstead, and John Lathbury. Appendices I, 'Latin Texts in Order of Quotation,' and II, 'Quotations from Lost or Previously Unknown Works,' provide a small anthology of quotations, many from works otherwise unprinted; and there is an index of 'pictures,' or mythographic motifs, on pp 393-4.

An index of mythographic motifs in certain early Christian writers, arranged alphabetically by subject, is included in PL 219, cols 365-92, '**Index mythologicus, seu de diis, deabus, et superstitionibus paganorum,**' with a list of the authors consulted in cols 391-2.

A useful anthology of Classical and medieval mythographic works, depending on several earlier editions, is edited finally by **Augustin van Staveren**, *Auctores mythographi Latini: Cajus Julius Hyginus, Fab. Planciad. Fulgentius, Lactantius Placidus, Albricus Philosophus, cum integris commentariis Jacobi Micylli, Joannis Schefferi, et Thomae Munckeri, quibus adcedunt Thomae Wopkensii emendationes ac conjecturae* (Leyden and Amsterdam 1742), including the

Fabulae and *Poeticon astronomicon* of Hyginus; the *Mythologiae, Expositio Virgilianae continentiae,* and *Expositio sermonum antiquorum* of Fulgentius; the *Narrationes fabularum* of Lactantius Placidus; and the *De deorum imaginibus libellus* here attributed to Albricus Philosophus, or Alberic of London. More recent editions of these works will be cited below. The collection is heavily annotated throughout with the comments of Renaissance scholars; a 24-page 'Index rerum et verborum' (following p. 963) seems based on these notes rather than on the texts.

In the following survey of individual mythographic works, the first section will include treatments of mythography at large, and the second section commentaries on individual authors.

Mythography at Large

A good bit of general mythographic lore is included in **Cicero's** *De natura deorum,* ed. **W. Ax** in *M. Tulli Ciceronis scripta quae manserunt omnia,* fasc. 45, Bibliotheca Teubneriana (2nd ed. Leipzig 1933, repr. Stuttgart 1961), with an index of names and subjects; trans. **H. Rackham,** Loeb Classical Library (Cambridge, Mass. 1961), with an index of subjects, and by **Horace C.P. McGregor** as *The Nature of the Gods* (Penguin Books 1972), with an index.

Another Classical mythographer is the compiler known to us as **Hyginus,** whose works seem to date from the second century A.D. with later revisions. His mythography is found in his *Fabulae,* ed. **W.J. Rose,** *Hygini fabulae* (Leyden [1934]), with an index of names; and in bk 2 of his *Poetica astronomica* or *De astronomia,* ed. **Bernhard Bunte,** *Hygini astronomica* (Leipzig 1875) and **Fabrizio Serra,** *Hyginus astronomus* (Pisa 1976), with an index of names. Both works are translated by **Mary A. Grant,** *The Myths of Hyginus* (Lawrence, Kansas 1960), with a convenient introduction, useful notes, and an index of subjects.

Mythographic material also appears, though by no means systematically, in the works of Macrobius (4th-5th C) and in bks 1 and 2 of Martianus Capella's *De nuptiis Philologiae et Mercurii* (5th C).

Macrobius is edited by **James Willis**, Bibliotheca Teubneriana (2nd ed. Leipzig 1970), 2 vols: I, the *Saturnalia*, an extended celebration of the learning of Vergil; and II, the *Commentarii in Somnium Scipionis*, on an episode of Cicero's *De re publica*. At the end of vol. II are very full indices of authors cited and of subjects, covering both works. The *Saturnalia* is translated by **Percival Vaughan Davies**, Records of Civilization, Sources and Studies 79 (New York 1969), with an index of citations from Homer, Lucretius, and Vergil, and an index of subjects; the *Commentarii* is translated by **William Harris Stahl**, *Macrobius: Commentary on the Dream of Scipio*, Records of Civilization, Sources and Studies 48 (New York 1952), with an informative introduction and a general index.

The *De nuptiis* of Martianus is edited by **Adolph Dick**, *Martianus Capella*, Bibliotheca Teubneriana (Leipzig 1925; repr. with corrections and addenda by **Jean Préaux**, Stuttgart 1969), with an index of subjects and names and an index of authors cited; this edition is now replaced by that of **James Willis**, *Martianus Capella*, Bibliotheca Teubneriana (Leipzig 1983), with an index of subjects and important words, an index of Greek words, and an index of authors cited. The important bk 2 is edited, with a valuable introduction and full annotation, by **Luciano Lenaz**, *De nuptiis Philologiae et Mercurii, liber secundus* (Padua 1975). The *De nuptiis* is translated by **William Harris Stahl** and **Richard Johnson** with **E.L. Burge**, *Martianus Capella and the Seven Liberal Arts*, Records of Civilization, Sources and Studies 84 (New York 1971-7), vol. II, with a brief index; vol. I is an elaborate introduction, including a 'Bibliographical Survey of the Seven Liberal Arts in Medieval and Renaissance Iconography' (pp 245-9). Commentaries on Martianus will be cited below in the section on individual authors.

The influential *Mythologiae* of **Fulgentius the Mythographer**, probably written in North Africa during the late fifth or early sixth century, is a compilation of fifty highly allegorized Classical fables. It is edited by **Rudolph Helm**, *Fabii Planciadis Fulgentii V. C. opera ...*, Bibliotheca Teubneriana (Leipzig 1898; repr. Stuttgart, with addenda by **Jean Préaux** 1970) pp 3-80, with indices of authors cited, names, and words; and translated by **Leslie George Whitbread**, *Fulgentius the Mythographer* (Columbus, Ohio 1971), with an informative general introduction and introductions to the individual works, valuable notes, indices of authors and names, and a table of contents of the *Mythologiae* on pp 39-40. Fulgentius's *Expositio Virgilianae continentiae* and *Super Thebaiden* will be taken up below in the section on individual authors.

A tremendously popular though non-allegorical exposition 'De diis gentium' is included by Isidore of Seville (6th-7th C) in bk 8, ch. 11 of his *Etymologiae* (ed. Lindsay, for which see p. 185 below); it appears also in a very useful edition by **Katherine Nell McFarlane**, *Isidore of Seville on the Pagan Gods (Origines VIII.11)*, Transactions of the American Philosophical Society 70/3 (Philadelphia 1980), with an introduction, an extremely detailed commentary, a bibliography (pp 36-8), and indices of 'Gods and Other Mythological or Supernatural Figures' and 'Classical and Patristic Authors' (38-40). This account is repeated, for example, by Rabanus Maurus (8th-9th C) in *De universo* 15.6, PL 111, cols 426-36.

Other early non-allegorical collections are the first two of the three so-called **'Vatican Mythographers,'** ed. **Georg Heinrich Bode**, *Scriptores rerum mythicarum Latini tres Romae nuper reperti* (Celle 1834, repr. Hildesheim 1968), 2 vols, including in vol. I a useful subject index, and in II notes which identify parallels in other authors. The compilation of the First Mythographer, which may date from the Merovingian period, contains a total of 234 myths; that of the Second Mythographer, possibly from Carolingian times and sometimes ascribed to Remigius of Auxerre, consists of a proem and 230 myths. Information on the Vatican Mythographers, including lists of manuscripts, is provided by **Kathleen O. Elliott** and **J.P. Elder**, **'A Critical Edition of the** *Vatican Mythographers,'* *Transactions of the American Philological Association* 78 (1947) 189-207.

A 64-line mythographic poem by **Theodulf of Orléans** (8th-9th C), **'De libris quos legere solebam et qualiter fabulae poetarum a philosophis mystice pertractentur,'** ed. **Ernst Dümmler** in *Poetae Latini aevi Carolini*, MGH Poetae 1 (Berlin 1881) I, 543-4, presents a few motifs.

The 352-line pastoral debate poem *Ecloga Theodoli* (9th or 10th C), which made its way into the school curriculum, opposes Classical myths to stories from the Old Testament. An early edition of the *Eclogue* by **Johann Osternacher**, *Quos auctores Latinos et sacrorum bibliorum locos Theodulus imitatus esse videatur* (Urfahr bei Linz

1907), is valuable for its extended lists of parallels from other authors; the *Eclogue* itself is also conveniently printed by **R.B.C. Huygens** on pp 9-18 of his edition of the important commentary on it by Bernard of Utrecht, *Bernard d'Utrecht, Commentum in Theodulum (1076-1099)*, Biblioteca degli 'Studi medievali' 8 (Spoleto 1977). Essential information about the *Eclogue* is provided by **Betty Nye Quinn**, 'ps. Theodolus,' in the *Catalogus translationum et commentariorum* ed. Kristeller and Cranz (see p. 116 below) II, 383-408.

Unlike the works of the first two Vatican Mythographers, that of the third (probably to be identified as **Alberic of London**, writing in the middle or late twelfth century and sometimes thought to be Alexander Neckham) is intensely allegorical; after a brief proem, it is made up of chapters on Saturn, Cybele, Jupiter, Juno, Neptune, Pluto, Proserpina, Apollo, Mercury, Pallas, Venus, Bacchus, Hercules, Perseus, and the signs of the Zodiac. It is edited by Bode, *Scriptores rerum mythicarum*, with index and notes as described above; essential information can be found in Elliott and Elder, 'Critical Edition,' including a list of manuscripts on pp 205-7.

A recently recognized mythographic work of the twelfth century, organized according to gods and other Classical motifs, is edited by **Virginia Brown**, **'An Edition of an Anonymous Twelfth-Century *Liber de natura deorum*,'** *Mediaeval Studies* 34 (1972) 1-70, with a list of chapters on pp 2-4; a commentary is planned for a subsequent number of the journal.

Mythographic material is scattered through Alexander Neckham's *De naturis rerum* and *De laudibus divinae sapientiae* (for which see pp 43 above and 192-3 below), though the index to the volume does not include Classical names.

Mythography is used extensively – though not, of course, according to any logical classification – in the philosophical poetry of the twelfth-century 'School of Chartres':

Bernard Silvestris' great allegory the *Cosmographia* (or *De mundi universitate*) is edited by **Peter Dronke**, *Bernardus Silvestris: Cosmographia*, Textus minores 53 (Leyden 1978), with introduction, notes, bibliography, and an 'Index nominum et verborum.' It is translated by **Winthrop Wetherbee**, *The Cosmographia of Bernardus Silvestris*, Records of Civilization, Sources and Studies 89 (New York

1973), with introduction and notes and an index of themes, images, and technical terms (pp 173-4).

The best edition of the *Anticlaudianus* of **Alain de Lille** (Alanus ab Insulis) is by **R. Bossuat**, Textes philosophiques du moyen âge 1 (Paris 1955), with an index of subjects; the best translation is by **James J. Sheridan**, *Anticlaudianus, or the Good and Perfect Man* (Toronto 1973). (Medieval commentary and adaptation of the *Anticlaudianus* – none very rich in mythographic lore – are included below in chapter 7.) Alain's *De planctu Naturae* exists in an early edition by **Thomas Wright**, *The Anglo-Latin Satirical Poets and Epigrammatists of the Twelfth Century*, Rolls Series 59 (London 1872) II, 429-522, with a rudimentary index of subjects embedded piecemeal in the general index at the end of vol. II; a still earlier edition is printed in PL 210, cols 431-82, with the same kind of index in cols 1013-40. The best edition is now that of **Nikolaus M. Häring**, 'Alan of Lille, *De planctu Naturae*,' *Studi medievali* 3rd ser. 19 (1978) 797-879, though with no indices; and the best translation, that of **James J. Sheridan**, *The Plaint of Nature*, Medieval Sources in Translation 26 (Toronto 1980), with indices of persons, subjects, and biblical citations on pp 249-56.

Another twelfth-century poem containing some mythography, along with a great deal of interesting miscellaneous lore, is **John of Hanville's** *Architrenius*, ed. **Paul Gerhard Schmidt** (Munich 1974), with indices of names, words, and authors cited; a helpful summary of the poem is provided by **Winthrop Wetherbee**, *Platonism and Poetry in the Twelfth Century: The Literary Influence of the School of Chartres* (Princeton 1972) pp 243-53.

An alphabetically organized handbook by **Konrad von Mure** (13th C), printed under the titles *Repertorium vocabulorum* (Basel: Berthold Ruppel, n.d.) and *Magnus elucidarius omnes historias & poeticas fabulas continens* ... (Paris: Iehan Petit [1516]), offers a full coverage of Classical subjects but no allegorical interpretation.

The English 'classicizing' friars of the first half of the fourteenth century (Thomas Walleys, John Ridevall, Robert Holkot, Thomas Ringstead, et al.) of course abound in mythographical lore. Fortunately, there is an excellent guide to them in Smalley's *English Friars;* let us notice particularly two examples:

1/ John Ridevall's *Fulgentius metaforalis* is a 're-moralization' of parts of Fulgentius's *Mythologiae,* based on an association of the Classical gods with the Christian virtues or their components; it is edited by **Hans Liebeschütz,** *Fulgentius metaforalis: Ein Beitrag zur Geschichte der antiken Mythologie im Mittelalter,* Studien der Bibliothek Warburg 4 (Leipzig 1926), with 23 illustrations from MS. Vat. Palat. lat. 1066, an extensive introduction, and a full index of names and subjects. Liebeschütz's version, however – made up of six chapters on idolatry, Saturn and prudence, Jupiter and benevolence, Juno and memory, Neptune and intelligence, and Pluto and providence – represents only about half of the common medieval text (found in many of the manuscripts listed by Liebeschütz himself, pp 47-53, as well as in MS. Oxford, Bodl. 571, fols 83r-137r), which includes additional chapters on Apollo and truth, Pheton and ambition, Mercury and eloquence, Dane and cupidity, Ganymede and sodomy, Perseus and fortitude/audacity, Alceste and conjugal continence, Paris and injustice, Minerva and contemplation, Juno and the active life, and Venus and the voluptuous life; the subject is covered in detail by **Judson B. Allen, 'Commentary as Criticism: The Text, Influence, and Literary Theory of the *Fulgentius Metaphored* of John Ridewall,'** in *Acta Conventus Neo-Latini Amstelodamensis: Proceedings of the Second International Congress of Neo-Latin Studies, Amsterdam 19-24 August 1973,* ed. **P. Tuynman, G.C. Kuiper,** and **E. Kessler,** Humanistische Bibliothek 1, Abhandlungen 26 (Munich 1979) pp 25-47.

2/ **Robert Holkot's** enormously popular commentary on the Book of Wisdom, ed. Ryter (for which see p. 29 above), with an index of subjects at the beginning, includes many bits of mythography – for example on Hercules (pp 86-7), on Juno (520), on Jupiter (527 and 541), etc. In addition, his *Moralizationum historiarum, siue explicationum moralium ... liber unus,* printed *ibid.* pp 703-50, contains mythographic themes including some of his famous 'pictures' (discussed by Smalley, *English Friars* pp 165-83, with an index on 393-4), a brief index of subjects (p. 708), and a rather erratic index of subjects and incipits (749-50).

Let us next turn to a group of complexly related late medieval treatments of the Classical gods, which, though obviously dependent on earlier mythography, are similar enough to one another to be thought of as a group:

Petrarch's famous description of the gods in *Africa* 3.111-262 and passim, ed. **Nicola Festa**, Edizione nazionale delle opere di Francesco Petrarca 1 (Florence 1926) pp 55-62 and passim, trans. **Thomas G. Bergin** and **Alice S. Wilson** as *Petrarch's "Africa"* (New Haven 1977) pp 45-50 and passim, presents a rich and influential cluster of mythographic detail, though it is without allegory.

Pierre Bersuire (Petrus Berchorius) added as the fifteenth book of his *Reductorium morale* (discussed on p. 46 above) an elaborate moralization of Ovid's *Metamorphoses* (see p. 125 below); the opening chapter of this book is an introductory description and moralization of the gods themselves, entitled *De formis figurisque deorum.* The whole of *Reductorium morale* bk 15 was detached from Bersuire's canon at an early date and attributed to Thomas Walleys; a redaction is published under the title *Metamorphosis Ouidiana moraliter a magistro Thoma Walleys ... explanata* (Paris 1509, 1511, 1515, etc.), with a 22-page alphabetical 'Tabula moralis interpretationis' preceding fol. 1; the 1509 edition is reprinted under the name of Bersuire, along with the *Libellus* attributed to 'Albricus'(see below) from the edition of Basel, 1543, and with introductory notes by **Stephen Orgel** (New York 1979). The 1509 edition has been transcribed and published under the supervision of **J. Engels**, with abbreviations expanded but retaining the original divisions of lines and folios, in the series 'Werkmateriaal uitgegeven door het Instituut voor Laat Latijn der Rijksuniversiteit Utrecht' (Utrecht 1960-2), 2 vols: vol. I is *De formis figurisque deorum (Reductorium morale, XV, 1)*; for II see p. 125 below. Vol. III of the same series (1966) is a critical text of the *De formis,* based on MS. Brussels, Bibl. Reg. 863-9, with an introduction on the development and relationships of Bersuire's mythography and a brief index of subjects; passages not found in the Paris edition are identified by a vertical line in the left margin, and sources are indicated in the right margin. Large excerpts from another manuscript version of the *De formis* (MS. Milan, Ambros. D 66 inf.) are printed by **Fausto Ghisalberti**, 'L'*Ovidius moralizatus* di Pierre Bersuire,' *Studj romanzi* 23 (1933) 87-101, with a list of manuscripts on pp 133-4.

A brief work entitled *De deorum imaginibus libellus*, attributed in its manuscript to '**Albricus**' but probably dating from around 1400, is essentially Bersuire's *De formis* without the moralizations. Besides the early edition in van Staveren's *Auctores mythographi* (discussed on pp 106-7 above), it is edited along with Ridevall's *Fulgentius metaforalis* on pp 117-28 of the Liebeschütz edition, followed by the 34 pen-drawings which accompany it in MS. Vat. Reg. lat. 1290; a valuable set of tables showing the parallels between it and various other mythographic works appears on pp 58-64. It is also included in the 1979 reprint of Bersuire's *Metamorphosis ... explanata.*

Finally, there are two fifteenth-century French summaries of the gods, both closely derived from Bersuire's *De formis:* 1/ the so-called 'Copenhagen Commentary' which precedes the *Ovide moralisé* in a manuscript in the Royal Library at Copenhagen, ed. **Jeannette Theodora Maria van 't Sant**, *Commentaire de Copenhague de l'*'*Ovide moralisé' avec l'édition critique du septième livre* (Amsterdam 1929) pp 19-64, and C. de Boer et al., *'Ovide moralisé'* (see p. 124 below) V, 387-429; and 2/ the 'first proem' to a prose reworking of the *Ovide moralisé* by **Colard Mansion**, *Ovide de Salmonen son livre intitule Metamorphoses translate et compile par Colard Mansion ...* (Bruges: Colard Mansion, 1484), [fols 1r-36r], with a table of chapters [fols 36r-40v], 17 large woodcuts of scenes from the *Metamorphoses,* and 17 smaller ones of individual gods and goddesses, passim (other eds Paris 1493, 1505, 1531, etc.). The relationships among these works are variously analyzed by Seznec, *Survival of the Pagan Gods* pp 170-9; Liebeschütz, *Fulgentius metaforalis* (in tables mentioned above); van 't Sant, *Commentaire de Copenhague* pp 5-18; and **Joseph Engels**, *Etudes sur l'Ovide moralisé* (Groningen 1945) pp 24-39.

Another text that should perhaps be included here is the introductory treatment of the gods in the first 31 chapters of bk 1 of Thomas Walsingham's *Arcana deorum* (pp 3-39 in the van Kluyve edition, for which see p. 125 below), chs 1-16 of which seem derived from the Third Vatican Mythographer, and chs 17-31 from Bersuire's *De formis.*

A much more extensive and tremendously influential fourteenth-century allegorization of the gods, organized around their genealogies, is **Giovanni Boccaccio's** *Genealogie deorum Gentilium libri*, ed. **Vincenzo Romano**, Scrittori d'Italia 200-1 (Bari 1951), 2 vols, with a detailed table of contents at the end of each volume, and an index of authors and works cited at the end of vol. II; alphabetical indices of proper names are included in some early editions (e.g. Vicenza: Simon de Gabis, Bevilaqua, 1487, fols cxlvii-clxviii; and for a listing of early editions see **Ernest H. Wilkins, 'The Genealogy of the Editions of the *Genealogia deorum*,' *Modern Philology*** 17 [1919-20] 425-38). A selection of the genealogical 'trees' which in manuscripts and some early editions precede each of the first thirteen books is reproduced by **Ernest Hatch Wilkins, *The Trees of the 'Genealogia deorum' of Boccaccio*** (Chicago 1923).

Another elaborate mythographic compilation, written from 1391 to 1406 by **Coluccio Salutati**, is the *De laboribus Herculis*, really a massive defense of poetry and mythology in which the Labours of Hercules are embedded; it is edited by **B.L. Ullman**, Thesaurus mundi 1/1-2 (Zurich [1951]), 2 vols, with the 'first edition' (a long letter to Joannes de Senis) in II, 585-635, and no index except an index of citations from other authors, arranged alphabetically by author and work.

A Spanish work on the same subject, apparently written independently of Salutati in 1417, is **Enrique de Villena's** *Los doze trabajos de Hércules*, ed. **Margherita Morreale**, Biblioteca selecta de clásicos españoles 2/20 (Madrid 1958); it is organized according to the Twelve Labours as enumerated in Boethius's *De consolatione*, with each Labour subjected to a fourfold explanation: 'Istoria nuda' (poetic exposition), 'Declaraçion' (allegory), 'Verdad' (euhemeristic interpretation), and 'Aplicaçion' (application of a moral lesson to society).

Around 1400 **Christine de Pizan** wrote her *Epître d'Othéa la déesse à Hector*, consisting of a hundred 'histoires,' each in three parts: a text recounting some classical story, a gloss, and an allegory or morality. The *Epître* exists in many manuscripts and a few early editions (listed by Bühler, below, p. xii, n. 2), and also in two fifteenth-century English translations: one by **Stephen Scrope**, ed. **Curt F. Bühler**, *The Epistle of Othea, Translated from the French Text of Christine de Pisan* ..., EETS 264 (Oxford 1970), with full notes, an 'Index of Biblical Quotations,' an 'Index of Patristic (and Other Religious) Quotations,' and an index of proper names; the other perhaps by **Anthony Babyngton**, ed. **James D. Gordon**, *The Epistle of Othea to Hector: A 'Lytil Bibell of Knyghthod'* (University of Pennsylvania diss. 1942), with notes, an index of names and subjects, and a convenient table analyzing the *Epistle* according to 'Narrative,' 'Chivalric Virtue,' and 'Morality' (pp ix-xiii).

Individual Authors

Let us turn now to commentaries on particular authors and texts, which offer the most promising approach when one is pursuing an allusion or echo from a known work. A comprehensive catalogue of 'Latin translations of ancient Greek authors and the Latin commentaries on ancient Latin (and Greek) authors up to the year 1600,' with descriptions and full bibliographical information, is being produced under the general editorship of **Paul Oskar Kristeller** and **F. Edward Cranz**, *Catalogus translationum et commentariorum: Medieval and Renaissance Latin Translations and Commentaries* (Union académique internationale, Washington, D.C. 1960ff), 6 vols through 1986. It is arranged according to Classical authors, and each volume includes whatever articles have been completed by that time, without regard to alphabetical order; alphabetical indices will presumably be added at some later point. Vol. I contains a useful general bibliography (pp XV-XXIII) and lists of Greek and Latin authors 'who wrote before 600 A.D. and whose works were available before 1600 A.D.' (pp 1-76). A much briefer catalogue of early scholia and commentaries, of limited use for present purposes, is compiled by **Paul Faider**, *Répertoire des éditions de scolies et commentaires d'auteurs latins*, Collection d'études latines 8 (Paris 1931).

Since one's initial problem is frequently that of finding out whether a particular concept, person, or motif appears in the works of a given poet or group of poets, indices and concordances are of fundamental importance for research of this kind. A basic index of authors and editions is provided by **Wolfgang Buchwald** et al., *Tusculum-Lexikon griechischer und lateinischer Autoren des Altertums und des Mittelalters* (3rd ed. Darmstadt and Munich 1982).

A convenient general guide to lexica, indices, and concordances for individual authors is **Henri Quellet**'s *Bibliographia indicum, lexicorum, et concordantiarum auctorum Latinorum: Répertoire bibliographique des index, lexiques, et concordances des auteurs latins* (Hildesheim 1980), arranged alphabetically, with indices of authors on pp 239-56. The principal concordances will also be cited for each of the authors treated below.

Though medieval mythographic material can be derived from a variety of Classical literary sources, the most important are probably the works of Vergil (especially the *Aeneid*), the works of Ovid (especially the *Metamorphoses*), Lucan's *De bello civili* (*Pharsalia*), and the works of Statius (especially the *Thebaid*); indexed editions of all are easily available. I will take them up in that order, followed by some later writers who generated a tradition of mythographic commentary. No attempt will be made to cover purely grammatical commentaries, like those assembled by **Heinrich Keil** in *Grammatici Latini* (Leipzig 1855-78, repr. 1961), 7 vols and suppl. Another important product of medieval scholarship which for present purposes can be bypassed with a nod is the *accessus*, or introductory summary intended to epitomize a work in various aspects. The best introduction to the *accessus* is by **Edwin A. Quain**, 'The Medieval *accessus ad auctores*,' *Traditio* 3 (1945) 215-64, now reprinted separately under the same title (New York 1986); the best collection of texts is by **R.B.C. Huygens**, *Accessus ad auctores; Bernard d'Utrecht; Conrad d'Hirsau, Dialogus super auctores* (Leyden 1970), with an index of proper names on pp 132-6.

Besides the commentaries cited below, mythographic detail is of course incorporated piecemeal into any number of works that are themselves not primarily mythographic in intent. An almost random example is **John of Salisbury**'s *Policraticus*, ed. Clement C.J. Webb (Oxford 1909, repr. Frankfurt 1965), 2 vols, with an 'Index auctorum' in II, 468-503; it is translated in part by **John Dickinson** as *The Statesman's Book of John of Salisbury* (New York 1927), and the translation is completed by **Joseph B. Pike** as *Frivolities of Courtiers and Footprints of Philosophers* (Minneapolis 1938). Another obvious example is **Dante**'s *Convivio*, ed **G. Busnelli** and **G. Vandelli**, rev. **Antonio Enzo Quaglio**, Opere di Dante 5 (2nd ed. Florence 1964), 2 vols, with an index of names and subjects; and ed. **Maria Simonelli**, Testi e saggi di letterature moderne, Testi 2 (Bologna 1966), with a summary index and an index of names. There are many translations – for example by **William Walrond Jackson**, *Dante's Convivio* (Oxford 1909).

VERGIL

A recent concordance to the works of Vergil is that of **Henrietta Holm Warwick**, *A Vergil Concordance* (Minneapolis 1975). In addition, there are a number of earlier indices and lexica which serve much the same purpose – for example **Monroe Nichols Wetmore**, *Index verborum Vergilianus* (New Haven 1911); **Hugo Merquet**, *Lexikon zu Vergilius mit Angabe sämtlicher Stellen*, ed. **Hans Frisch** (Leipzig 1912); and **Wilhelm Ott**, *Rückläufiger Wortindex zu Vergil: Bucolica, Georgica, Aeneis* (Tübingen 1974). Others are cited by Quellet, *Bibliographia* pp 223-8.

The classic study of Vergil in medieval tradition is **Domenico Comparetti's** *Virgilio nel medio evo*, first published in 1872, revised by the author in 1895, and edited with revisions by **Giorgio Pasquali**, Il pensiero storico (Florence [1937-41]), 2 vols, of which vol. I deals with literary tradition and ch. 8 of that volume (pp 128-46) with allegorical interpretation; the second edition was translated by **E.F.M. Benecke** as *Vergil in the Middle Ages* (London 1895). Though it can be used with caution, the author's extreme contempt for medieval allegory makes it much less useful for present purposes than might be expected. Medieval allegory of the famous fourth Eclogue is conveniently surveyed by **Pierre Courcelle**, 'Les Exégèses chrétiennes de la quatrième Eglogue,' *Revue des études anciennes* 59 (1957) 294- 319; and patristic commentary on *Aeneid* bk 6 by **Courcelle**, 'Les Pères de l'église devant les enfers virgiliens,' *Archives d'histoire doctrinale et littéraire du moyen âge* 30 (1955) 5-74, with an index of authors on pp 71-4. *L'Année philologique* (see p. 105 above), beginning with vol. 24 (1955 [for 1953]), includes under 'Auteurs et textes' a section 'Vergilii commentatores, traductores, imitatores.'

The *Saturnalia* of Macrobius (4th-5th C), essentially a celebration of the learning of Vergil, has been mentioned in the section above. The fullest and most influential Vergilian commentary is that attributed to the non-Christian grammarian **Servius** (4th-5th C), including the *Aeneid,* the *Eclogues,* and the *Georgics*. It survives in two versions: a shorter version, presumably the work of Servius himself, and a longer, resulting from later accretions (sometimes called 'Servius Danielis' after Pierre Daniel, who first printed it); though the part attributed to

Servius is by no means devoid of allegory, the accretions contain proportionately more. The latest complete edition is that of **Georg Thilo** and **Hermann Hagen**, *Servii Grammatici qui feruntur in Vergilii carmina commentarii* (Leipzig 1881-1902, repr. Hildesheim 1961), 3 vols in 4. Vols I-II contain the commentary on the *Aeneid;* III/i, the commentary on the *Eclogues* and the *Georgics;* and III/ii, a collection of other commentaries to be mentioned below. Throughout the Servian commentary, the shorter version attributed to Servius himself is printed in roman type, with the later accretions in italic; further brief additions are often included in the footnotes, which should always be checked. Though the edition itself has no indices, there are two substantial indices based on it: **Earl LeVerne Crum**, *Index of Proper Names in Servius*, University of Iowa Humanistic Studies 4/1 (Iowa City 1927); and a more elaborate index of subjects and names by **J.F. Mountford** and **J.T. Schultz**, *Index rerum et nominum in scholiis Servii et Aelii Donati tractatorum*, Cornell Studies in Classical Philology 23 (Ithaca, N.Y. 1930). In addition, **J.W. Jones, Jr**, 'Allegorical Interpretation in Servius,' *The Classical Journal* 56 (1961) 217-26, includes on p. 226 a 'Table of Allegorical Notes' arranged by lines in the *Aeneid*. A new edition of the Servian commentary is underway, ed **Edward Kennard Rand** et al., *Servianorum in Vergilii carmina commentariorum editio Harvardiana*, Special Publications of the American Philological Association 1 (Lancaster, Pa and Oxford 1946ff), vols II-III through 1965, covering *Aeneid* bks 1-5; vol. I, which will appear last, will contain the commentary on the *Eclogues* and the *Georgics* along with a prolegomenon. Where the shorter and longer versions differ, they are printed in parallel columns.

There are a number of other early commentaries and collections of scholia on the works of Vergil, which, though less useful for present purposes than the Servian commentary, are nevertheless worth mentioning along with it. A onetime commentary by Aelius Donatus seems to survive only in pieces incorporated by other commentators. That of **Aemilius Asper** (2nd C) on the *Eclogues, Georgics,* and *Aeneid,* preserved mostly in other commentaries and reconstructed by **Alfred Thomsin**, *Etude sur le commentaire virgilien d'Aemilius Asper*, Bibliothèque de la Faculté de philosophie et lettres de l'Université de Liège 125 (Paris 1952) pp 125-43, is literary in intent but includes no allegory. The extensive commentary of **Tiberius Claudius Dona-**

tus (5th C or earlier) on the *Aeneid*, ed. **Heinrich Georges**, *Tiberi Claudi Donati ad Tiberium Claudium Maximum Donatianum filium suum interpretationes Vergilianae*, Bibliotheca Teubneriana (Leipzig 1905-6, repr. Stuttgart 1969), 2 vols, with an index of names and subjects, is primarily rhetorical in its approach.

A number of commentaries and collections of scholia on the *Eclogues* and *Georgics*, ed. Thilo and Hagen, *Servii ... commentarii* III/ii, contain a good bit of mythological explanation and occasionally allegory: the *Explanatio* of **Junius Philargyrius** on the *Eclogues*, extant in two versions (pp 1-189), an *Anonymi brevis expositio Vergilii Georgicorum* (191-320), a commentary on the *Eclogues* and the *Georgics* attributed to **Probus** (321-90), and the '**Scholia Veronensia**' on the *Eclogues* (391-450).

A collection of scholia on the *Eclogues* and the *Georgics* employing several of the above works, and like them including substantial mythological information along with some allegory, is the '**Scholia Bernensia**' preserved in manuscripts of the ninth and tenth centuries, ed. **Hermann Hagen**, *Scholia Bernensia ad Vergili Bucolica atque Georgica*, Jahrbuch für classische Philologie, Suppl. 4 (Leipzig 1867), with three appendices and an 'Epimetrum' containing excerpts from other manuscripts (pp 984-1006), and indices of authors cited, mythological references, and names of men, places, and peoples.

This whole group of commentaries and scholia is conveniently surveyed by **Martin Schanz**, *Geschichte der römischen Literatur bis zum Gesetzgebungswerk des Kaisers Justinian*, 4th ed. rev. **Carl Hosius**, Handbuch der Altertumswissenschaft 8 (Munich 1927-35, repr. 1959-67) II, 102-10.

Much more important is the *Expositio Virgilianae continentiae*, written in the fifth or sixth century by the same **Fulgentius** who compiled the *Mythologiae* (for which see p. 108 above); after a few summarizing statements about the *Eclogues* and the *Georgics*, Fulgentius calls up the shade of Vergil himself, who presents an intensely allegorical interpretation of the *Aeneid* as the successive stages of man's life. The *Expositio* is edited by Helm, *Fulgentii ... opera* pp 83-107, with indices of authors cited, names, and words. It is translated, with notes, by **Terrence Anthony McVeigh**, '**The Allegory of the Poets: A Study of Classical Tradition in Medieval Interpretation of Virgil**' (Fordham University unpublished diss. 1964) pp 201-53, and by Whitbread,

Fulgentius the Mythographer, with a useful introduction and notes, and indices of authors and names. An edition with an Italian translation by **Tullio Agozzino** and **Ferruccio Zanlucchi,** Accademia Patavina di scienze, lettere, ed arti, Collana accademica 4 (Padua 1972), includes notes citing many parallels in other authors.

A fragment of an anonymous commentary preserved in a tenth-century manuscript, covering the *Eclogues* and the first *Georgic,* is edited by **A. Boucherie,** *Fragment d'un commentaire sur Virgile,* Publications de la Société pour l'étude des langues romanes (Montpellier 1875), with a glossary.

An important later commentary covering the first six books of the *Aeneid,* written in the twelfth century and traditionally ascribed to **Bernard Silvestris,** follows Fulgentius's allegory of the stages of life, interpreting bk 1 as infancy, bk 2 as boyhood, bk 3 as adolescence, bk 4 as early manhood, and bk 5 as the age of full virility; an inferior edition by **W. Riedel,** *Commentum super sex libros Eneidos Virgilii* (Greifswald diss. 1924), which for years was the only printed version, is now superseded by that of **Julian Ward Jones** and **Elizabeth Frances Jones,** *Commentum quod dicitur Bernardi Silvestris super sex libros Eneidos Vergilii: The Commentary on the First Six Books of the Aeneid of Vergil Commonly Attributed to Bernardus Silvestris* (Lincoln, Nebr. 1977), with indices of authors cited and of names and subjects. There is a translation by **Earl G. Schreiber** and **Thomas E. Maresca,** *Commentary on the First Six Books of Virgil's Aeneid* (Lincoln, Nebr. 1979), with an index of subjects.

Similar interpretations of the *Aeneid* are summarized briefly by John of Salisbury, *Policraticus* 8.24, ed. Webb, II, 415-17 (817a-818a), trans. Pike, *Frivolities of Courtiers* pp 402-4; and by Dante, *Convivio* 4.26.8-15 (II, 332-7 in the Busnelli and Vandelli edition, pp 208-10 in Simonelli), trans. Jackson pp 284-6. Some notes on bk 6 of the *Aeneid,* possibly from the eleventh century, are edited by **J.J.H. Savage,** '**Mediaeval Notes on the Sixth *Aeneid* in Parisinus 7930,**' *Speculum* 9 (1934) 204-12. An interesting cumulative gloss from the twelfth century is edited by **Christopher Baswell, 'The Medieval Allegorization of the *Aeneid:* MS. Cambridge, Peterhouse 158,**' *Traditio* 41 (1985) 181-237.

OVID

A concordance to the works of Ovid has been compiled by **Roy J. Deferrari** et al., *A Concordance of Ovid* (Washington, D.C. 1939). Other works that can be used in similar ways are **Otto Eichert**, *Vollständiges Wörterbuch zu den Verwandlungen des Publius Ovidius Naso* (7th ed. Hanover 1878; repr. Hildesheim 1972); **Johannes Siebelis**, *Wörterbuch zu Ovids Metamorphosen*, ed. **Friedrich Polle** (5th ed. Leipzig 1983, repr. Wiesbaden 1969); and **Julianus Maschietto**, *Onomasticon Ovidianum* (Passau 1970). Others are cited by Quellet, *Bibliographia* pp 130-4. Some useful general studies of Ovid in medieval tradition are those of **Lester K. Born**, 'Ovid and Allegory,' *Speculum* 9 (1934) 362-79; **Salvatore Battaglia**, 'La tradizione di Ovidio nel medioevo,' *Filologia romanza (Filologia e letteratura)* 6 (1959) 185-224; **Franco Munari**, *Ovid im Mittelalter* (Zurich 1960); **Paule Demats**, *Fabula: Trois études de mythographie antique et médiévale*, Publications romanes et françaises 122 (Geneva 1973); and **Kenneth J. Knoespel**, *Narcissus and the Invention of Personal History*, Garland Publications in Comparative Literature (New York 1985) pp 23-58.

Though commentary on Ovid develops later than that on Vergil – not getting well underway until the twelfth century – it is much more plentiful during the later Middle Ages than Vergilian commentary. The *Metamorphoseon narrationes* or *Narrationes fabularum Ovidianarum*, attributed to the mysterious **Lactantius Placidus** (5th-6th C?), is a summary of the fables in the *Metamorphoses,* with incorporations from elsewhere; besides appearing in many early editions of Ovid and in van Staveren's *Auctores mythographi*, it is edited by **Hugo Magnus**, *Metamorphoseon libri XV, Lactanti Placidi qui dicitur narrationes fabularum Ovidianarum* (Berlin 1914) pp 625-721, and by **D.A. Slater**, *Towards a Text of the Metamorphosis of Ovid* (Oxford 1927) appendix.

A brief and apparently jocular versified interpretation of the amours of the gods as the union of monks and nuns, preserved in a twelfth-century manuscript, is edited by **Wilhelm Wattenbach**, '**Mittheilungen aus zwei Handschriften der k. Hof- und Staatsbibliothek,**' *Sitzungsberichte der philosophisch-philologischen und historischen*

Classe der k. b. Akademie der Wissenschaften zu München 3 (1873) 685-747.

The first major commentary on the *Metamorphoses* is a brief but interesting *Allegoriae super Ovidii Metamorphosin* written in the twelfth century by **Arnulf of Orléans**, edited in part by **Fausto Ghisalberti**, '**Arnolfo d'Orléans: Un cultore di Ovidio nel secolo XII,**' *Memorie del R. Istituto lombardo di scienze e lettere: Classe di lettere, scienze morali e storiche* 24/4 (1932) 157-234, with sizeable excerpts from the text of the *Allegoriae* and valuable accompanying notes on pp 201-29, an index of names and sources on 230-3, and a long, informative introduction, including many extended quotations from mythographic works in manuscripts and detailed information about annotated manuscripts of Ovid on 157-200.

Albrecht von Halberstadt's commentary on the *Metamorphoses*, written in German rhymed couplets and dating from the early thirteenth century, survives only in fragments; it was edited and revised in Early Modern German in 1544 by **Jörg Wickram**, whose edition provided the basis for **Karl Bartsch's** *Albrecht von Halberstadt und Ovid im Mittelalter*, Bibliothek der gesammten deutschen National-Literatur 38 (Quedlinburg 1861, repr. Amsterdam 1965), where it appears as a poem of over 10,000 lines, with marginal references to the corresponding book- and line-numbers of the *Metamorphoses*, useful notes, a word-index, and a long introduction that is valuable despite its date.

Another versified allegorization of the *Metamorphoses*, written in the thirteenth century by **John of Garland**, is the 520-line *Integumenta super Ovidium Metamorphoseos*, ed. **Fausto Ghisalberti**, *Integumenta Ovidii: Poemetto inedito del secolo XIII*, Testi e documenti inediti o rari 2 (Messina 1933), with an index of proper names, an informative introduction, and extremely valuable notes including many parallels from other authors, sometimes quoted from manuscript. Though on the whole the *Integumenta* is rather jejune, it is distinguished by its allegories drawn from science and medicine – for example in lines 109-10 (p. 44), where Pan pursuing Syrinx (Latin *Syringa*) is interpreted as a man looking for a syringe to relieve his bladder!

Brief excerpts from two thirteenth-century commentaries, the *Versus Bursarii Ouidii* (covering nearly all the works of Ovid) and the *Liber Titan* (covering the *Metamorphoses*) are printed by E.H. Alton, 'Ovid in the Mediaeval Schoolroom,' *Hermathena* 95 (1961) 70-82. The allegorical part of the Ovidian commentary by **Giovanni del Virgilio**, dating from the early fourteenth century and employing both verse and prose, is edited by **Fausto Ghisalberti** under the title *Allegorie librorum Ovidii Metamorphoseos*, in 'Giovanni del Virgilio espositore delle *Metamorfosi*,' *Giornale Dantesco* 34 N.S. 4 (1933 for 1931) 1-110, with the text of the *Allegorie* on pp 43-107, an index of allegories on 108-10, and an index of manuscripts on 39-42; the rest of Giovanni's commentary is being edited under the direction of Virginia Brown.

The most elaborate interpretation of Ovid produced by the Middle Ages is the *Ovide moralisé*, a paraphrase and moralization of the *Metamorphoses* written in French octosyllabic couplets, probably between 1316 and 1328. It is edited by **C. de Boer** et al., *'Ovide moralisé': Poème du commencement du quatorzième siècle*, Verhandelingen der Koninklijke Akademie van Wetenschappen te Amsterdam, Afdeeling Letterkunde N.R. 15, 21, 30 no. 3, 37, 43 (Amsterdam 1915, 1920, 1931, 1936, 1938), 5 vols. Vol. I contains a general introduction and bks 1-3; vol. II, bks 4-6; vol. III, bks 7-9; vol. IV, bks 10-13; and vol. V, bks 14-15 along with two appendices: a passage from bk 14 found in a single manuscript, and the 'Copenhagen Commentary' mentioned on p. 114 above. Each book of the *Ovide* is an expanded paraphrase of the corresponding book of the *Metamorphoses*, interrupted at fairly regular intervals by extended allegorical and/or moral interpretations – thus producing a continuous pattern of paraphrase followed by interpretation. In the de Boer edition, each book is preceded by a 'Sommaire,' relating lines of the *Ovide* to the corresponding passage in the *Metamorphoses*. Even without an initial clue, then, the *Ovide moralisé* can be mechanically checked for a given mythographic motif by first using a concordance or an indexed edition to find out where (or whether) it appears in the *Metamorphoses* itself, and then consulting the 'Sommaire' for the relevant book to find the corresponding passage in the *Ovide*. It should be noted that the *Ovide moralisé* contains a good bit of apparently original interpretation, so that its value as a 'repository of tradition' is open to serious question; on the other hand, the influence of it and its progeny seems to have been tremendous, thus making it in itself a plausible source of tradition for later literary works. One fifteenth-century prose resumé is edited by de Boer, *Ovide moralisé en prose (texte du quinzième siècle)*, Verhandelingen der Koninklijke Nederlandse Akademie van Wetenschappen, Afd. Letterkunde N.R. 61 no. 2 (Amsterdam 1954), with an index of proper names. Other items are cited by Bossuat, *Manuel bibliographique* pp 510-11, *Supplément* p. 107, and *Second supplément* p. 105.

Another full and immensely popular exposition of the *Metamorphoses*, dating from the second quarter of the fourteenth century, is the *Ovidius moralizatus* written by **Pierre Bersuire** (Petrus Berchorius) as bk 15, chs 2-15, of his *Reductorium morale*. As we have seen in the previous section, the whole of bk 15 (including also ch. 1, *De formis figurisque deorum*) was detached from Bersuire's canon at an early date and attributed to Thomas Walleys; for published editions see p. 113 above. In the Engels-supervised transcription of the 1509 edition, the *Ovidius moralizatus* occupies vol. II (1962). The critical text (based on MS. Brussels, Bibl. Reg. 863-9) will presumably appear in vol. IV; in the meantime, a critical text of ch. 2 only (covering *Metamorphoses* bk 1) has been edited by **Maria S. van der Bijl**, 'Petrus Berchorius, *Reductorium morale* liber XV: *Ovidius moralizatus cap. ii*,' *Vivarium* 9 (1971) 25-48. Large excerpts from chs 1-10 (containing moralizations of *Metamorphoses* bks 1-9), from the version found in MS. Milan, Ambros. D 66 inf. (see again p. 113 above), are published on pp 102-32 of Ghisalberti's article in *Studj romanzi* 23.

An early fifteenth-century paraphrase and explication of the *Metamorphoses*, preserved in a single manuscript, is **Thomas Walsingham**'s *Archana deorum*, ed. **Robert A. van Kluyve** (Durham, N.C. 1968), with indices of authors cited and of proper names; following an introductory description of the gods in 1.1-31 (see also p. 114 above), the interpretation of the *Metamorphoses* begins with 1.32 (p. 39).

There are also many commentaries on Ovid's *Fasti*, all of them unpublished. Excerpts from several are printed by **E.H. Alton**, 'The Medieval Commentators on Ovid's *Fasti*,' *Hermathena* 20 (1930) 119-51, particularly the marginalia from MS. Brussels, Bibl. Reg. 5369-73, on pp 129-46; selections are also quoted by Ghisalberti in the introduction and notes to his 'Arnolfo d'Orléans,' passim. The most prominent commentary on the *Fasti* seems to have been that by the twelfth-century **Arnulf of Orléans**, which is edited by **Jean Holzworth**, '**An Unpublished Commentary on Ovid's *Fasti* by Arnulfus of Orléans**' (Bryn Mawr unpublished diss. 1940), and quoted in excerpts by her in '**Hugutio's *Derivationes* and Arnulfus's Commentary on Ovid's *Fasti*,**' *Transactions of the American Philological Association* 73 (1942) 259-76, as well as by Alton, 'Medieval Commentators' pp 124-8. A study of certain unedited *accessus* and commentaries on the *Ars amatoria* and *Heroides*, including some excerpts, is contributed by **Lucia Rosa**, '**Su alcuni commenti inediti alle opere di Ovidio**,' *Annali della Facoltà di lettere e filosofia dell'Università di Napoli* 5 (1955) 191-231.

Finally, the use of Ovid in medieval scientific writing, which can provide the stuff of figurative language, is surveyed by **Simone Viarre**, *La Survie d'Ovide dans la littérature scientifique des XIIe et XIIIe siècles*, Publications du CESCM 4 (Poitiers 1966), with many quotations in the text, indices of citations from Ovid and from other authors, and an extensive bibliography.

LUCAN

The concordance to Lucan is by **Roy J. Deferrari** et al., *A Concordance of Lucan* (Washington, D.C. 1940); also useful is **George William Mooney**, *Index to the Pharsalia of Lucan*, *Hermathena* 44, 1st suppl. (Dublin 1927). Other such works are cited by Quellet, *Bibliographia* pp 106-8. Medieval glosses and commentaries on Lucan are conveniently surveyed by **Berthe M. Marti**, *Arnulfi Aurelianensis glosule super Lucanum*, Papers and Monographs of the American Academy in Rome 18 (Rome 1958) pp XXX-XXXI.

Besides a set of unrewarding scholia from the sixth century or earlier, ed. **Hermann Genthe**, *Scholia vetera in M. Annaei Lucani Bellum civile* (Berlin 1868), there are three published medieval commentaries on Lucan. A rather jejune set of glosses from before the tenth century, the *Adnotationes super Lucanum*, is edited by **Johann Endt**,

Bibliotheca Teubneriana (Leipzig 1909, repr. Stuttgart 1969), with an index of authors and a general index; a supplement, based on many additional manuscripts and covering bks 1-7 of the poem to date, is being edited by **G.A. Cavajoni**, *Supplementum adnotationum super Lucanum*, Testi e documenti per lo studio dell'antichità 63 (Milan 1979 ff), 2 vols through 1984. A commentary preserved in a tenth-century manuscript, and including some mythographic material, is edited by **Hermann Usener**, *M. Annaei Lucani commenta Bernensia*, Scholia in Lucani *Bellum civile* 1 (Leipzig 1869, repr. Hildesheim 1967), with an index of authors. The fullest commentary of all, however, is that by Arnulf of Orléans (12th C), ed. Marti (above), with a useful introduction and an index of words and names.

STATIUS

The concordance to the works of Statius is by **Roy J. Deferrari** and **Sister M. Clement Eagan**, *A Concordance of Statius* (Brookland, D.C. 1942); other such works are cited by Quellet, *Bibliographia* pp 191-3. Commentaries will be treated by Paul M. Clogan in a forthcoming volume of *Catalogus translationum et commentariorum* ed. Kristeller and Cranz. The fullest commentary on the *Thebaid* is that of the scholar known as **Lactantius Placidus** (5th-6th C?); it is edited, apparently inadequately, by **Richard Jahnke**, *Lactantii Placidi qui dicitur commentarios in Statii Thebaida et commentarium in Achilleida*, Bibliotheca Teubneriana (Leipzig 1898), with an index of parallels to the Vatican Mythographers and an index of names. A brief *Super Thebaiden* traditionally attributed to **Fulgentius**, ed. Helm, *Opera* pp 180-6, and trans. with an introduction by Whitbread, *Fulgentius* pp 239-44, probably belongs to the twelfth century, as maintained by **Brian Stock**, 'A Note on *Thebaid* Commentaries: Paris, BN lat. 3012,' *Traditio* 27 (1971) 468-71. Glosses on the *Thebaid* (not to be included in the *Catalogus*) are listed by **Clogan**, 'Medieval Glossed Manuscripts of the *Thebaid*,' *Manuscripta* 11 (1967) 102-12; and a full account of the manuscript commentaries on both the *Thebaid* and *Achilleid* is presented by **Robert Dale Sweeney**, *Prolegomena to an Edition of the Scholia to Statius*, *Mnemosyne* suppl. 8 (Leyden 1969), with a *specimen criticum* of Lactantius Placidus's commentary on *Theb.* 3.205-386 on pp 94-110. A commentary on the *Achilleid* by

Lactantius Placidus is included in the edition by Jahnke, and is covered by his indices mentioned above. And the medieval text of the *Achilleid,* differing substantially from the text which is now standard, is edited by **Clogan,** *The Medieval Achilleid of Statius* (Leyden 1968), along with the accompanying glosses.

JUVENAL

There are two concordances to the satires of Juvenal: **Lucile Kelling** and **Albert Suskin,** *Index verborum Iuvenalis* (Chapel Hill, N.C. 1951); and **Michel Dubrocard,** *Juvenal-Satires: Index verborum, Relevés statistiques,* Alpha-Omega 28 (Hildesheim 1976). Other indices are cited by Quellet, *Bibliographia* pp 100-1. Commentaries and glosses are covered by **Eva M. Sanford,** 'Juvenalis Decimus Junius,' in *Catalogus translationum et commentariorum* ed. Kristeller and Cranz, I, 175-238. Early scholia on Juvenal are edited by **Paul Wessner,** *Scholia in Iuvenalem vetustiora,* Bibliotheca Teubneriana (Leipzig 1941), with an index of names, subjects, and words. The twelfth-century glosses of **Guillaume de Conches,** *Glosae in Iuvenalem* ed. **Bradford Wilson,** Textes philosophiques du moyen âge 18 (Paris 1980), with an index of names and words (pp 201-3), contain occasional bits of mythography.

CLAUDIAN

Indices to Claudian are enumerated by Quellet, *Bibliographia* pp 51-2. Commentaries are covered by **Amy K. Clarke** and **Harry L. Levy,** 'Claudius Claudianus,' in *Catalogus translationum et commentariorum* ed. Kristeller and Cranz, III, 141-71. The fullest is that of **Geoffrey of Vitry** (12th C) on the *De raptu Proserpinae,* ed. **A.K. Clarke** and **P.M. Giles,** *The Commentary of Geoffrey of Vitry on Claudian, 'De raptu Proserpinae,'* Mittellateinische Studien und Texte 7 (Leiden 1973), with an index of names and an appendix of *accessus* to the *De raptu* (pp 122-4). A commentary on Claudian's *In Rufinum,* possibly by Geoffrey of Vitry, exists in three fragments – two edited by Clarke and Giles, *ibid.* pp 125-7, the other by **Emile Chatelain** and **C.-A. Pret,** 'Fragments de scholies sur Claudien,' *Revue de philologie de littérature et d'histoire anciennes* N.S. 8 (1884) 81-99.

MARTIANUS CAPELLA

Indices to Martianus (except for that in the recent edition by Willis, cited on p. 107 above) are enumerated by Quellet, *Bibliographia* p. 118. Commentaries on the *De nuptiis Philologiae et Mercurii* are surveyed by **Cora E. Lutz**, '**Martianus Capella**,' in *Catalogus translationum et commentariorum* ed. Kristeller and Cranz, II, 367-81; and more briefly by Stahl et al., *Martianus Capella and the Seven Liberal Arts*, I, 55-71. Three ninth-century commentaries are edited by **Lutz**: **Dunchad** (Martin of Laon), *Glossae in Martianum*, Philological Monographs Published by the American Philological Association 12 (Lancaster, Pa 1944), with an index of names and places; **Scotus Eriugena**, *Iohannis Scotti annotationes in Marcianum* (Cambridge, Mass. 1939), with an index of names and places; and **Remigius of Auxerre**, *Remigii Autissiodorensis commentum in Martianum Capellam* (Leyden 1962-5), 2 vols, with a full introduction and indices of names and important subjects in I, and an index of names in II. The commentary of Scotus Eriugena has been edited more recently by **Edouard Jeauneau**, *Quatre thèmes érigéniens*, Conférence Albert-le-Grand 1974 (Montreal 1978) pp 101-66, with indices of Greek words, authors, proper names, and subjects on pp 177-84. The Old High German commentary by **Notker of St Gall** (9th-10th C), ed. **E.H. Sehrt** and **Taylor Stark**, *Notkers des Deutschen Werke ... zweiter Band: Marcianus Capella, De nuptiis Philologiae et Mercurii*, Altdeutsche Textbibliothek 37 (Halle 1935), is in great part a translation and reworking of the commentary of Remigius. A late twelfth-century commentary on bks 1-2 of *De nuptiis* (MS. Vat. Barb. lat. 10), drawn mainly from Remigius, is edited by **Ann Rose Raia**, '**Barberini Manuscripts 57-66 and 121-30**' (Fordham University unpublished diss. 1965) pp 205-323. A commentary on the *De nuptiis* attributed to Bernard Silvestris is edited by **Haijo Jan Westra**, *The Commentary on Martianus Capella's 'De nuptiis' Attributed to Bernard Silvestris: A Critical Edition* (University of Toronto diss. 1979), to appear in the series Studies and Texts of the Pontifical Institute of Mediaeval Studies. Excerpts are printed by **Edouard Jeauneau**, '**Note sur l'Ecole de Chartres**,' *Studi medievali* 3rd ser. 5 (1964) 855-64, with an introduction on pp 844-9 and references to other Chartrian commentaries on Martianus, Macrobius, and Boethius, passim (reprinted in his *'Lectio philosophorum': Recherches sur l'Ecole de Chartres* [Amsterdam 1973] pp 5-49); and by Wetherbee, *Platonism and Poetry* pp 267-72.

7

Commentaries on Major Authors

There are certain major authors or works which, while not precisely classifiable under any of the headings we have considered so far, inspire traditions of commentary that can be fruitful for the study of medieval imagery. In practical terms, if a concept or image that one is interested in happens to appear in such an author or work, its medieval associations can sometimes be found by way of the commentaries. Once again, concordances will be potentially useful.

Plato, *Timaeus*

The complete concordance to the Greek text of Plato is by **Leonard Brandwood**, *A Word Index to Plato*, Compendia: Computer-Generated Aids to Literary and Linguistic Research 8 (Leeds 1976). More useful for present purposes is a 64-page alphabetical index to the *Dialogues*, compiled by **Evelyn Abbott**, *A Subject-Index to the Dialogues of Plato, being An Index to the Matters and Names Contained in the Dialogues of Plato according to the Pages of Stephens's Edition* (New York 1875, repr. 1971 in the Burt Franklin Bibliography and Reference Series 424, Philosophy Monograph Series 63). A convenient smaller guide is **Morris Stockhammer's** *Plato Dictionary* (New York 1963). All of these works, of course, include the *Timaeus* as part of the entire Platonic corpus.

For the Middle Ages, the basic commentary on the *Timaeus* is that by **Chalcidius** (probably from the early fifth century, though the date has been much disputed), edited along with his Latin translation of the *Timaeus* by **J.H. Waszink**, *Timaeus a Calcidio translatus commentarioque instructus*, Corpus Platonicum medii aevi, ed. Raymond

Klibansky, Plato Latinus 4 (2nd ed. London 1975), with various indices, including a brief index of mythological names on p. 397. In addition, Macrobius's commentary on the *Somnium Scipionis* and Martianus Capella's *De nuptiis* (treated in chapter 6 above) include a substantial amount of unsystematized commentary on the *Timaeus*. The important twelfth-century commentary by **Guillaume de Conches** is edited by **Edouard Jeauneau**, *Glosae super Platonem*, Textes philosophiques du moyen âge 13 (Paris 1965), with various indices, including indices of biblical citations, authors cited, proper names, and notable words; the footnotes contain occasional quotations from Guillaume's unprinted *Glosae super Macrobium*.

Other glosses and commentaries on the *Timaeus* are listed by **Raymond Klibansky, *The Continuity of the Platonic Tradition during the Middle Ages* (London 1939) pp 29-31; and by **Margaret Gibson, 'The Study of the *Timaeus* in the Eleventh and Twelfth Centuries,' *Pensamiento* 25 (1969) 186-8. Various brief extracts are edited by **Tullio Gregory, *Platonismo medievale: Studi e ricerche*, Istituto storico italiano per il medio evo, Studi storici fascs 26-7 (Rome 1958) passim.

Prudentius

The concordance to the works of Prudentius is by **Roy Joseph Deferrari** and **James Marshall Campbell**, *A Concordance of Prudentius*, Mediaeval Academy of America 9 (Cambridge, Mass. 1932). A bibliography of commentaries is included by **Maurice Lavarenne**, *Etude sur la langue du poète Prudence* (Paris 1933) pp 620-1; the dates and relationships of the various commentaries are treated by **Hubert Silvestre, 'Aperçu sur les commentaires carolingiens de Prudence,' *Sacris erudiri* 9 (1957) 50-74.

Medieval commentaries on Prudentius are characteristically jejune and likely not to be very rewarding for present purposes. The two on which almost all others depend are an apparently ninth-century work possibly by **John Scotus Eriugena**, ed. **John M. Burnam**, *Glossemata de Prudentio, edited from the Paris and Vatican Manuscripts*, University Studies Published by the University of Cincinnati ser. 2, I, 4 (Cincinnati 1905), consisting of brief glosses on the *Cathemerinon, Apotheosis, Hamartigenia, Psychomachia, Contra Symmachum,* and *Dittochaeon;* and a somewhat later and fuller commentary often attributed to **Remigius of Auxerre** (d. 908), ed. **Burnam,** *Commentaire anonyme sur Prudence d'après le manuscrit 413 de Valenciennes* (Paris 1910), including glosses on these same poems plus the *Peristephanon,* with a running list of parallels in other authors (pp 227-80) and indices of Greek and Latin words (287-300).

Two other commentaries on the works of Prudentius, traditionally attributed to **Iso of St Gall** or his student **Salomon** (d. 919), were first edited by **Johann Weitz,** *Aurelii Prudentii Clementis V. C. opera, noviter ad MSC. fidem recensita ... cum glosis veteribus* (Hanau 1613), and conflated by **Faustinus Arevalus,** *M. Aurelj Clementis Prudentj V. C. carmina ... glossis Isonis magistri et aliis veterum ... illustrata* (Rome 1788-9), 2 vols, in which form they are reprinted as 'Glossae veteres' in PL 59, cols 767-1078 and 60, cols 11-594.

Selected scholia from a tenth-century manuscript (Vat. lat. 3859) are included in the footnotes of **Albert Dressel,** ed., *Aurelii Prudentii Clementis quae exstant carmina* (Leipzig 1860) passim.

An eleventh-century commentary on the beginning and the end of the *Psychomachia,* '**Glose in prima et extrema parte Sichomachie Prudentii,**' is edited by Silvestre, 'Aperçu' pp 65-74.

Illustrations of Prudentius's works are treated by **Richard Stettiner,** *Die illustrierten Prudentiushandschriften* (Kaiser-Wilhelms-Universität Strassburg diss., Berlin 1895), with a separately published 'Tafelband' (Berlin 1905), containing 695 illustrations; it is supplemented by **Helen Woodruff,** *The Illustrated Manuscripts of Prudentius* (Cambridge, Mass. 1930), with 142 illustrations, including some that are not in Stettiner.

Augustine, *De civitate Dei*

A concordance to the *De civitate Dei,* geared to the CCL edition, appears under the title *Catalogus verborum quae in operibus Sancti Augustini inveniuntur* (Eindhoven 1976ff), vols XLVII-XLVIII. Medieval commentary on the *De civitate Dei* is a product of the fourteenth century.

The earliest two commentaries are those of **Nicholas Trevet** (Trivet/Triveth, d. 1328) and **Thomas Walleys** (d. 1340), which appear together in many fifteenth- and early sixteenth-century editions of the *De civitate* (see *NUC* 26, 142-3).

The *Additiones* of **Jacopo Passavanti** (d. 1357) and the *Theologicae veritates* of **François de Mayronis** (Meyronis/Maronis, d. 1327) are printed along with the commentaries of Trevet and Walleys in at least two editions (Basle: Adam Petri de Langendorff for Joh. Koberger, 1515; and Lyon: Jacobus Sacon, 1520); the same two editions, incidentally, include a 62-folio index to the *De civitate*, entitled 'Principalium materiarum librorum Sancti Augustini *De ciuitate Dei* summaria annotatio.'

A French translation and commentary on the *De civitate Dei* by **Raoul de Presles** (Praelles/Pratellis), dating from 1371-5, was printed at Abbeville by Pierre Gérard and Jean Dupré, 1486-7, 2 vols; and again under the title *Le Premier-Second Volume de monseignour Sainct Augustin de la Cité de Dieu, translate de latin en françoys* (Paris: J. Petit, 1531), 2 vols.

A commentary by **John Ridevall** (fl. 1330), of which only bks 1-3 and 6-7 survive, remains unprinted except for some excerpts quoted by Smalley, *English Friars* pp 314-21.

The commentaries of Trevet, Walleys, and Ridevall are discussed by Smalley, *English Friars* pp 58-65, 88-100, and 121-32; that of Raoul de Presles, by **A. de Laborde**, *Les Manuscrits à peintures de la Cité de Dieu* (Paris 1909) I, 41-71. Illustrations of the *De civitate Dei* are studied thoroughly by de Laborde, *ibid.,* 3 vols, with 137 plates in III and a general index at the end of II.

Boethius

The concordance to the works of Boethius is by **Lane Cooper,** *A Concordance of Boethius: The Five Theological Tractates and the Consolation of Philosophy,* Mediaeval Academy of America 1 (Cambridge, Mass. 1928).

For medieval commentary on the *De consolatione philosophiae* – most of which remains unprinted – the best guide is **Pierre Courcelle,** *La Consolation de philosophie dans la tradition littéraire: Antécédents et postérité de Boèce* (Paris 1967), especially the descriptive catalogue of commentaries on pp 239-332; among various indices are an index to the manuscripts of the different commentaries (pp 403-18), an index of proper names (419-30), and a lexical index (pp 435-6). The most important commentaries on the *De consolatione* are probably the ninth-century 'Anonymous of St Gall' (Courcelle, pp 275-8, 403-4), an edition of which is being prepared by Petrus W. Tax; the early tenth-century commentary by **Remigius of Auxerre** (Courcelle, pp 278-90, 405-6), some partial editions of which are listed by Courcelle (p. 406), and the work preliminary to a full edition of which is being done by Joseph S. Wittig; the twelfth-century commentary by **Guillaume de Conches** (Courcelle, pp 302-3, 408-10); the twelfth-century 'Erfurt Anonymous' (Courcelle, pp 304, 411-12), edited as a ninth-century work by **Edmund Taite Silk**, *Saeculi noni auctoris in Boetii Consolationem philosophiae commentarius*, Papers and Monographs of the American Academy in Rome 9 (Rome 1935), with an appendix of excerpts from the commentary of Remigius (pp 305-43) and an index of proper names covering both; and the early fourteenth-century commentary of **Nicholas Trevet** (Courcelle, pp 318-19, 412-13). Another fourteenth-century commentary which is easily available is that once attributed to Thomas Aquinas, and now hesitantly ascribed to William Whetley, Thomas Walleys, or one Marquard (Courcelle, pp 322-3, 414-15); it is printed in many early editions of Aquinas, most recently as *Commentum super lib. Boetii De consolatu philosophico* in *Doctoris angelici divi Thomae Aquinatis ... opera omnia*, ed. S.E. Fretté and P. Maré (Paris: Vivès, 1874-1889) XXXII, 425-657.

Illustrations of the *De consolatione* are covered by Courcelle, pp 67-99, 141-58, 185-99, and 233-8, with 132 illustrations (plus frontispiece), arranged topically, and two indices to the sources of the illustrations, arranged alphabetically and topically (pp 437-45).

The commentaries of **John Scotus Eriugena** (9th C) and **Remigius of Auxerre** (9th-10th C) on the 'Opuscula sacra' of Boethius are edited by **Edward Kennard Rand**, *Johannes Scottus*, Quellen und Untersuchungen zur lateinischen Philologie des Mittelalters 1/2 (Munich 1906).

The twelfth-century commentaries on the 'Opuscula sacra' by **Gilbert of Poitiers** and by **Thierry of Chartres** and his followers are edited by **Nikolaus M. Häring**, *The Commentaries on Boethius by*

Gilbert of Poitiers and *Commentaries on Boethius by Thierry of Chartres and his School*, Pontifical Institute of Mediaeval Studies, Studies and Texts 13 and 20 (Toronto 1966 and 1971), both with glossarial indices.

A Chartrian commentary on the *De Trinitate* alone is that by **Clarembald of Arras** (12th C), ed. **Wilhelm Jansen,** *Der Kommentar des Clarenbaldus von Arras zu Boethius De Trinitate: Ein Werk aus der Schule von Chartres im 12. Jahrhundert,* Breslauer Studien zur historischen Theologie 8 (Breslau 1926), with indices of persons and subjects.

Aquinas' *Expositio super librum Boetii De Trinitate* is edited by **Bruno Decker,** Studien und Texte zur Geistesgeschichte des Mittelalters 4 (Leyden 1955), with indices of biblical citations, authors, and proper names.

Alain de Lille, *Anticlaudianus*

The fullest medieval commentary on the *Anticlaudianus* was written in the thirteenth century by **Ralph of Longchamp** (Radulphus de Longo Campo), *In Anticlaudianum Alani commentum*, ed. **Jan Sulowski,** Źródła do Dziejów Nauki i Techniki 13 (Wrocław 1972), with various indices, including an index of names and an index of subjects. Glosses on the *Anticlaudianus* are described by **Denise Cornet,** *Les Commentaires de l''Anticlaudianus' d'Alain de Lille d'après les manuscrits de Paris* (Paris, Ecole nationale des chartes diss. 1945), ch. 1, summarized in *Ecole nationale des chartes: Positions des thèses soutenues par les élèves de la promotion de 1945* ... (Nogent-le-Rotrou 1945) pp 78-9.

The *Anticlaudianus* was also subjected to a number of medieval adaptations. A thirteenth-century Latin version by **Adam de la Bassée,** the *Ludus super Anticlaudianum*, ed. **Paul Bayart** (Tourcoing 1930) with an index of chapters (pp 329-36), transforms the *Anticlaudianus* and parts of the *De planctu Naturae* into a series of short poems, often in the famous goliardic meter and sometimes accompanied by music; excerpts of a related French version, either preceding the *Ludus* or derived from it, are printed by Bayart, pp lxxxix-cvi. An extremely free thirteenth-century adaptation, based only very generally on the

Anticlaudianus, is **Ellenbaut's** *Anticlaudien,* ed. **Andrew J. Creighton** (Catholic University of America diss.; Washington, D.C. 1944), with a convenient summary (pp 5-7), notes, an index of proper names, and a complementary word list and glossary. The *Compendium Anticlaudiani,* an influential short version of the *Anticlaudianus* preserved in over thirty fourteenth- and fifteenth-century manuscripts, is edited with an introduction by **Peter Ochsenbein,** '**Das Compendium Anticlaudiani: Eine neu entdeckte Vorlage Heinrichs von Neustadt,**' *Zeitschrift für deutsches Altertum und deutsche Literatur* 98 (1969) 81-109. This *Compendium* is in turn adapted as the first section of **Heinrich von Neustadt's** early fourteenth-century poem *Gottes Zukunft,* ed. **S. Singer,** *'Apollonius von Tyrland'* ..., Deutsche Texte des Mittelalters 7 (Zurich 1906, repr. Dublin and Zurich 1967) pp 329-50, with a general index covering all three poems in the volume.

The *Prophetia Merlini*

The *Prophetia Merlini* is a brief text attached to Geoffrey of Monmouth's *Historia regum Britanniae,* purporting to be the words of Merlin himself. It is included here because it is the subject of an extended commentary erroneously attributed to Alain de Lille, containing a great deal of traditional material: *Prophetia Anglicana & Romana, hoc est, Merlini Ambrosii Britanni ... una cum septem libris explanationum in eandem prophetiam ... Alani de Insulis ...* (Frankfurt 1603, 1608, 1649), with a brief index, slightly expanded in the 1608 and 1649 editions.

Dante, *Divina Commedia*

There are many concordances and indices to the *Commedia.* The most recent concordance is by **Luciano Lovera** et al., *Concordanza della Commedia di Dante Alighieri* (Turin 1975), 4 vols, with an index of proper names at the end of III; vol. IV contains Giorgio Petrocchi's critical text and a dictionary of rhymes. A brief index of persons, places, names, and subjects is by **Pasquale Trasi,** *Indice analitico della 'Divina Commedia'* (Bergamo 1964).

The early commentators on the *Commedia*, though their interpretations of Dante's text cannot always be taken seriously, are of immense value as reflections of what meanings particular images would have carried for late medieval readers. If a traditional image that one is interested in happens to turn up in the *Commedia* (and how many do not?), an idea of its common figurative associations can often be gathered from what the early commentators have to say about it. A useful study of the commentaries until 1340 is **Bruno Sandkühler's** *Die frühen Dantekommentare und ihr Verhältnis zur mittelalterlichen Kommentartradition*, Münchner romanistische Arbeiten 19 (Munich 1967) pp 77-239, with a few texts on pp 239-66 and a catalogue of manuscripts on pp 267-80. In the following list of major commentaries, all are from the fourteenth century except that of Giovanni da Serravalle, which was written in 1416-17.

1/ **Jacopo Alighieri**, *Chiose alla cantica dell' 'Inferno' di Dante Alighieri*, ed. Jarro, i.e. **G. Piccini** (Florence 1915). *Inferno* only.

2/ The 'anonymous Lombard' (ps.-Jacopo Alighieri), *Chiose di Dante le quale fece il figliuolo co le sue mani*, ed. **F.P. Luiso** (Florence [1904]) vol. II. Only the part on the *Purgatorio* is published (see Sandkühler, pp 116-31).

3/ **Graziolo de' Bambaglioli**, *Il commento dantesco di Graziolo de' Bambaglioli*, ed. **Antonio Fiamazzo** (Savona 1915). *Inferno* only.

4/ An 'anonymous theologian,' ed. Sandkühler, pp 239-51. *Inferno* I-IV and *Paradiso* XI, 64 only.

5/ **Guido da Pisa** (Guido Sodalis), *Expositiones et glose super Comediam Dantis, or Commentary on Dante's Inferno*, ed. **Vincenzo Cioffari** (Albany, N.Y. 1974), with a glossary of variant forms of words on pp XLV-LXI. *Inferno* only.

6/ *Chiose anonime alla prima cantica della Divina Commedia di un contemporaneo del poeta*, ed. **Francesco Selmi** (Turin 1865). *Inferno* only.

7/ **Jacopo della Lana**, *Commedia di Dante degli Allagherii col commento di Jacopo della Lana*, ed. **Luciano Scarabelli**, Collezione di opere inedite o rare 38-40 (Bologna 1866), 3 vols.

8/ *L'ottimo commento della Divina Commedia* [ed. **Alessandro Torri**] (Pisa 1827-9), 3 vols, with an index of subjects at the end of each volume. Two introductions and a gloss on *Inferno* XIII, 64 are added by Sandkühler, pp 251-6.

9/ **Pietro Alighieri**, *Petri Allegherii super Dantis ipsius genitoris*

Comoediam commentarium, ed. **Vincenzo Nannucci** (Florence 1845), with an index of authors cited in the commentary. Pietro's commentary is analyzed topically by **John Paul Bowden**, *An Analysis of Pietro Alighieri's Commentary on the Divine Comedy* (Columbia University diss. 1949; New York 1951), with an index of names and subjects.

10/ **Giovanni Boccaccio**, *Esposizione sopra la Commedia di Dante*, ed. **Giorgio Padoan**, Tutte le opere di Giovanni Boccaccio 6 ([Turin] 1965), with indices of names and subjects, and two indices of words. *Inferno* through XVII, 17 only.

11/ *Chiose sopra Dante* [ed. **Vincenzo Nannucci**] (Florence 1846).

12/ **Benvenuto da Imola**, *Benevenuti de Rambaldis de Imola Comentum super Dantis Aldigherij Comoediam*, ed. **J.P.** **Lacaita** (Florence 1887), 5 vols. Benvenuto is generally agreed to be the most learned and intelligent of the early commentators.

13/ **Francesco da Buti**, *Commento di Francesco da Buti sopra la Divina Commedia*, ed. **Crescentino Giannini** (Pisa 1858-62), 3 vols, with an index of proper names at the end of III.

14/ *Commento alla Divina Commedia d'anonimo Fiorentino del secolo XIV*, ed. **Pietro Fanfani**, Collezione di opere inedite o rare 13-15 (Bologna 1866-74), 3 vols.

15/ **Filippo Villani**, *Il comento al primo canto dell' 'Inferno,'* ed. **Giuseppe Cugnoni**, Collezione di opuscoli danteschi inediti o rari 31-[32] (Città di Castello 1896). *Inferno* I only.

16/ **Giovanni da Serravalle** (Giovanni Bertoldi), *Translatio et comentum totius libri Dantis Aldigherii* [ed. **Fr. Marcellino da Civezza** and **Teofilo Domenichelli**] (Prato 1891).

Large selections from medieval and later commentary on the *Commedia*, along with selected illustrations, are edited by **G. Biagi** et al., *La Divina Commedia nella figurazione artistica e nel secolare commento* (Turin 1924-39), 3 vols. The fullest treatment of manuscript illustrations is by **Peter Brieger, Millard Meiss**, and **Charles S. Singleton**, *Illuminated Manuscripts of the Divine Comedy*, Bollingen Series 81 (Princeton 1969), 2 vols. Vol. I contains an analysis of the illustrations, canto by canto (pp 115-208), a catalogue of manuscripts and their illustrations (209-339), 130 'comparative illustrations,' an iconographic index (353-67), and a general index (368-78); II contains 483 pages of illustrations following the order of the *Commedia,* 16 plates in colour, and an iconographic index (pp 525-39).

8

Miscellaneous

Introductory

There are of course many important bodies of imagery which, while they may relate in various ways to one or more of the fields already discussed, really constitute worlds of their own, and so can be approached much more rewardingly by other, more direct methods. An obvious example is the symbolism of beasts and birds, which, though it is covered to some extent in the encyclopedias, receives its fullest treatment in the bestiaries. Probably the best introduction to the bestiaries is by **Florence McCulloch**, *Medieval Latin and French Bestiaries* (rev. ed. Chapel Hill, N.C. 1962), which includes an extended, alphabetically organized analysis of 'principal subjects' (pp 78-192); 48 line-drawings of bestiary illustrations (193-6 and pls I-X); and a good bibliography (205-10).

A particularly elaborate example is the twelfth-century illustrated bestiary reproduced in an easily legible facsimile by **M.R. James**, *The Bestiary: Being a Reproduction in Full of the Manuscript Ii.4.26 in the University Library, Cambridge, with Supplementary Plates of English Origin* ..., Roxburghe Club (Oxford 1928), translated amusingly but without serious violation of the meaning by **T.H. White**, *The Bestiary: A Book of Beasts* (New York 1954), including the illustrations.

Another important bestiary is the *De bestiis et aliis rebus* once attributed to Hugh of St Victor, bk 1 of which is by **Hugh of Folieto** and bks 2-4 by anonymous authors, PL 177, cols 9-164, with an alphabetical index (cols 9-14), a subject-index to the entire volume (1223-42), and a table of contents (1243-6).

A similar type of compilation is the lapidary, or book of symbolic stones and gems. A monumental study of the lapidaries is being published by **Christel Meier**, *Gemma spiritalis: Methode und Gebrauch der Edelsteinallegorese vom frühen Christentum bis ins 18. Jahrhundert*, Münstersche Mittelalter-Schriften 34 (Munich 1977ff), 2 vols, of which I has already appeared; what promises to be the most important section for our purposes – the fourth, 'Die Tradition der Edelsteinallegorese in Texten von Beda Venerabilis bis zum Ende des 18. Jahrhunderts' – will appear in vol. II, along with an index to both volumes.

The most important single lapidary of the Middle Ages is by **Marbode** (Marbod) **of Rennes** (11th-12th C), *Liber de lapidibus* or *Liber de gemmis*, PL 171, cols 1737-70, with a parallel medieval French translation, and various lesser or doubtful works of Marbode on stones in cols 1771-80; the most fully annotated and useful edition, however, is by **John M. Riddle**, *Marbode of Rennes's (1035-1123) De lapidibus, Considered as a Medical Treatise*, Sudhoffs Archiv: Zeitschrift für Wissenschaftsgeschichte, Beiheft 20 (Wiesbaden 1977), including a full introduction, the letters found in some manuscripts attributing the work to Evax, king of Arabia (pp 28-33), the text of the *De lapidibus* with a parallel English translation and a very full commentary (34-118), various minor works of Marbode on stones with parallel translation (119-29), and a bibliography (140-4).

Still another great world of medieval imagery is the hexaemeral tradition, concerning God's six days of creation. A recent valuable study is **Johannes Zahlten**'s *Creatio mundi: Darstellungen der sechs Schöpfungstage und naturwissenschaftliches Weltbild im Mittelalter*, Stuttgarter Beiträge zur Geschichte und Politik 13 (Stuttgart 1979), whose main sections are 'Bestandsaufnahme der Schöpfungsdarstellungen,' 'Schriftliche Quellen zum Sechstagewerk,' and 'Die Ikonographie und Ikonologie des Sechstagewerkes'; besides other apparatus, it includes 401 illustrations, an alphabetical list of commentaries on Genesis (pp 284-97), an alphabetical list of other works dealing with the days of creation (297-300), and an extensive bibliography.

Among many important medieval hexaemera, I mention **Basil**'s *Homilies on the Hexameron* (4th C), translated into Latin by **Eustathius** before 400, PG 30, cols 869-968; the *Hexaemeron* of **Ambrose** (4th C), PL 14, cols 133-288, adapted from Basil; **Bede**'s *Hexae-*

meron, PL 91, cols 9-190; **Bonaventura**'s highly spiritualized *Collationes in Hexaemeron, sive illuminationes ecclesiae*, in *Opera omnia* V, 329-454 (with a subject-index to the entire volume on pp 585-606), trans. **José de Vinck** in *The Works of Bonaventura* (Paterson, N.J. [1960-70]), vol. V (with scriptural references in the margins throughout, a list of non-scriptural references on pp 383-98, and detailed outlines of the *Collations* in a pocket at the end); and the *Hexaëmeron* of **Robert Grosseteste** (13th C) ed. **Richard C. Dales** and **Servus Gieben**, Auctores Britannici medii aevi 6 (London 1982), with indices of names, authors cited, and important words on pp 357-74.

For our purposes, such miscellaneous bodies of imagery can be divided into two broad classes: those whose unifying element is the 'tenor,' or thing signified by the image; and those whose unifying element is the 'vehicle,' or image that does the signifying. Though there are probably enough examples of both types to fill several volumes, I will restrict myself here to five of the most prominent but untidy groups: among those of the first type, the imagery of Mary, the imagery of the Cross, and eschatological imagery; and among those of the second type, the imagery of numbers and colours. All are, of course, vast and complex fields, so that the following surveys themselves must of necessity be highly selective.

Mary

My analysis of medieval Mariology will be organized around three large subjects: general bibliography and indices, medieval works, and later works.

BIBLIOGRAPHY AND INDICES

The most important periodical devoted to Mariology is the annual *Marianum* (1939ff), individual volumes of which include more or less regularly a 'Nuntia bibliographica' and a list of books received. Particularly valuable is the 'Bibliografia mariana' by **Giuseppe M. Besutti**, attached as appendices to volumes of *Marianum* as follows: pt I (covering 1948-50), appendix to vol. 12 (1950); II (1950-51), appendix to 14 (1952); III (1952-7), appendix to 20 (1958); IV (1958-66), appendix to 28 (1966); and V (1967-72), appendix to 35 (1973). Each part has an alphabetical index of names and subjects. Pt IV is also printed separately under the name of Besutti as *Bibliografia mariana 1958-1966* (Rome [1968]). A useful 'Schede di bibliografia' covering 1958-77, by **Davide M. Montagna**, *Marianum* 39 (1977) 174-59 and 491-6, adds (p. 174), 'È in preparazione il proseguimento per gli anni 1973-1978 (di probabile edizione nel 1979)'; but this continuation seems not yet to have appeared.

A dictionary of Mary has been compiled by **Gabriel M. Roschini**, *Dizionario di Mariologia* (Rome 1961), with an 'Indice sistematico' on pp 505-11 and an 'Indice delle voci' on pp 513-17. The first volume of a *Lexikon der Marienkunde*, ed. **Konrad Algermissen** et al. (Regensburg 1967ff), has appeared, containing the entries 'Aachen' to 'Elisabeth.'

Probably the most useful index to Marian imagery is **Anselm Salzer's** *Die Sinnbilder und Beiworte Mariens in der deutschen Literatur und lateinischen Hymnenpoesie des Mittelalters, mit Berücksichtigung der patristischen Literatur* (Linz 1893, repr. Darmstadt 1967) – a very full collection, drawing on medieval German literature, Latin hymns, and the Greek and Latin Fathers. Since the imagery of the Virgin is to a great extent universal, its examples can be used with some confidence in interpreting other medieval literature as well. The work is divided into four large parts: 'Maria, die jungfräuliche Gottesmutter,' 'Maria in ihrer Tugendschönheit,' 'Maria in ihrer Erhabenheit,' and 'Maria in ihrer Beziehung zu den Menschen.' Each part is elaborately subdivided; the smallest subdivisions are individual symbols and epithets for Mary. There are two complementary indices of German designations (pp 601-10) and Latin designations (610-17).

An older work that can be used in somewhat the same way for Latin ecclesiastical literature is that of **Jean Jacques Bourassé**, *Summa aurea de laudibus beatissimae Virginis Mariae* (Paris 1866), 13 vols. In particular, vol. XIII, cols 889-1234, is an elaborate set of indices to the first 12 volumes, the most relevant of which are iv (cols 965-1004), 'Scriptura sacra Mariae'; v (1003-36), 'Figurae, tituli Mariani'; vi (1035-42), 'Carmina et iconographia Mariana'; and viii (1063-1210), 'Maria et omnia.' Index x (cols 1233-94) is a special index to vol. XIII itself; and xi (1293-1332), entitled 'Inventio accelerata,' is a sort of skeleton-key to the whole work. Vols IX, cols 857-1512 and X, cols 10-596 contain an 'Encomia Mariana' – an alphabetical dictionary of epithets for Mary, mostly figurative, annotated with their medieval sources (this 'Encomia' is a reprinting of the *Polyanthea Mariana* by **Hippolyto Marracci** [Rome 1648 etc.]). Vols V, cols 539-1390 and VI, cols 9-1502 contain a 'Testimonia Mariana ss patrum,' with indices in VI, 1503-28. Vol. III contains a 'Liturgica Mariana' in two parts: 'SS patrum liturgia Mariana' (cols 1527-1696) and 'Excerpta ex antiquis liturgiis' (1695-1832), with an outline of their contents in cols 1835-6.

Finally, the PL includes several relevant indices: in vol. 218, cols 1009-11, **'De Virgine Maria Dei genitrice'**; in 219, cols 493-528, **'Index in Mariana,'** especially sec. 7 'Encomiastica' (cols 502-22); and in 220, cols 473-4, **'De vigiliis B. Mariae Virginis'** and cols 491-497, **'De festis B. Mariae Virginis.'**

MEDIEVAL WORKS

The most elaborate medieval encyclopedia on Mary is by **Richard of St Laurence** (13th C), *De laudibus Beatae Mariae Virginis* (ps.-Albertus Magnus), included in *B. Alberti Magni ... opera omnia* ed. **A.** and **E. Borgnet** (Paris: Vivès, 1890-99) XXXVI, 1-841, with an 'Index capitum contentorum' (pp 843-9), an 'Index rerum notabilium' (851-63), and an 'Index locorum sacrae scripturae' (865-79). The *De laudibus* is divided into 12 books: 1, 'In quo exponitur Angelica Salutatio'; 2, on serving Mary; 3, 'De duodecim privilegiis'; 4, 'De virtutibus Mariae'; 5, 'De pulchritudine Mariae'; 6, 'De appellationibus Mariae'; 7, 'Quomodo Maria designatur per coelestia et superiora'; 8, 'De his quae pertinent ad terram, et possunt figurare Mariam'; 9, 'De receptaculis aquarum, quae figurant Mariam'; 10, 'De aedificiis quibus Maria figuratur in biblia'; 11, 'De munitionibus et navigiis quae possunt signare Mariam'; and 12, 'De horto concluso, cui sponsus comparat Mariam, in Canticis.' For present purposes, bks 6-12 are particularly rewarding.

A shorter but very useful work by **Albertus** himself is the *Biblia Mariana*, ed. Borgnet in *Opera omnia* XXXVII, 365-443, with an index of the biblical books on p. 445. The *Biblia* is arranged by books of the Bible; within each book it proceeds chapter by chapter, explaining all references, both literal and allegorical, to Mary.

Two brief treatises by **Eadmer of Canterbury** (11th-12th C) are the *De excellentia Virginis Mariae*, PL 159, cols 557-80, dealing with many aspects of Mary; and the *De quatuor virtutibus quae fuerunt in Beata Maria, ejusque sublimitate*, PL 159, cols 579-86, on her possession of the four Cardinal Virtues.

The *Mariale* by **Adam of Perseign** (12th C), PL 211, cols 699-744, consists of five sermons on various feasts of Mary; there is also a *Fragmenta Mariana* by Adam, PL 211, cols 743-54. Notes on both of these works, citing many parallels in other authors, appear in cols 753-80, with an index to the two works as well as the notes in cols 1315-20.

Another great repository of Marian imagery is medieval interpretation of the *sponsa* of Canticles as Mary – a product particularly of the later Middle Ages. The following commentators, all of the twelfth century, are noteworthy for their Marian emphasis:

1/ **Rupert of Deutz**, *Commentaria in Canticum canticorum*, ed. Haacke (see p. 24 above); PL 168, cols 839-962.

2/ **Honorius Augustodunensis**, *Sigillum Beatae Mariae*, PL 172, cols 495-518.

3/ **Philip of Harvengt**, *Commentaria in Cantica canticorum*, PL 203, cols 181-490.

4/ **Alain de Lille**, *In Cantica canticorum ... elucidatio*, PL 210, cols 51-110.

5/ **William of Newburgh**, *Explanatio sacri epithalami in matrem Sponsi: A Commentary on the Canticle of Canticles (12 C)*, ed. John C. Gorman, Spicilegium Friburgense 6 (Fribourg, Switz. 1960), with a convenient introduction to the subject.

Medieval hymns to the Virgin are also, of course, intensely figurative, and much of what has been said above in my chapter on hymns will apply here. A list of hymns to Mary in the *Analecta hymnica* can be found in the *Register* to AH ed. Lütolf (cited on p. 74 above), II, 85-90, 'BMV.' We may notice particularly a type of hymn 'De nominibus Beatae Mariae Virginis,' which consists entirely of figurative epithets for Mary – exemplified in AH XXXI, 132-3, hymns 130 and 131; and AH XL, 104-5, hymn 105.

MODERN WORKS

Among modern studies of Mariology at large, the most elaborate is **Hubert du Manoir**, gen. ed., *Maria: Etudes sur la Sainte Vierge* (Paris 1949-71), 8 vols, of which I and II are the most relevant for medieval subjects. Vol. I contains four books: 1, 'Marie dans la Sainte Ecriture et la littérature patristique'; 2, 'Marie dans la liturgie'; 3, 'Marie dans le dogme et la théologie'; and 4, 'Spiritualité et apostolat.' Vol. II contains two books: 5, 'Marie dans les lettres et dans les arts'; and 6, 'Etudes d'histoire du culte et de la spiritualité marials' (medieval and early Renaissance). Vol. VIII includes an index of scriptural texts (pp 101-17) and a general index for vols I-VII (118-90), similar indices for vol. VIII (193-201), and a table of contents for the whole work (203-13).

A particularly useful survey is that of **Gabriel M. Roschini**, *Mariologia* (2nd ed. Rome 1947-8), 2 vols in 4. For present purposes, the most valuable parts are likely to be the list of 'Scriptores occidentales' on Mary in I, 211-76 (through the fifteenth century); the surveys 'De significatione nominis Mariae' (through the fifteenth century) and 'De prophetiis, figuris, et symbolis B.M.V. in genere,' in II/i, 58-63 and 69-137. An 'Index rerum et nominum' appears in II/iii, 293-347.

Patristic writings on Mary in Greek, Syriac, and Latin are assembled by **Sergius Alvarez Campos**, *Corpus Marianum patristicum* (Burgos 1970), 7 vols in 9. For the West, the relevant volumes are I, 'Scriptores qui usque ad Nicaenum Concilium fuerunt'; III, 'Scriptores occidentales qui a Concilio Nicaeno usque ad Concilium Ephesenum fuerunt'; and VI, 'Scriptores occidentales qui a Concilio Epheseno usque ad finem saeculi VII fuerunt.'

Among the innumerable more popular treatments of Mary, I mention three.

1/ *Mariology*, ed. **Juniper B. Carol** (Milwaukee 1955-61), 3 vols, is organized topically, with chapters by various scholars. Though written from a modern standpoint, it pays a good bit of attention to earlier tradition. It is best approached by way of the table of contents.

2/ A convenient historical survey by **Hilda Graef** appears in two forms: *Mary: A History of Doctrine and Devotion*, vol. I, *From the Beginnings to the Eve of the Reformation* (New York 1963), with indices of subjects and names; and *Maria: Eine Geschichte der Lehre und Verehrung* (Freiburg i.B. 1964), three-fourths of which is devoted to the Middle Ages.

3/ Yrjö Hirn, *The Sacred Shrine: A Study of the Poetry and Art of the Catholic Church* (2nd ed. London 1958), includes several valuable chapters (X-XXI) on aspects of Mary – particularly XXI, 'The Symbols of the Virgin' – along with useful notes and bibliography.

This sketch of the bibliography of Mary implies at least a glance in the direction of St Joseph. The journal devoted to his tradition is *Cahiers de Joséphologie* (1953 ff). In particular, each number of vols 3-10 (1955-62), and occasional numbers thereafter, include a selection of **'Textes patristiques sur Saint Joseph,'** ed. **G.-M. Bertrand** and G. **Ponton;** and a convenient analysis by **Bertrand, 'Saint Joseph dans les écrits des Pères,'** appears in 14 (1966) 9-201.

There is a bibliography by **Aimé Trottier,** *Essai de bibliographie sur Saint Joseph* (4th ed. Montreal 1968); pp 424-61 contain an 'Index thematique,' an index of 'Hierarchie et instituts religieux,' and an 'Index chronologique.'

The Cross

The most elaborate medieval work on the figurative associations of the Cross is the *De laudibus sanctae crucis* of **Rabanus Maurus,** PL 107, cols 133-294 – basically a series of 28 hexameter poems relating the Cross to other large Christian or Christianized concepts (e.g. the four Cardinal Virtues, the four elements, the seven Gifts of the Holy Ghost, various numbers bearing spiritual meanings, etc.) and further embellished by visual images, somewhat in the manner of 'shaped' poems. Bk 1 contains the poems themselves, each arranged as a large rectangle whose component letters, when read in a normal manner (starting at the top, and within each line from left to right), make up a hexameter poem on the Cross. Some of the letters in each rectangle, however, also form separate patterns, in which the participating letters form some kind of visual cross while at the same time spelling out separate pronouncements about the Cross. In the words of Zöckler, *Kreuz Christi* (see p. 149 below), trans. Evans, *Cross of Christ* pp 206-7,

The twenty-eight divisions or hexameter-groups of the poem are constructed in such-wise that one part of the letters, without injury to the connection in other respects, yields alone a special sense, which refers to the virtues and glories of the sacred cross. And indeed these separate letters (in the manuscripts and editions ordinarily printed in red, and enclosed by red lines) form on each occasion a cross of simpler or more complicated structure; simplest in the third figure, where great uncial letters – each enclosing within itself several smaller ones – yield together the crosswise interpenetrating words *Crux* and *Salus* –

C

R

S A L V S

V

X

Each poem is followed by a 'Declaratio figurae,' or explanation of the figure that appears within the rectangle; and the PL edition includes, between the rectangle and the 'Declaratio,' a reduction of each poem into conventional hexameter lines. Bk 2 (cols 265-94) is made up of 28 encomia on aspects of the Cross – themselves highly figurative – corresponding to the poems and figures of bk 1. A convenient table of contents for the entire work appears in cols 1155-8. A useful guide to the complexities of the *De laudibus* is provided by **Hans-Georg Müller,** *Hrabanus Maurus, De laudibus sanctae crucis: Studien zur Überlieferung und Geistesgeschichte mit dem Faksimile-Textabdruck aus Codex Reg. Lat. 124 der vatikanischen Bibliothek,* Beiheft zum 'Mittellateinischen Jahrbuch' 11 (Ratingen 1973).

A briefer medieval assembly of traditional appellations for the Cross is a litany of 50 figurative epithets included in a homily *De cruce dominica* or *In venerabilem crucem,* written originally in Greek, translated into Latin as early as the fifth century, and included in a collection of 38 Latin homilies attributed to John Chrysostom. This early Latin translation appears in some old editions of Chrysostom, for example *Opera D. Joannis Chrysostomi ...* (Basle 1547) III, 839-40, and *Divi Ioannis Chrysostomi ... divina opera* (Venice 1574) III, 306r; the Greek text is printed, with a later and for our purposes irrelevant translation, in PG 50, col. 819. The rather complicated history of this homily is outlined by **André Wilmart, 'La Collection des 38 homélies latines de Saint Jean Chrysostome,'** *Journal of Theological Studies* 19 (1917-18) 305-6 and 315; and **Berthold Altaner, 'Beiträge zur**

Geschichte der altlateinischen Übersetzungen von Väterschriften,'
Historisches Jahrbuch 61 (1941) 217-22. A brief but sometimes useful index of 'Allegoriae quae ad crucem spectant' in medieval writers is included in PL 219, cols 141-3. Further medieval imagery of the Cross can be found by way of the secondary works cited below.

The most inclusive study ever made of the Cross and its related traditions, including much medieval material, is that of **Jacob Gretser** (1560-1625), *De sancta cruce*, printed most recently among his *Opera omnia* (Ratisbon 1734) vols I-III. By far the most useful part for our purposes is vol. I, which is divided into five books: 1, 'De ipsa sancta cruce'; 2, 'De imaginibus s. crucis'; 3, 'De apparitionibus s. crucis'; 4, 'De signo s. crucis'; and 5, 'De cruce spirituali.' The chapters in each of these books are listed in a 7-page index (itself unpaginated) between p. 21 of the preface and p. 1 of the text; a 73-page alphabetical subject-index (unpaginated) follows p. 482 of the text; and the rest of the volume contains 129 pages of appendices, with an 8-page alphabetical subject-index. Vol. II is made up of extracts from various works, mostly Greek, dealing with the Discovery of the Cross, the Exaltation of the Cross, the Adoration of the Cross, and other subjects, with a table of contents on pp 11-12 and a 7-page scriptural index following p. 457. Vol. III contains five books, the most relevant of which is bk 5 (pp 285ff), which 'Hymnos & encomia metrica Graecorum & Latinorum in s. crucem comprehendit' – particularly pp 352-9, 'Hymni et cantica Latinorum in sanctam crucem.' An index of the chapters in each book appears on pp 14-16. Though Gretser's massive compilation should not be ignored in any study involving the imagery of the Cross, I have never found it the most immediately profitable way of attacking a specific problem; a more rewarding approach seems to be to use modern scholarship and its documentation (to be surveyed below) as a guide to the voluminous medieval literature of the Cross.

Let us first, however, glance briefly at three other Renaissance treatises.

1/ **John Martiall**, in *A Treatyse of the Crosse Gathered out of the Scriptures, Councelles, and Auncient Fathers of the Primitive Church* (Antwerp 1564), assembles a good bit of traditional material, along with references to its sources in the Fathers – particularly in a section entitled 'That the Crosse of Christe was praefigured in the lawe of nature, foreshewen by the figures of Moyses his lawe, denounced by the prophetes and shewed from heauen in the time of grace' (fols 24v-36v). There is an index of authors cited (fols 10r-11v), and a table of contents occupying 24 sides following fol. 169r.

2/ A treatise by the famous **Justus Lipsius** (1547-1606), *De cruce* (1st ed. Antwerp 1594; last, Leiden 1695), is concerned primarily with the historical facts of crucifixion, and so is less useful than might be supposed; but it does include occasional testimony from early writers, as for example in 1.9.

3/ A particularly valuable compilation, dealing with the inscription INRI at the top of the Cross, is that of **Honorat Nicquet** (1585-1667), *Titulus sanctae crucis* or *Historia et mysterium tituli sanctae crucis* (1st ed. Antwerp 1670; last, Leiden 1695), usually bound with Lipsius's *De cruce,* but containing much more traditional material, and including an 'Index auctorum' and 'Index rerum et verborum.' The inscription at the top of the Cross is treated more briefly by Gretser, *De sancta cruce* 1.28-30 (vol. I, pp 41-6).

Among modern scholarly works containing references to medieval writings on the Cross, a rewarding if now rather antiquated general treatment is **Otto Zöckler's** *Das Kreuz Christi: Religionshistorische und kirchlich-archäologische Untersuchungen, zugleich ein Beitrag zur Philosophie der Geschichte* (Gütersloh 1875), trans. **Maurice J. Evans** as *The Cross of Christ: Studies in the History of Religion and the Inner Life of the Church* (London 1877).

Adolf Jacoby, 'Kreuzbaum, Kreuzholz,' in *Handwörterbuch des deutschen Aberglaubens* ed. E. **Hoffmann-Krayer** and **Hanns Bächtold-Stäubli** (Berlin 1927-42) V, 487-99, is valuable particularly for its presentation of apocryphal and other out-of-the way material.

The symbolism of the Cross in early Christianity is covered by **Aloys Grillmeier,** *Der Logos am Kreuz: Zur christologischen Symbolik der älteren Kreuzigungsdarstellung* (Munich 1956), with a bibliography on pp 131-42; by Rahner, *Griechische Mythen* trans. Battershaw (see p. 106 above), chs 2 and 7; and again by **Rahner,** *Symbole der Kirche: Die Ekklesiologie der Väter* (Salzburg 1964) pp 304-431 and passim.

Articles containing massive bibliography oriented to their own subjects are **Gerhart B. Ladner,** 'St Gregory of Nyssa and St Augustine on the Symbolism of the Cross,' in *Late Classical and Medieval*

Studies in Honor of Albert Mathias Friend, Jr ed. **Kurt Weitzmann** (Princeton 1955) pp 88-95, and 'Vegetation Symbolism and the Concept of Renaissance' in *De artibus opuscula* XL: *Essays in Honor of Erwin Panofsky* ed. Millard Meiss (Zurich 1960, New York 1961) I, 303-22; **Eleanor Simmons Greenhill,** 'The Child in the Tree: A Study of the Cosmological Tree in Christian Tradition,' *Traditio* 10 (1954) 323-71; and **R.E.** Kaske, 'A Poem of the Cross in the Exeter Book: "Riddle 60" and "The Husband's Message",' *Traditio* 23 (1967) 41-71. Medieval exegeses of the famous Ephesians 3:18 with reference to the Cross are assembled by Zöckler, *Kreuz Christi* and Evans, *Cross of Christ*, appendix VII; by Schönbach, *Altdeutsche Predigten* (see p. 83 above) II, 177-87; and by **Robert L. Füglister,** *Das lebende Kreuz: Ikonographisch-ikonologische Untersuchung der Herkunft und Entwicklung einer spätmittelalterlichen Bildidee und ihrer Verwurzelung im Wort* (Freiburg i.d. Schweiz diss., Einsiedeln 1964) pp 184-215.

The Sign of the Cross is treated exhaustively in all aspects in a heavily documented series of articles by **Franz Joseph Dölger,** 'Beiträge zur Geschichte des Kreuzzeichens, I-IX,' *Jahrbuch für Antike und Christentum* 1 (1958) 5-19, 2 (1959) 15-29, 3 (1960) 5-16, 4 (1961) 5-17, 5 (1962) 5-22, 6 (1963) 7-34, 7 (1964) 5-38, 8/9 (1965-6) 7-52, and 10 (1967) 7-29. The most useful division for our purposes is likely to be pt IX, in 10 (1967) – particularly sections 34, 'Die Verklärung des Kreuzes und der Lobpreis des Kreuzes'; 35, 'Die Kreuzesmystik vom Baum des Lebens'; and 37, 'Die kreuzförmige Ausbreitung des Logos im Weltall. Das Kreuz der Feldmesser und die Ausbreitung der Weltseele in Chi-Form.'

The legendary earlier history of the Cross is conveniently surveyed by **Esther Casier Quinn,** *The Quest of Seth for the Oil of Life* (Chicago 1962), with an extensive bibliography on pp 165-87. The Cross in Old English literature and Anglo-Saxon culture is covered in an antiquated but still useful study by **William O. Stevens,** *The Cross in the Life and Literature of the Anglo-Saxons*, Yale Studies in English 22 (New York 1904; repr. Hamden, Conn. 1977), with a greatly outdated bibliography on pp 104-9 and a new bibliographical preface by Thomas D. Hill on pp 3-6 of the reprint.

The Cross is of course a favourite subject in medieval hymns, many of them highly figurative. The best introduction to the subject is **Joseph Szövérffy's** *Hymns of the Holy Cross: An Annotated Edition with Introduction*, Medieval Classics: Texts and Studies 7 (Brookline, Mass. 1976), partly repeated from his article '**"Crux fidelis ...":** **Prolegomena to a History of the Holy Cross Hymns,'** *Traditio* 22 (1966) 1-41. An index to the hymns of the Cross in the AH can be found in the *Register* ed. Lütolf, II, 102, '**Crux**' etc.

Eschatology

The enormous field of medieval eschatology may, for present purposes, be considered under three main headings: eschatology generally, Joachim of Fiore and Joachist eschatology, and the Antichrist and his times.

ESCHATOLOGY GENERALLY

A bibliography of sorts, limited to the period from the Apostolic Fathers to Jerome, is compiled by **Sean Conlon, 'A Select Bibliography of Modern Studies (1850-1977) on Eschatology in the Western Church of the First Four Centuries,'** *Ephemerides Carmeliticae* 28 (1977) 351-72.

The most convenient indices of pre-Joachistic eschatological motifs are those in the *Patrologia Latina*. PL 218, col. 1225, contains a brief index '**De fine mundi et Antichristo.'** Among the Special Indices in PL 220 are three eschatological ones, all organized topically and elaborately subdivided: CXXXII, '**Index de Antichristo'** (cols 265-78; see the section on the Antichrist, below); CXXXIII, '**Index de resurrectione mortuorum'** (cols 277-90); and CXXXIV, '**Index de judicio universali et ultimo'** (cols 291-308).

Among the many scholarly treatments of medieval eschatology at large, the most immediately valuable for our purposes is probably **Ernst Wadstein,** *Die eschatologische Ideengruppe: Antichrist – Weltsabbat – Weltende und Weltgericht, in den Hauptmomenten ihrer christlich-mittelalterlichen Gesamtentwickelung* (Leipzig 1896), which is divided into two large parts and subdivided topically as follows: I. Antichrist, Weltende, und Weltgericht: **A**. Weltende und Weltgericht, including (1) Eschatologische Zeitstimmung, (2) Dogmatische Behandlung, and (3) Künstlerische Behandlung; **B**. Antichrist, including (1) Ethisch-kirchlicher Pessimismus, (2) Polemische Richtungen, (3) Dogmatische Behandlung, and (4) Künstlerische Behandlung. II. Weltsabbat: **A**. Theoretischer Chiliasmus; **B**. Praktischer Chiliasmus, including (1) Cäsaristischer, (2) Papistischer, and (3) Anarchistischer-revolutionärer. Though Wadstein's study is of course long out of date and must accordingly be used with a great deal of caution, its breadth and thoroughness of coverage, its workable organization, and especially its inclusion of out-of-the-way details, quotations, and references make it a particularly rewarding treatment for the student of eschatological material in literature.

Some of the same qualities can be found in a brief study by **Wilhelm Kamlah**, *Apokalypse und Geschichtstheologie: Die mittelalterliche Auslegung der Apokalypse vor Joachim von Fiore*, Historische Studien 285 (Berlin 1935, repr. Vaduz 1965), an extremely useful survey of commentary on the Apocalypse through the twelfth century; an appendix (pp 130-1) summarizes commentary on the *mulier amicta sole* of Apoc. 12.

Two articles that can be plundered for bibliography on medieval eschatology generally are those of **R.E. Kaske**, 'Dante's "DXV" and "Veltro",' *Traditio* 17 (1961) 185-254; and **Robert E. Lerner**, 'Refreshment of the Saints: The Time after Antichrist as a Station for Earthly Progress in Medieval Thought,' *Traditio* 32 (1976) 97-144.

An excellent anthology of 35 selections from medieval eschatological writings is compiled by **Bernard McGinn**, *Visions of the End: Apocalyptic Traditions in the Middle Ages*, Records of Civilization, Sources and Studies 96 (New York 1979), with useful notes (pp 287-346) and a sizeable bibliography (347-63). A more popular collection by **McGinn**, containing almost no duplications, is *Apocalyptic Spirituality: Treatises and Letters of Lactantius, Adso of Montier-en-Der, Joachim of Fiore, the Franciscan Spirituals, Savonarola*, Classics of Western Spirituality (New York 1979), with briefer notes and bibliography (pp 277-316).

A thorough study of the chiliastic element in medieval eschatology, with emphasis on the twelfth and thirteenth centuries, is presented by **Bernhard Töpfer**, *Das kommende Reich des Friedens: Zur Entwicklung chiliastischer Zukunftshoffnungen im Hochmittelalter*, Forschungen zur mittelalterlichen Geschichte 11 (Berlin 1964), with a bibliography on pp 333-41.

A more popular account of 'revolutionary millenarianism' is that of **Norman Cohn**, *The Pursuit of the Millennium: Revolutionary Millenarians and Mystical Anarchists of the Middle Ages* (3rd ed. rev. Oxford 1970), with bibliographies of medieval sources and modern scholarship on pp 372-98.

The standard treatment of the signs preceding the Last Judgment is by **William W. Heist**, *The Fifteen Signs before Doomsday* (East Lansing, Mich.· 1952), with two appendices listing versions of the legend (pp 204-14) and a bibliography (215-23).

Pictorial representation of the Apocalypse was covered rather summarily by **Montague Rhodes James**, *The Apocalypse in Art*, Schweich Lectures of the British Academy, 1927 (London 1931), with a list of illustrated Apocalypses in manuscripts and in other media (pp 1-25), notes which include lists of the subjects illustrated in several prominent Apocalypses (82-113), and an index of relevant libraries (114-15). James's survey is being replaced by **Richard Kenneth Emmerson** and Suzanne Lewis, **'Census and Bibliography of Medieval Manuscripts Containing Apocalypse Illustrations, ca. 800-1500,'** *Traditio* 40 (1984) 337-79, 41 (1985) 367-409, and 42 (1986) 443 ff.

Though anything like a complete list of medieval eschatological works would be manifestly impossible, I list some of the most important and useful (excluding Joachistic works and those dealing specifically with the Antichrist, which will be taken up below). Perhaps the most important single statement of orthodox medieval eschatology is **Augustine**'s letter to Bishop Hesychius, **'De fine saeculi'** (*Epistola* 199), ed. **Al. Goldbacher** in *S. Aureli Augustini ... Epistulae*, CSEL 57 (Vienna 1911) IV, 243-92 (PL 33, cols 904-25); trans. **Sister Wilfrid Parsons** in *Saint Augustine, Letters*, Fathers of the Church 30 (New York 1955) IV, 356-401. Augustine's eschatology appears also in the final books of *De civitate Dei*, especially bk 20, ed. **Bernard Dombart** and **Alfons Kalb**, CCL 14 (Turnhout 1955) II, 699-758.

Another great foundation of medieval eschatology is **Jerome**'s commentary on Daniel, *Commentariorum in Danielem libri III ⟨IV⟩*, ed. **F. Glorie** in *S. Hieronymi presbyteri opera*, CCL 75A (Turnhout 1964) pt I, vol. 5, with an index of scriptural citations on pp 992-1001 and an index of authors cited on pp 1014-23 (PL 25, cols 491-584); trans. **Gleason L. Archer, Jr** as *Jerome's Commentary on Daniel* (Grand Rapids, Mich. 1958), including on pp 159-89 a translation of the PL footnotes. Still another is Gregory's moralization of Job 39-41, *Moralia in Iob* (see p. 25 above) 30.10.36 to the end of bk 34, in PL 76, cols 543-750; trans. in *Morals on the Book of Job* III/ii, 388-661.

An important eschatological prophecy known as the **Tiburtine Sybil** or **Tiburtine Oracle**, translated from Greek into Latin in the fourth century and much revised in the eleventh and twelfth, is edited by **Ernst Sackur**, *Sybillinische Texte und Forschungen* (Halle 1898, repr. Turin 1963) pp 177-87, with a full introduction; another known as *Revelationes Sancti Methodii*, by **Pseudo-Methodius**, evidently written in Syriac in the seventh century and eventually translated into Latin in the eighth, is also edited by Sackur, pp 59-96, with a full introduction.

A highly influential anti-Joachistic eschatological work of the thirteenth century is **William of St Amour**'s *De periculis novissimorum temporum*, the best edition of which appears in *Magistri Guilielmi de Sancto Amore ... opera omnia quae reperiri potuerant* (Constance 1632) pp 17-72, with headings summarizing the contents of the individual chapters; *De periculis* is also included by Matěje z Janova (Matthew of Janov, 14th C) in his *Regulae Veteris et Novi Testamenti*, for which see pp 163-4 below.

A brief treatise on the Last Judgment once attributed to Thomas Aquinas, *De praeambulis ad Judicium et de ipso Judicio et ipsum concomitantibus*, is edited by Fretté in *Doctoris ... Thomae Aquinatis ... opera omnia* XXVIII, 629-53.

Since the great cornerstone of medieval eschatology is interpretation of the Apocalypse, and since an uncommonly large number of the important commentaries on it either are not included or are represented only inadequately in the PL (indexed in PL 219, col. 114), I list those commentaries – both traditional and Joachistic – which must be read outside the PL, omitting also those found in the *Glossa ordinaria* and the commentaries on the whole Bible by Hugh of St Cher, Peter Aureoli, Nicholas of Lyre, Denis the Carthusian, and others (see pp

19-20 and 21-3 above; according to Beryl Smalley in 'John Russel O.F.M.,' *Recherches de théologie ancienne et médiévale* 23 [1956] 305, the Apocalyptic commentary included among the works of Hugh of St Cher is 'of doubtful authenticity').

1/ **Victorinus of Pettau** (3rd-4th C), *Commentarii in Apocalypsin* along with Jerome's recension of it and later accretions, ed. **Johannes Haussleiter** in *Victorini Episcopi Petavionensis opera*, CSEL 49 (Vienna 1916), with indices of scriptural citations, names, and words.

2/ **Ambrosius Autpertus** (8th C), *Expositio in Apocalypsin*, ed. **Robert Weber** in *Opera*, CCLCM 27-27A (Turnhout 1975), 2 vols.

3/ **Beatus of Liébana** (8th C), ed. **Henry A. Sanders**, *Beati in Apocalipsin libri duodecim*, Papers and Monographs of the American Academy in Rome (Rome 1930), with an index of biblical and other citations on pp 646-57. The commentary itself includes elaborate tables (between pp 500 and 501) analyzing the connections between the number 666 (Apoc. 13:18) and the Antichrist.

4/ A pseudo-Isidorian, pseudo-Augustinian, pseudo-Hieronymian commentary of uncertain date (8th-9th C?), apparently of Irish derivation, ed. **Grazia Lo Menzo Rapisarda**, *Incerti auctoris commentarius in Apocalypsin*, Miscellanea di studi di litteratura cristiana antica 16 (Catania 1966-7), with indices of scriptural citations (pp 121-4), authors cited (125-31), names (133), and notable words (pp 135-7); the text is reprinted in PLS 4, cols 1850-63.

5/ **Joachim of Fiore** (12th-13th C), *Expositio magni prophete abbatis Joachim in Apocalipsim* (Venice 1527); preceding fol. 1 are 4 pages of diagrammatic illustrations, and a 55-page 'Tabula principalium dictorum' (both omitted from the reprint by Minerva, Frankfurt a.M., 1964).

6/ **Alexander the Minorite** (sometimes called Alexander of Bremen or of Bexhövede, 13th C), *Expositio in Apocalypsim*, ed. **Alois Wachtel**, MGH Quellen zur Geistesgeschichte des Mittelalters 1 (Weimar 1955), with indices of scriptural citations (pp 511-16), authors cited (517-20), names (521-46), and words and subjects (pp 547-76). This is the most intensely political medieval interpretation of the Apocalypse.

7/ **Adenulph of Anagni** (ps.-Albertus Magnus, 13th C), *In Apocalypsim B. Joannis apostoli luculenta expositio*, ed. Borgnet in *B. Alberti Magni ... opera omnia* XXXVIII, 465-826, with an index of chapters (pp 793-6), an analytical index (797-9), a subject index (pp 800-18), and an index of scriptural citations (819-26).

8/ **Pseudo-Thomas Aquinas**, *Expositio I super Apocalypsim* (13th C), ed. Fretté in *Doctoris ... Thomae Aquinatis ... opera omnia* XXXI, 469 to XXXII, 86.

9/ **Pseudo-Thomas Aquinas**, *Expositio II super Apocalypsim*, ed. Fretté in *Doctoris ... Thomae Aquinatis ... opera omnia* XXXII, 104-424.

10/ **Nicholas de Gorran** (13th C), *In Acta apostolorum, et singulas apostolorum, Iacobi, Petri, Iohannis & Iudae canonicas epistolas, & Apocalypsin commentarij* (Antwerp 1620) pp 178-304, with a 6-page subject-index to the whole volume following p. 304.

11/ **Peter Olivi** (13th C), *Postilla super Apocalypsim* – an important Joachistic commentary, which for the most part remains unprinted. The best MSS are Rome, Bibl. Angelica 382, fols 1-232, and Florence, Bibl. Laurenziana, Conv. Soppr. 397, fols 3-230; the former is much more legible. Extracts are printed by **Ignaz von Döllinger**, *Dokumente vornehmlich zur Geschichte der Valdesier und Katharer*, Beiträge zur Sektengeschichte des Mittelalters 2 (Munich 1890) XLIV, 527-85; and **Etienne Baluze**, *Miscellanea*, ed. **J.D. Mansi** (Lucca 1761-4) II, 258-70. Olivi's commentary on Apoc. 17 is edited by **Felice Tocco**, *Lectura Dantis: Il Canto XXXII del Purgatorio* (Florence 1902) Appendix II, pp 39-53.

12/ **Vital du Four** (Vitalis de Furno, 13th-14th C; ps.-Alexander of Hales, Stegmüller, *Repertorium* II, 428, #2964), *Alexander de Hales ... eruditissimi commentarij ... in Apocalypsim Sancti Ioannis* (Paris 1647), with a 20-page subject index and a 12-page index of scriptural citations following p. 422.

13/ *L'Apocalypse en française au XIIIe siècle (Bibl. nat. fr. 403)*, ed. **L. Delisle** and **P. Meyer**, Société des anciens textes français (Paris 1901) – the Apocalypse in French, accompanied by a French commentary, with an elaborate list of the subjects pictured in 16 important manuscripts of the Apocalypse plus the tapestry of Angers (pp XII-LIX), a list of illustrated manuscripts of the Apocalypse (pp CXCVIII-CC), and a large supplementary volume of illustrations.

14/ *An English Fourteenth Century Apocalypse Version with a Prose Commentary, Edited from MS. Harley 874 and Ten Other MSS*, ed. **Elis Fridner**, Lund Studies in English 29 (Lund 1961), with the French original (a version of that edited by Delisle and Meyer) printed parallel, and a bibliography on pp 285-90.

JOACHISTIC ESCHATOLOGY

Eschatology of the later Middle Ages was profoundly altered by the teachings of Joachim of Fiore (ca 1135-1202) and his followers, which accordingly demand separate treatment. The basic bibliographic guide to Joachim and Joachism (now unhappily thirty-odd years out of date) is **Francesco Russo**, *Bibliografia Gioachimita*, Biblioteca di bibliografia italiana 28 (Florence 1954), including pts I, 'L'uomo: Vita e opere' (pp 11-120); II, 'L'eredità di Gioacchino: L'ordine florense' (121-8); III, 'Gli influssi' (129-36); IV, 'Gioacchino e Dante' (137-48); V, 'Per la storia del Gioachinismo' (149-87); an 'Indice dei manoscritti citati' (189-96); an 'Indice degli incipit' (197-200); and an 'Indice degli autori ricordati' (201-11). A valuable supplementary survey, now also somewhat antiquated, is provided by **Morton W. Bloomfield**, **'Joachim of Flora: A Critical Survey of his Canon, Teachings, Sources, Biography, and Influence,'** *Traditio* 13 (1957) 249-311, with an appendix 'The Relations Between Joachim, the Joachites, and Dante' (pp 310-11).

The most important study on Joachim and his influence is by **Marjorie Reeves**, *The Influence of Prophecy in the Later Middle Ages: A Study in Joachimism* (Oxford 1969), with three useful appendices – 'The Genuine and Spurious Works of Joachim' (pp 511-24), 'Some Short Prophecies Attributed to Joachim or Associated with Joachist Prophecies' (525-33), and 'Examples of Prophetical Anthologies' (534-40) – and a selected bibliography (541-6). Reeves's shorter study, *Joachim of Fiore and the Prophetic Future* (London and New York 1976), presents a more popular treatment, with a selected bibliography on pp 198-202. Joachim's exegetical influence is surveyed by de Lubac, *Exégèse médiévale* (for which see p. 15 above) II/i, 437-559. The most thorough study of Joachim's *Figurae* (see below) is by **Marjorie Reeves** and **Beatrice Hirsch-Reich**, *The Figurae of Joachim of Fiore*, Oxford-Warburg Studies (Oxford 1972), with 47 illustrations at the end. The adoption of Joachistic eschatology by the Franciscan Spirituals is detailed by **Ernst Benz**, *Ecclesia spiritualis: Kirchenidee und Geschichtstheologie der franziskanischen Reformation* (Stuttgart 1934).

Though the eschatological writings of Joachim and his followers are of course vast in scope and varied in kind, I cite here some of the most promising for our purposes. The two most important eschatological works of Joachim himself are his *Liber de concordia Noui ac Veteris Testamenti* ed. E. **Randolph Daniel**, Transactions of the American Philosophical Society 73/8 (Philadelphia 1983), with a 'Glossary of Old Testament Individuals' (pp 436-42), indices of biblical and other citations (445-8), an index of persons (449-53), and a subject index (454-5); and his *Expositio in Apocalypsim* (item 5 in the list on p. 154 above). Joachim's *Figurae* – an elaborate set of illustrations schematizing his eschatology in pictorial form – are edited by **Leone Tondelli, Marjorie Reeves**, and **Beatrice Hirsch-Reich**, *Il libro delle figure dell'abbate Gioachino da Fiore* (2nd ed. Turin 1953), vol. I text, vol. II plates, with a convenient 'Table of Manuscripts relating to the *Liber figurarum*' in II, 13. Other works of Joachim are conveniently listed by Russo, *Bibliografia* pp 13-25, and by Reeves, *Influence* pp 512-18 and *Joachim* pp 198-9.

From the sizeable body of pseudo-Joachistic works I mention three prominent examples, all from the thirteenth century.

1/ A commentary on Jeremias was printed most recently under the title *Abbatis Ioachim diuina prorsus in Ieremiam prophetam interpretatio* (Cologne 1577), with an elaborate table of contents in 77 unnumbered pages following p. 386, and many diagrams, passim, on unnumbered pages preceding p. 6.

2/ A commentary on Isaias is printed as *Eximii profundissimique sacrorum eloquiorum perscrutatoris ac futurorum prenunciatoris abbatis Joachim Florensis scriptum super Esaiam prophetam* (Venice: Lazarus de Soardis, 1517), with an alphabetical index of subjects on eight unnumbered sides preceding fol. 1, illustrative diagrams filling six unnumbered sides, and elaborate diagrams also on fols 11r-17v.

3/ An *Oraculum angelicum Cyrilli cum expositione abbatis Joachim* is edited most recently by **Paul Piur** in *Briefwechsel des Cola di Rienzo* ed. **Konrad Burdach** and **Paul Piur**, Vom Mittelalter zur Reformation 2/4 (Berlin 1912) pp 241-327, with a 'Wortverzeichnis' on pp 331-43. Other pseudo-Joachistic works are listed by Russo, *Bibliografia* pp 27-62, and by Reeves, *Influence* pp 518-24 and *Joachim* p. 199.

In the wilderness of more generally Joachistic literature, a particularly rich collection of neo-Sibylline and other highly figurative prophecies, some including glosses, is edited by **O. Holder-Egger, 'Italienische Prophetieen des 13. Jahrhunderts,'** *Neues Archiv der Gesellschaft für ältere deutsche Geschichtskunde* 15 (1890) 141-78 (pt I), 30 (1905) 321-86 (pt II), and 33 (1908) 95-187 (pt III) – all with biblical and other echoes carefully identified in footnotes.

Many texts reflecting the Joachistic eschatology of the **Franciscan Spirituals** are edited by **Heinrich Denifle** and **Franz Ehrle** in *Archiv für Litteratur- und Kirchengeschichte des Mittelalters* 1-4 (1885-8). A monument of early fourteenth-century Franciscan Joachistic eschatology is **Ubertino da Casale's** *Arbor vite crucifixe Jesu* (Venice: Andreas de Bonetis of Pavia, 1485; repr. Turin 1961), with a table listing the chapters in each book on fol. 248r-v/pp 497-8, and a useful introduction and bibliography by Charles T. Davis on pp III-VIII of the reprint; of particular eschatological interest is bk 5, whose first chapter (fols 204r-209v/pp 409-20) contains an elaborate list of schemes for dividing history into periods. A colourful and influential fourteenth-century prophecy by the Franciscan **Telesforus of Cosenza,** *De causis, statu, ac fine praesentis schismatis et tribulationum futurarum*, is edited most recently by **Emil Donckel, 'Studien über die Prophezeiung des Fr. Telesforus von Cosenza, O.F.M. (1365-1386),'** ch. 6 'Der Widmungsbrief des Teleforus an den Dogen von Genua,' *Archivum Franciscanum historicum* 26 (1933) 282-314, with an elaborate introduction on pp 29-104 under the same title. And an equally colourful eschatological treatise by another fourteenth-century Franciscan, **Jean de Roquetaillade** (Joannes de Rupescissa), the *Vade mecum in tribulatione*, is edited by **Ortwin Gratius** in *Fasciculus rerum expetendarum et fugiendarum*, ed. **Edward Brown** (London 1690) II, 496-508.

ESCHATOLOGY CENTERING ON THE ANTICHRIST

So prominent is the role of the Antichrist in medieval eschatology that works organized around him or his times can best be treated as a separate category. We should begin by noticing that the complex body of medieval lore concerning the Antichrist is based largely on particular parts of the Bible – especially the four explicit references to him in 1 John 2:18 and 22, 1 John 4:3, and 2 John 7; the detailed account of his career and death developed in exegesis of 2 Thess. 2:3-11; the description of him in exegesis of Apoc. 13, ending with the famous number 666 in verse 18; his killing of Enoch and Elias in exegesis of Apoc. 11:3-13; his role in the final great battle between good and evil in exegesis of Apoc. 17:9-14, Apoc. 20, and Ezech. 38-9; exegesis of Christ's apocalyptic speeches in Matt. 24, Mark 13, and Luke 21; exegesis of the prophecies in Dan. 7-12; and exegesis of miscellaneous biblical passages like Gen. 49:16-17, Deut. 33:22, Jer. 8:16 and 9:14-16, Is. 25:6-8, Job 40:10 to 41:25, and John 5:43 (see Emmerson, *Antichrist in the Middle Ages* pp 35-46; and Rauh, *Bild des Antichrist* pp 24-97 [both discussed below]). Inevitably, medieval commentaries on these and other passages contain a great deal of potentially relevant material; for most problems, however, there are more convenient ways to begin.

For works found in the PL, there are the two indices mentioned on p. 151 above: the 'De fine mundi et Antichristo,' PL 218, col. 1225; and the much fuller and more useful 'Index de Antichristo,' PL 220, cols 265-78, which is organized topically into i, 'Signa adventus Antichristi praenuntia'; ii, 'Signa adventum Antichristi concomitantia'; and iii, 'Signa subsequentia Antichristi regnum, et finis persecutionum ultimarum' – each of which is divided into many subtopics (e.g. 'Jesus Christus occidendo Antichristum spiritu oris, finem regno ejus et potentiae imponet'), so that particular motifs can be checked fairly easily.

Among post-medieval scholarly works on the Antichrist, a monumental study is that of **Thomas Malvenda, *De Antichristo*** (Rome 1604), in 11 books and 548 pages, later expanded into 13 books and 849 pages (Lyon 1647), 2 vols. The books of this second edition are 1, a survey of previous opinion about the Antichrist; 2, 'De tempore adventus Antichristi'; 3, 'De ortu & initiis Antichristi'; 4, 'De praedicatione Evangelij in toto orbe, quod est signum adventus Antichristi'; 5, 'De altero signo antecessuro Antichristum, quod erit Romani Imperij desolatio'; 6, 'De regno, bellis, & monarchia Antichristi'; 7, 'De vitiis Antichristi'; 8, 'De doctrina & miraculis Antichristi' and pt 2, 'De miraculis Antichristi'; 9, 'De persecutione Antichristi adversus ecclesiam'; 10, 'De Henoch & Elia tempore Antichristi venturis'; 11, 'De conversione Iudaeorum ad fidem Christi sub finem saeculi'; 12, 'De regno Christi mille annorum, de solutione Diaboli in fine mundi, de Baelio, Gog, & Magog'; 13, 'De morte Antichristi.' The major expansions are that bks 1-2 of the first edition become bks 1-3 of the second; and bk 10 of the first edition becomes bks 12-13 of the second. The first edition includes headings summarizing the subjects of the books and chapters throughout, an index of scriptural citations on two unnumbered pages following p. 548, a brief subject-index on five unnumbered pages, and an appendix of additions on pp 541-8. The second edition includes, preceding p. 1 of vol. I, a 6-page table of contents of books and chapters in that volume; following p. 603 of I, a 13-page index of that volume; preceding p. 1 of vol. II, a 4-page table of contents of books and chapters in that volume; and following p. 246 of II, an 8-page subject index of that volume. Though reflecting partly the views of its own time rather than those of the Middle Ages, and necessarily innocent of modern scholarship on the Antichrist, Malvenda's work is a rich repository of medieval lore and can be used profitably with the usual caution.

Probably the most convenient modern introduction is **Richard Kenneth Emmerson**'s *Antichrist in the Middle Ages: A Study of Medieval Apocalypticism, Art, and Literature* (Seattle 1981), which provides a comprehensive treatment of the medieval Antichrist and a chapter on his survival into the Renaissance, along with very full annotation, bibliographies of primary and secondary sources, and indices of biblical texts (pp 339-41) and illustrated manuscripts (342-4).

A thorough study, extending from the beginnings through the twelfth century and not including Joachim, is **Horst Dieter Rauh**'s *Das Bild des Antichrist im Mittelalter: Von Tyconius zum deutschen Symbolismus*, Beiträge zur Geschichte der Philosophie und Theologie des Mittelalters, Texte und Untersuchungen N.F. 9 (Münster 1973), with full bibliographies of primary and secondary sources (pp 541-50). A brief survey of the Antichrist in Joachistic tradition is included by de Lubac in *Exégèse médiévale* II/i, 527-58, 'L'Antichrist.'

Apart from medieval commentaries on biblical passages like those mentioned above, there are various medieval treatises and other compilations dealing specifically with the Antichrist. Jerome's commentary on Daniel, ed. Glorie (discussed on p. 154 above), includes as its exegesis of Dan. 11:21 to 12:13 (pp 914-44) a 'De Antichristo in Danielem [IV].'

A brief but tremendously influential tenth-century treatise by **Adso of Montier-en-Der** (Adso Dervensis), which provides much of the basis for later medieval developments of the Antichrist, is edited by **D. Verhelst**, *De ortu et tempore Antichristi, necnon et tractatus qui ab eo dependunt*, CCLCM 45 (Turnhout 1976), along with several different versions of it – a *Descriptio cuiusdam sapientis de Antichristo*, a *De Antichristo quomodo nasci debeat, auctore Albuino*, a *Sermo Sancti Augustini de Antichristo*, a *Vita Antichristi ad Carolum Magnum ab Alcuino edita*, a *De tempore Antichristi*, an *Epistola Methodii de Antichristo* from the *Liber floridus* by Lambert of St Omer, and a *Liber Anselmi de Antichristo* – as well as indices of scriptural citations (pp 169-70), authors cited (171-4), and words (175-80); Adso's *De ortu et tempore* is translated by **John Wright** in *The Play of Antichrist* (Toronto 1967) pp 100-10.

A treatise containing an unusual amount of political interpretation is the *De investigatione Antichristi* by **Gerhoh of Reichersberg** (11th-12th C), ed. **Ernst Sackur**, MGH Libelli de lite imperatorum et pontificum saeculis XI et XII, 3 (Hanover 1897) pp 304-95, with indices of names and authors cited for the entire volume.

Raoul of Flaix, in bk 18 of his massive commentary on Leviticus (see p. 28 above), includes as his exposition of Lev. 24:10 a chapter 1 'De Antichristo dominio' (ed. La Bigne in *Maxima bibliotheca veterum patrum* XVII, 217-22), containing a wealth of unusual material.

Perhaps the fullest medieval account of the Antichrist is a thirteenth-century treatise apparently written either by William of St Amour or by one of his followers (Nicholas of Lisieux?), the *Liber de Antichristo et ejus ministris*, ed. **Edmond Martène** and **Ursin Durand** in *Veterum scriptorum et monumentorum historicorum, dogmaticorum, moralium, amplissima collectio* (Paris 1724-33; repr. New York 1968 in Burt Franklin: Research & Source Works Series 276 [Essays in History, Economics, & Social Science 26]) IX, 1271-1446 (attributed to Nicholas Oresme), with a list of chapter-subjects at the beginning of each of its four books (cols 1277, 1336, 1364, 1404), a subject-index to the whole of vol. IX on 17 unnumbered pages following col. 1470, and scriptural citations in the margins throughout; a new edition by Robert Adams is nearing completion. The *Liber de Antichristo*, which is organized generally around the career of the Antichrist, contains practically all of the important eschatological motifs, and is in my experience the richest and most rewarding single eschatological work of the Middle Ages.

A brief treatise once attributed to Thomas Aquinas, *De adventu et statu et vita Antichristi*, is edited by Fretté in *Doctoris ... Thomae Aquinatis ... opera omnia* XXVIII, 610-28.

The important and controversial *Tractatus de tempore adventus Antichristi* by **Arnold of Villanova**, known to us in a revision of 1300, is excerpted by **Heinrich Finke**, *Aus den Tagen Bonifaz VIII.: Funde und Forschungen*, Vorreformationsgeschichtliche Forschungen 2 (Münster i.W. 1902) pp CXXIX-CLIX, with an index of names for the entire volume on pp CCXII-CCXXII.

A brief treatise reflecting a wealth of eschatological learning is the *Tractatus de Antichristo* written in 1300 by **John of Paris** (John Quidort), printed along with the *Expositio magni prophete Joachim in librum Beati Cirilli de magnis tribulationibus et statu Sancte Matris Ecclesie ...* (Venice: Lazarus de Soardis, 1516) fols 44r-51v; a new edition and translation has been completed by **Sara Beth Peters Clark**, 'The *Tractatus de Antichristo* by John of Paris: A Critical Edition, Translation, and Commentary' (Cornell University diss. 1981).

Another unusually rewarding work is the *De victoria Christi contra Antichristum* by **Hugo de Novo Castro** (Hugh of Neuchâtel or Newcastle, 13th-14th C), printed along with a brief *Coniectura de ultimis diebus mundi* by **Nicholas of Cusa** ([Nuremberg: Joh. Sensenschmidt] 1471); each of the two books of the *De victoria* is preceded by a table listing the contents of its chapters.

An interesting though rather neglected source is the section 'Antechristus' in the still unprinted fourteenth-century encyclopedia *Omne bonum*, written in England by an unidentified '**Jacobus**' (BL MS. Royal 6. E. VI, fols 100v-104r).

Finally, the fourteenth-century Czech scholar **Matěje z Janova** (Matthew of Janov) includes a long and sometimes wildly original treatise *De Antichristo* as lib. 3, tract. 5, dist. 5-10, ch. 10 of his *Regulae Veteris et Novi Testamenti* ed. **Vlastimil Kybal** (Innsbruck 1908-26) III, 1-251, with a list of the contents of chapters (pp xxv-xxxiv) and indices of scriptural citations and other authors (pp 382-7), names (388-92), and subjects (393-438). In addition, dist. 10, chs 11-16, of the *Regulae* (III, 252-332) contain the complete text of the *De periculis* of William of St Amour (see p. 154 above), with a valuable subject-index on pp 439-48; dist. 11, chs 1-6 (pp 333-57) contain a brief tract entitled by the editor, '**De successiva revelacione Antichristi a fidelibus predicatoribus**'; and chs 6-8 (pp 358-67) contain a brief eschatological '**Narracio de Milicio**' (i.e. the fourteenth-century Czech reformer **Jan Milic**). Another brief tract by Milic, entitled *Milicii libellus de Antichristo*, appears on pp 368-81, with indices of scriptural citations, names, and subjects on pp 449-55.

Number

Medieval number-symbolism is derived ultimately from Greek arithmetical lore stemming from Pythagoras, and allegorical interpretation of the numbers in Scripture following the model of Philo Judaeus. Apart from the simple use of 'round numbers' (e.g. the use of 100 to mean 'a great many'), it can appear in literature in broadly two ways. On the one hand, numbers can be used with primary emphasis on their symbolic significance itself (e.g. 3 symbolizing the Trinity, or 4 symbolizing the four elements and through them the material world); on the other, they can be used architectonically, to create symmetrical or otherwise meaningful patterns in a literary work (e.g. Dante's pattern $1 + 33 + 33 + 33 = 100$ in the cantos of the *Divine Comedy*). The following discussion, oriented as it is to the finding of raw material for interpretation rather than to the interpretation itself, will take no account of this distinction; instead, it will take up first some important post-medieval sources of medieval number-symbolism, and then some medieval ones.

By far the most elaborate compilation of numerical symbolism is that of **Pietro Bongo** (Petrus Bungus, 16th-17th C), which appeared in progressively expanding editions, under various titles, beginning in 1583. The final expansion, entitled *Numerorum mysteria* (Bergamo 1599), containing a 77-page appendix of additional material, is reprinted under the editorship of **Ulrich Ernst** (Hildesheim 1983), with an informative 34-page introduction by Ernst; the edition of Paris 1618, sometimes described as the definitive one, is in fact the same as that of Bergamo 1599, though the pagination – especially in the appendix – sometimes differs considerably. The *Numerorum mysteria* is organized numerically, with abundant references to earlier writers in the margins. Preceding p. 1 are a 6-page index of authors cited, a 44-page index of scriptural citations, and a 6-page index of scriptural citations in the appendix; following the appendix is a 120-page subject index to both main text and appendix, including under 'Numerus' a 25-page index of the significances of individual numbers.

A much briefer but nevertheless useful treatise is that of **Josse van Clichtove** (15th-16th C), *De mystica numerorum significatione opusculum, eorum presertim qui in sacris litteris vsitati habentur, spiritualem ipsorum designationem succincte elucidans* (Paris 1513), also organized numerically, with references to Scripture and the Fathers in the margins; following fol. 41r are a 2-page index of the contents of its 28 chapters, and a 4-page index of the most prominent meanings of the numbers 1-25 and important numbers after that.

An early work more difficult to use is that of **Henry Cornelius Agrippa von Nettesheim**, *De occulta philosophia libri tres* 2.2-21, with the significances of particular numbers in chs 4-15 ([Cologne] 1533) pp 101-45; repr. ed. **Karl Anton Nowotny** (Graz 1967) pp 113-157; trans. **J. F.** as *Three Books of Occult Philosophy, Written by Henry Cornelius Agrippa, of Nettesheim* (London 1651) pp 170-238. Agrippa's treatment includes a chapter for each number through 12, then one chapter for numbers above 12; though he clearly reflects earlier interpretations, he does not cite them as such.

In the modern scholarship on medieval number-symbolism, probably the best single work to date is **Heinz Meyer**'s *Die Zahlenallegorese im Mittelalter: Methode und Gebrauch* (Münstersche Mittelalter-Schriften 25 (Munich 1975). Pt A, 'Die Methoden der allegorische Deutung von Zahlen im Mittelalter,' includes for example a discussion of then unpublished treatises on number by Odo of Morimond, Thibault of Langres, and William of Auberive (pp 47-53), all of which have since been published (see below); twelve basic rules for the symbolic interpretation of numbers (pp 53-77); and a particularly rewarding section entitled 'Zur Anwendung der Zahlendeutung in der Exegese' (pp 77-108). Pt B is a catalogue of the meanings of individual numbers in the works of Gregory, Bede, and Honorius Augustodunensis (pp 109-99). There is a good bibliography of primary and secondary literature (pp 205-11) and a very useful index of the allegorical meanings of numbers, arranged alphabetically by meanings (pp

212-14). Plans for a 'Lexikon der Zahlenbedeutungen' (to which Meyer's *Zahlenallegorese* is a preliminary) are outlined by **Meyer** and **Rudolph Suntrup,** '**Zum Lexikon der Zahlenbedeutungen im Mittelalter: Einführung in die Methode und Probeartikel, Die Zahl 7,**' *Frühmittelalterliche Studien: Jahrbuch des Instituts für Frühmittelalterforschung der Universität Münster* 11 (1977) 1-73; the 'Probeartikel' (pp 18-73) is a full treatment of the number 7, including meanings of the number itself (pp 22-9), symbolic occurrences of 7 following the order of the Bible (pp 29-66), and indices of the meanings of the number 7 (pp 67-8), symbols that are themselves sevenfold (pp 68-70), relevant symbols that are themselves not sevenfold (pp 70-2), and extensions of meaning (p. 72).

Another basic study is **Hanne Lange**'s *Les Données mathématiques des traités du XIIe siècle sur la symbolique des nombres,* Cahiers de l'Institut du moyen-âge grec et latin 32 (Copenhagen 1979), a detailed analysis of the principles underlying the numerical symbolism of the later Middle Ages.

Among other modern scholarly works, **Ursula Grossmann**'s '**Studien zur Zahlensymbolik des Frühmittelalters,**' *Zeitschrift für katholische Theologie* 76 (1954) 19-54, though it contains no systematic treatment of the significances of individual numbers, presents a wealth of such interpretations, particularly from the works of Augustine, Hincmar of Rheims, and Alcuin.

Burkhard Taeger, *Zahlensymbolik bei Hraban, bei Hincmar – und im 'Heliand'?: Studien zur Zahlensymbolik im Frühmittelalter,* Münchener Texte und Untersuchungen zur deutschen Literatur des Mittelalters 30 (Munich 1970), provides exhaustive treatments of the number-symbolism in Rabanus's *De laudibus sanctae crucis* (pp 3-86) and Hincmar's *Ferculum Salomonis* (pp 89-192), and a discussion of its possible significance for the *Heliand* and for the numerical construction of early medieval poetry at large (pp 195-228), with indices to his discussions of particular parts of the *De laudibus* and the *Ferculum* (pp 235-40) and to his references to particular numbers (pp 241-3).

Hennig Brinkmann includes in his *Mittelalterliche Hermeneutik* (see p. 67 above) a closely packed survey 'Die Zahlen' (pp 86-93), valuable particularly for its extensive bibliographical footnotes.

Henri de Lubac's section 'Symboles numériques' in *Exégèse médiévale* II/ii, 7-40, is an excellent survey of the subject, full of specific examples.

Dorothea Forstner, in *Die Welt der Symbole* (discussed on p. 47 above), includes a section 'Zahlen' (pp 49-63) containing epitomes of the significances – not only medieval – of the numbers 1-10, 12, 40, 50, 100, and 1,000.

Ernst Hellgardt, in *Zum Problem symbolbestimmter und formalästhetischer Zahlenkomposition in mittelalterlicher Literatur, mit Studien zum Quadrivium und zur Vorgeschichte des mittelalterlichen Zahlendenkens* (Munich 1973), presents a very thorough study including, for example, discussions of Augustine's number-theory (pp 157-251) and of many aspects of the use of numbers in literature (pp 253-302), along with unusually full bibliographies: I on the history of mathematics, II on the ontology and aesthetics of number, III on numerical exegesis and number-symbolism, IV on pictorial art, and V (pp 316-47) a particularly full bibliography of number-symbolism and numerical composition in medieval German literature – mostly on individual works, organized broadly by period and within that pattern by individual work – with a brief bibliographical appendix (pp 348-51) on numerical composition in Classical and non-German medieval literature.

A book-length study that was once the standard treatment of the subject, though it is now in great part superseded, is **Vincent Foster Hopper**'s *Medieval Number Symbolism: Its Sources, Meaning, and Influence on Thought and Expression*, Columbia University Studies in English and Comparative Literature 132 (New York 1938), including a convenient appendix, 'Number Symbols of Northern Paganism' (pp 203-11).

Christopher Butler's general survey, *Number Symbolism*, Ideas and Forms in English Literature (London 1970), contains a brief chapter 'The Early Medieval Period: Biblical Exegesis and World Schemes' (pp 22-46), which, though generally not very useful for our purposes, includes a convenient summary of Martianus Capella on numbers (pp 33-5, and see p. 169 below).

Among studies relating number-symbolism to literature, **Ernst Robert Curtius**'s famous seminal excursuses in *Europäische Literatur und* *lateinisches Mittelalter* (Bern 1948), Exkurse XV, 'Zahlenkomposition' and Exkurse XVI, 'Zahlensprüche' (pp 493-504), trans. **Willard R. Trask** in *European Literature and the Latin Middle Ages* (London 1953) pp 501-14, are packed with examples – mostly from the Romance languages – and still immensely valuable.

An excellent brief survey by **Edmund Reiss**, '**Number Symbolism and Medieval Literature,**' *Medievalia et humanistica* N.S. 1 (1970) 161-74, covers both primary and secondary sources, with illustrative examples from medieval literature and abundant bibliographical references in the footnotes.

The works of Taeger and Hellgardt have been mentioned above. **Johannes Rathofer's** *Der Heliand: Theologischer Sinn als tektonische Form, Vorbereitung und Grundlegung der Interpretation* (Cologne 1962), which offers a thorough numerical analysis of the *Heliand,* can be consulted for the significance of numbers themselves by way of the entries on individual numbers in the index (pp 610-11).

Reinildis Hartmann in *Allegorisches Wörterbuch* (for full discussion see p. 40 above), pp 510-33 'Zahlen,' assembles extensive lists of interpretations, by other early writers, of the numbers mentioned by Otfried: 2-7, 10-12, 38, 40, 46, 77, 153, 960.

Michael S. Batts, '**Numerical Structure in Medieval Literature,**' in *Formal Aspects of Medieval German Poetry: A Symposium* ed. **Stanley N. Werbow** (Austin 1969) pp 95-121, includes a bibliography on the use of number in medieval literature, especially German (pp 113-19), with an index to the bibliography (120-1).

Number symbolism is, of course, related also to other large bodies of medieval learning. Its connection with the symbolism of church-building is analyzed by Joseph Sauer, *Symbolik des Kirchengebäudes* (see p. 67 above) – particularly in the section 'Die Zahlensymbolik' (pp 61-87), which is heavily annotated with specific examples, gives great emphasis to liturgical writers like William Durandus and Sicard of Cremona, and includes (pp 69-85) a list of the significances of the numbers 1-10 and selected numbers thereafter; references to individual numbers are also listed in the general index under 'Zahl' (p. 485).

Another convenient key to number-symbolism in the liturgy is provided by **Rudolph Suntrup**, *Die Bedeutung der liturgischen*

Gebärden und Bewegungen in lateinischen und deutschen Auslegungen des 9. bis 13. Jahrhunderts, Münstersche Mittelalter-Schriften 37 (Munich 1978), who in his index under 'Zahlen' (pp 499-500) cites references to liturgically symbolic uses of the numbers 1-12.

The many appearances of numbers in popular lore are best approached through the index-volume (X) of the *Handwörterbuch* ed. Hoffmann-Krayer and Bächtold-Stäubli – both the references to 'Zahl' on p. 408 and the names of the individual numbers, 'eins,' 'zwei,' 'drei,' etc.

Medieval writers who in one way or another incorporate number-symbolism are of course legion; I list those whose presentation of it seems to me the fullest, most important, or most useful for our purposes.

For the PL as a whole, a brief index is included under the entry 'Numerus' in the '**Index directivus**,' PL 221, col. 1033.

Augustine's many explications of numbers can be found most easily by way of the index just mentioned; by way of the index to Augustine in PL 46, cols 464-5, under 'Numerus'; or by way of the *Concordantiae Augustinianae* by **David Lenfant** (Paris 1656), under 'Numerare, numerus.' The most important references are probably *De doctrina Christiana* 2.16.25 and 3.35.51 (PL 34, cols 48 and 86); *Tractatus in Joannem* 25.6 (CCL 36, p. 251; PL 35, col. 1599); *De civitate Dei* 11.30-1 (CCL 48, pp 350-1; PL 41, cols 343-5), 15.20 (ibid. pp 483-6 or cols 462-5), and 18.44 (ibid. pp 640-1 or col. 605); *De Trinitate* 4.4.7 to 6.10 (CCL 50, pp 169-75; PL 42, cols 892-5); and *Contra Faustum* 12.14-21 (PL 42, cols 262-5).

Macrobius's influential analysis of numbers appears in the *Commentarii in Somnium Scipionis* 1.6, ed. Willis pp 18-34; trans. Stahl, *Commentary on the Dream of Scipio* pp 99-117.

A rather jejune but equally important survey, including the significances of the numbers 1-10, is presented by Martianus Capella in *De nuptiis* 7.732-60, ed. Willis pp 263-79; trans. Stahl et al., *Martianus Capella and the Seven Liberal Arts* II, 277-94.

The number-symbolism of Gregory the Great is conveniently outlined by Meyer, *Zahlenallegorese* pp 109-99; of particular interest is his interpretation of the numbers in Job 42:12-13, *Moralia in Iob* 35.16.42 (PL 76, cols 772-4).

Isidore of Seville, in a brief *Liber numerorum qui in sanctis scripturis occurrunt*, PL 83, cols 179-200, interprets the numbers 1-20, 24, 30, 40, 46, 50, and 60.

An eighth-century Irish *Liber de numeris*, once attributed to Isidore, is primarily a gathering of topoi, proverbs, and miscellaneous material organized in numerical sequences (e.g. 'one God,' 'four divisions at Judgment,' 'five senses,' 'ten windows of the soul'), thus providing a good bit of information on common numerical patterns; though the *Liber de numeris* is printed only fragmentarily (PL 83, cols 1293-1302), it is the subject of a valuable analysis by **Robert E. McNally**, *Der irische Liber de numeris: Eine Quellenanalyse des pseudo-isidorischen Liber de numeris* (University of Munich printed diss. 1957), which includes many such patterns in its quotations, passim.

Aldhelm's *Liber de septenario, de metris, aenigmatibus, ac pedum regulis* opens with an extended analysis of biblical 'sevens,' PL 89, cols 161-70.

The extensive but scattered number-symbolism of Bede is conveniently outlined by Meyer, *Zahlenallegorese* pp 109-99.

Rabanus Maurus's great encyclopedia *De universo*, bk 18, ch. 3 'De numero,' PL 111, cols 489-95, offers interpretations of the numbers 1-17, 20, 22, 24, 25, 28, 30, 32, 40, 60, 70, 72, 75, 80, 100, 120, 150, 300, 500, 1,000, 1,200, 7,000, 600,500, 10,000, and 144,000.

The probably eighth-century *Clavis scripturae*, bk 12 'De numeris,' ed. Pitra in *Spicilegium Solesmense* III, 282-9, or bk 5 'De numeris,' ed. Pitra in *Analecta sacra* II, 22-8, contains a broadly similar selection: 1-17, 20, 22, 24, 25, 28, 30, 33, 40, 42, 50, 60, 70, 72, 75, 80, 100, 153, 300, 500, 1,000, 1,200, 7,000, 600,550, 10,000, and 144,000.

The *Explanatio in ferculum Salomonis* and *Responsio* by **Hincmar of Rheims** (9th C), PL 125, cols 817-34 and 1197-1200, present a wealth of number-symbolism, though not in numerical order (on Hincmar, see also Grossmann, 'Studien zur Zahlensymbolik' and Taeger, *Zahlensymbolik*.

Otloh of St Emmeram (11th C), in his *Dialogus de tribus quaestionibus* chs 34-41, PL 146, cols 103-19, analyzes the relation of 1, 2, and 3 in the Trinity (cols 103-12), and epitomizes the significances of the numbers 2-10 (cols 112-19).

In *Poetae Latini aevi Carolini* ed. **Ludwig Traube**, MGH Poetae 3 (Berlin 1896) III, 799, a subject-index by **Karl Neff** lists allegorical uses of fourteen different numbers in the poems contained in that volume.

The number-symbolism of Honorius Augustodunensis can be surveyed by way of the outline in Meyer's *Zahlenallegorese* pp 109-99, or by skimming the chapter-headings of his works in PL 172, cols 1447-69.

Hugh of St Victor, in *De scripturis et scriptoribus sacris*, ch. 15 'De numeris mysticis sacrae scripturae,' PL 175, cols 22-3, proposes seven ways in which a number can be significant in Scripture, giving one or more specific examples of each.

John of Salisbury's *De septem septenis*, PL 199, cols 945-64, is an elaborate explication of seven key 'sevens,' including much traditional lore concerning 7 and other numbers.

Three especially interesting twelfth-century treatises on number-symbolism are edited by **Hanne Lange**, *Traités du XIIe siècle sur la symbolique des nombres*, Cahiers de l'Institut du moyen-âge grec et latin 29 (Copenhagen 1978): 1/ **Geoffrey of Auxerre**, *De sacramentis numerorum a tredenario usque ad vicenarium*, a detailed analysis of the numbers 13-20 (pp 3-21); 2/ **Geoffrey**, *De creatione perfectorum et sacramento*, basically an analysis of the 'perfection' in the numbers 6, 28, 496, 8,128, and 130,816, though the process involves a wealth of other number-symbolism (pp 23-8); and 3/ **Thibault of Langres**, *De quatuor modis quibus significationes numerorum aperiuntur*, which, though it offers no systematic interpretation of individual numbers, is full of complex and rewarding number-symbolism (pp 31-108). Though there are no indices, the footnotes throughout are a mine of relevant sources and parallels.

A letter by **William of Auberive** (12th C), *De sacramento quadragenarii*, along with rather unrevealing excerpts from his treatise *De sacramentis numerorum a ternario usque ad duodenarium*, are printed by **Jean Leclercq, 'L'Arithmétique de Guillaume d' Auberive,'** in *Analecta monastica: Première série*, Studia Anselmiana 20 (Rome 1948) pp 197-202. William's *Regule arithmetice*, which includes no systematic account of individual numbers but is full of number-symbolism, is edited along with two more of his letters by Lange, *Données mathématiques* pp 86-117.

A fuller twelfth-century treatise by **Odo of Morimond**, *Analetica numerorum et rerum in theographyam (I)*, also edited by **Hanne Lange**, Cahiers de l'Institut du moyen-âge grec et latin 40 (Copenhagen 1981), includes, for example, brief analyses of the numbers 50, 45, 40, 30, 20, and 10 (pt 2, sec. 3, chs 18-23; pp 150-5), and a more elaborate exposition of the meanings of the number 1 (pt 3, chs 13-24; pp 169-82).

Finally, some number symbolism is included by Pierre Bersuire (14th C) in both his *Reductorium morale* and his *Repertorium morale*. In the *Reductorium* bk 13, chs 26-8 (*Opera omnia* [Cologne 1730-1] II, 558-61), ch. 26 'De numeris' (p. 558) deals with numbers generally, ch. 27 'De unitate' (pp 558-60) with the number 1, and ch. 28 'De dualitate' (pp 560-1) with 2-13, 40, and 50. In the *Repertorium* (*Opera omnia* vols III-VI), numbers appear individually in their proper alphabetical places, and can be located also by way of the index at the end of vol. VI.

And Jerónimo Lloret, *Sylva allegoriarum* (see p. 39 above) pp 1069-96, includes an appendix 'De numeris' containing interpretations of 1-18, 20-2, 24-5, 27-30, 33, 37-8, 40, 42, 45-6, 50, 60, 66, 70, 75, 77, 80, 86, 90, 98-100, 110, 120, 127, 130, 137, 140, 144, 147, 150, 153, 175, 180, 200, 250, 273, 300, 318, 390, 400, 430, 500, 600, 666, 700, 1,000, and many higher numbers.

Colour

Of all the bodies of external lore that are available for the interpretation of medieval literature, colour seems by general agreement to be the most difficult to apply. Like number-symbolism but to a much greater degree, colour-symbolism does not lend itself very well to independent demonstration, but usually must depend to some extent on the convincing interpretation of other less elusive patterns or motifs in the same work. One important reason, no doubt, is that colour offers less of a rational basis for symbolic meaning than almost any other body of material one can think of, so that any symbolism involving it will necessarily offer more possibilities for subjective or arbitrary meanings. Probably for this reason, colour-symbolism – even in the intensely allegorical climate of the Middle Ages – seems never to have developed the complex rationale evident in, say, the numerical treatises of Geoffrey of Auxerre, Thibault of Langres, and Odo of Morimond. A further preliminary difficulty is of course created by the fact that in both Latin and the medieval vernaculars, the very names of colours are often difficult to identify with any certainty and seem not always to be used consistently.

In this brief outline I will concentrate on the figurative meanings of colours, omitting factual or scientific treatments of them – like, for example, Isidore's *Etymologiae* 19.17 and 28, Bartholomaeus Anglicus's *De rerum proprietatibus* 19.1-36 (Frankfurt 1601, pp 1135-62), and Vincent of Beauvais's *Speculum naturale* 2.56-71 (*Speculum quadruplex* vol. I [Douai 1624, repr. Graz 1964] cols 114-125). On the other hand, since colour is itself a quality existing for the most part in objects that have their own identity, the study of its figurative meanings inevitably shades off into other large categories – the symbolism of stones and gems, the symbolism of flowers, heraldry, and so on. The following sketch will try, as far as possible, to confine itself to works and references concerning the meaning of colours as such, in the following order: general, colours associated with the elements and the rainbow, liturgical colours, colours of love, and miscellaneous.

GENERAL

Though at present there is no general lexicon of medieval colour symbolism, **Christel Meier, 'Das Problem der Qualitätenallegorese,'** *Frühmittelalterliche Studien* 8 (1974) 388 n. 13, refers to a *Lexikon der Farbenbedeutungen* that is in preparation.

A bibliography, not confined to the Middle Ages and now somewhat out of date, is compiled by **Sigmund Skard,** *The Use of Color in Literature: A Survey of Research* (Philadelphia 1946) pp 204-41, organized topically (individual languages and authors are on pp 210-41), with an index of names, including names of medieval authors and anonymous works, on pp 242-9; the most rewarding parts for medieval material are probably pp 188-90 and 221ff.

Perhaps the fullest survey of the subject, extending from the beginning into the twelfth century, is by **A. Hermann** in the article **'Farbe,'** pt C 'Christlich,' in *Reallexikon* ed. Klauser et al. (see p. 105 above) VII,

413-43, divided into i, 'Neues Testament' (cols 413-16); ii, 'Apokryphen' (416); iii, 'Patristik' (417-35); and iv, 'Kunst' (435-43). 'Patristik,' the most important section for our purposes, is subdivided into a/ 'Heidnische Zustände und Meinungen' (417-18); b/ 'Kosmos und Natur' (418-20); c/ 'Mensch,' including 'Kaiser,' 'Priester,' 'Laien,' and 'Zirkusastrologie' (420-31); and d/ 'Symbolik' (431-5). Of particular relevance is the subsection 'Symbolik,' a packed survey organized by individual colours – the single colours white, red, black, yellow, and violet/purple; the groups red-white, white-gold, and violet-red-white; and multicolour. An elaborate bibliography occupies cols 443-7.

Another valuable survey, though much more selective, is that of **Peter Dronke, 'Tradition and Innovation in Medieval Western Colour-Imagery,'** in *The Realms of Colour: Die Welt der Farben: Le Monde des couleurs* ed. **Adolf Portmann** and **Rudolf Ritsema,** Eranos Jahrbuch 41 (Leiden 1972) pp 51-107, with useful bibliography throughout – particularly in nn 1-6 (pp 51-2).

A very full and well-documented study of colour-symbolism in Christian visual art is provided by **Gottfried Haupt,** *Die Farbensymbolik in der sakralen Kunst des abendländischen Mittelalters (Ein Beitrag zur mittelalterlichen Form- und Geistesgeschichte)* (Universität Leipzig diss., Dresden 1941); of special interest for our purposes is pt II, 'Der Farbenwert als Symbol christlicher Verkündigungsinhalte,' which is divided into two sections, both containing specific references to medieval writers in the footnotes: 1/ 'Die Elementqualitäten der Farben' (pp 50-65), and 2/ 'Der "geistige Farbenwert"' (65-117), including analyses of the individual colours gold, white, red, blue, green, and black with its adjacent colours. A particularly valuable appendix (pp 130-40) assembles 77 excerpts, mostly from the PL, of medieval statements concerning colours; and the full bibliography (141-6) is still useful.

Christel Meier, *Gemma spiritalis* (see p. 140 above) vol. I, includes a long and thoroughly documented discussion of colours (pp 142-236), containing sections on 'Die einfachen Farben' (146-203), 'Komplexe Farbenbezeichnungen' (203-26), and 'Besonderheiten der Edelsteinfarben' (227-36).

Dorothea Forstner in *Welt der Symbole,* pp 123-32 'Farben,' offers brief epitomes of the symbolic meanings (not only medieval) of blue, yellow, green, red, purple/violet, black, and white.

A rich body of unusual material is assembled by **C. Mengis** in the article **'Farbe'** in the *Handwörterbuch* ed. Hoffmann-Krayer and Bächtold-Stäubli, II, 1189-1215, including in col. 1194 a convenient table showing the connection of the colours red, yellow, black, and white with the signs of the Zodiac, the seasons, the ages of man, the elements, the geographical directions, the qualities of the elements, their physical states, the humours, and the complexions. The *Handwörterbuch* also contains substantial entries on individual colours: blue, I, 1366-86; yellow, III, 570-83; green, III, 1180-6; red, VII, 792-834; black, VII, 1431-55; and white, IX, 337-58.

Studies on the use of colour in particular literatures or individual authors often include information on colour-symbolism at large. Though such studies are of course legion, I mention those that seem to me the most useful. A wealth of examples, mostly from medieval German literature, appear in the text and footnotes of **Wilhelm Wackernagel**, **'Die Farben- und Blumensprache des Mittelalters,'** in his *Kleinere Schriften*, Abhandlungen zur deutschen Alterthumskunde und Kunstgeschichte (Leipzig 1872) I, 143-240, with a brief summary of what he takes to be the meanings of the various colours on pp 238-240.

I.V. Zingerle, in **'Farbensymbolik,'** *Germania: Vierteljahrsschrift für deutsche Alterthumskunde* 8 (1863) 497-505, assembles explicit references to the symbolism of colours in German poetry of the fourteenth and fifteenth centuries; in **'Farbenvergleiche im Mittelalter,'** *Germania* 9 (1864) 385-402, he lists comparisons to colours in medieval German literature.

Minna Jacobsohn's *Die Farben in der mittelhochdeutschen Dichtung der Blütezeit*, Teutonia: Arbeiten zur germanischen Philologie 22 (Leipzig 1915) is a convenient checklist of colours in this important body of literature, with an index of colours on pp 175-7.

Christel Meier's **'Die Bedeutung der Farben im Werk Hildegards von Bingen,'** *Frühmittelalterliche Studien* 6 (1972) 245-355, is an exhaustive treatment of Hildegard's colour-symbolism (including also brief accounts of Hugh of St Victor, Adam Scotus, and Joachim of Fiore), in three parts: I, 'Die einzelnen Farben' (pp 251-92) white, black, pallid, gray, yellow, blue, red, gold and other metallic colours, and green, with a convenient summary on pp 290-2; II, 'Die Farben der göttlichen Kräfte' (292-320); and III, 'Die Farben der Heilsgeschichte' (320-55).

Friedrich Ohly, 'Probleme der mittelalterlichen Bedeutungs-forschung und das Taubenbild des Hugo de Folieto' in his *Schriften zur mittelalterlichen Bedeutungsforschung* (Darmstadt 1977) pp 32-92, offers, along with a rewarding brief discussion of 'Farbenbe-deutung' (pp 37-40), an extended analysis of the colours of the dove in the *De bestiis et aliis rebus* (pp 56-86).

Karl Knauer's 'Studien zur Geschichte der Farbenbestimmung im Französischen von den Anfängen bis gegen Ende des 18. Jahr-hunderts,' *Archivum Romanicum* 17 (1933) 205-58, though con-cerned primarily with the designation of colours rather than their sym-bolism, and though not confined to medieval writers, is full of refer-ences to colours, some of them medieval, with an index of authors, subjects, and words on pp 254-8.

COLOURS ASSOCIATED WITH THE ELEMENTS AND THE RAINBOW

Various interpretations connecting the colours to aspects of the physi-cal world are surveyed by Hermann, 'Farbe' (*Reallexikon* VII) pp 418-20; Dronke, 'Tradition and Innovation' pp 67-71; Haupt, *Farben-symbolik* pp 50-65; and Mengis, 'Farbe' (*Handwörterbuch* II), with the schematic representation in col. 1194. I add here a few of the more prominent references associating them with the four elements and the rainbow.

Jerome, in his letter to Fabiola (*Epistola 64*, 19), PL 22, cols 617-619), interprets the *byssus, purpura, hyacinthus,* and *coccus* worn by the high priest in Exodus 25:4 as referring to the four elements, earth, water, air, and fire respectively; this interpretation is repeated by **Bede**, *De tabernaculo et vasis ejus* 3.10, PL 91, col. 485, who in *De templo Salomonis* 15 (PL 91, col. 771), gives the four colours allegorical meanings evidently growing out of their connection with the elements.

Isidore, in *De natura rerum* 31, ed. Fontaine, *Traité de la nature* (for which see p. 200 below) pp 285-6 (with parallels from other authors in the notes on p. 285), allegorizes the four colours of the rainbow, red, purple, white, and black; and a long additional passage found in some manuscripts (PL 83, col. 1003, footnote) presents a much fuller allegorization.

Bede, *De natura rerum* 31, PL 90, col. 252 (see pp 201-2 below for full discussion), identifying the colours of the rainbow as red, purple, hyacinth, and green, associates them with the four elements.

Ivo of Chartres (11th-12th C), *Sermo 3*, PL 162, col. 521, connects the colours of Exodus 25:4 with the elements. **Bruno of Asti** (11th-12th C), *Expositio in Exodum*, makes the same connection, adding also the meaning of the four cardinal virtues (PL 164, cols 306-7); and further such interpretations can be found in commentaries on Exodus 25:4 generally.

LITURGICAL COLOURS

Probably the best general account of liturgical colour-symbolism is that of **Joseph Braun**, *Die liturgische Gewandung im Occident und Orient, nach Ursprung und Entwicklung, Verwendung und Symbolik* (Freiburg i.B. 1907) pt v, ch. 2 'Die liturgischen Farben,' pp 728-60 – particularly pp 749-52, 'Ursprung und Symbolik der liturgischen Farbenregel.'

Convenient brief surveys are presented by **H. Leclercq**, 'Couleurs liturgiques,' in *DACL* III/ii, 2999-3004; and by Hermann, 'Farbe' (*Reallexikon* VII) in the subdivision 'Priester,' pp 421-6.

A particularly useful study of the liturgical colours in the English church is that of **J. Wickham Legg**, *Notes on the History of the Liturgical Colours* (London 1882), including a prefatory table identifying the colours used for 33 feasts or periods in the liturgical year in four English rites, six French, two Spanish, two German, and one Italian rite, ranging from the thirteenth to the eighteenth century; sections entitled 'A Comparison of the Colours in Use in Various Western Rites' (pp 12-35) and 'English Liturgical Colours' (35-55), both full of specific references to the use of colours in particular liturgies; and a bibliography (56-9) consisting entirely of editions of liturgical documents. The only copy I know of in the United States is that in the Rare Book Room of the University of Minnesota library, which practically deserves mention as a reference-work in itself – containing as it does a wealth of handwritten additions and modifications that appear to be the author's own; a critical review by **H.G. Morse**, *English Liturgical Colours: Observations on Notes on the History of the Liturgical Colours by Dr. J. Wickham Legg* ... (London 1882), itself including after p. 14 a 'Table of Liturgical Colours according to the Use of Certain Dioceses in France'; handwritten letters on the subject by other scholars; a number of brief additions from contemporary journals, chiefly the *Church Review;* and two other short studies by Legg, entitled 'Notes on the Liturgical Colours from the Lebrun Papers' and 'On an Early Sequence of Liturgical Colours.'

The English liturgical colours are also treated by **John David Chambers**, *Divine Worship in England in the Thirteenth and Fourteenth Centuries* (London 1877) Appendix I, pp iii-xv.

Among medieval liturgists, the most influential statement is that of William Durandus (13th C) in his *Rationale* (see pp 62-3 above), bk 3, ch. 18 'De quatuor coloribus, quibus ecclesia in ecclesiasticis utitur indumentis' (pp 129-32 in the Naples 1859 edition), explaining the significance of the four colours white, red, black, and green, to which is added violet and its significance; in 1.3.39-41 of the *Rationale* (p. 30), Durandus allegorizes the same four colours plus *lividus* ('leaden') and *subalbus* ('whitish').

Honorius Augustodunensis (12th C) in his *Sacramentarium* 29, 'De vestibus presbyteri,' PL 172, cols 762-3, allegorizes the seven colours of the panther as the colours of the priest's seven vestments, each signifying a different virtue; in his *Gemma animae* 1.162, 'De oleo et altari,' PL 172, col. 594, the odours of various flowers – each having also a distinctive colour – signify various kinds of good works.

Other twelfth-century examples of symbolic liturgical colours are found in **pseudo-Hugh of St Victor**, *Speculum de mysteriis ecclesiae* 6, 'De vestimentis sacris,' PL 177, cols 352-6; and Sicard of Cremona, *Mitrale* 2.5 and 7, 'De vestibus sanctis,' PL 213, cols 72 ff and 83-4.

The full explanation of the four basic liturgical colours (white, red, black, and green) by Innocent III (12th-13th C) in his *De sacro altaris mysterio* 1.65, 'De quatuor coloribus principalibus, quibus secundum proprietates dierum vestes sunt distinguendae,' PL 217, cols 799-802, is generally accepted as the first fully developed canon of liturgical colours.

A tract in the Irish *Lebar Brecc*, quoted with translation by **Whitley Stokes**, *The Tripartite Life of Patrick with Other Documents Relating to that Saint*, Rolls Series 89 (London 1887) I, clxxxvii-cxc, presents an elaborate and apparently indigenous explanation of the significances of eight liturgical colours derived from those of Aaron's robe: yellow, blue, white, green, brown, red, black, and purple.

COLOURS OF LOVE

The colours of love, often presented as colours of the lover's clothing, form the subject of a German play and group of poems from the fourteenth and fifteenth centuries. Versions of the play are printed as #103 'Di siben varb,' by **Adalbert von Keller**, *Fastnachtspiele aus dem fünfzehnten Jahrhundert*, Bibliothek des litterarischen Vereins in Stuttgart 29 (Stuttgart 1853) II, 774-81; and as #XIV '**Von den 7 varben**,' by **Vigil Raber**, *Fünfzehn Fastnachts-Spiele aus den Jahren 1510 und 1511*, ed. **Oswald Zingerle**, Wiener Neudrucke 9 (Vienna 1886) I, 246-62.

Walther Gloth, *Das Spiel von den sieben Farben*, Teutonia 1 (Königsberg i.Pr. 1902) pp 58-88, presents a detailed analysis of the meanings of the colours green, red, blue, black, white, yellow, brown, and gray, with many examples.

A more recent discussion, with valuable documentation, is by **Ingeborg Glier**, *Artes amandi: Untersuchung zu Geschichte, Überlieferung, und Typologie der deutschen Minnereden* (Munich 1971) pp 106-9 and passim.

Among the poems on colours, a poem of 1178 lines evidently representing a Low German version of an originally High German composition is edited by **W. Seelmann**, 'Farbentracht,' *Jahrbuch des Vereins für niederdeutsche Sprachforschung* 28 (1902) 129-56, with a list of 13 other medieval German and Dutch works on colours.

A poem on the six colours green, red, blue, white, black, and yellow is edited in various forms by **Christoph Heinrich Myller**, '**Fragmente und kleinere Gedichte**,' in *Samlung deutscher Gedichte aus dem XII. XIII. und XIV. Jahrhundert* (Berlin 1784-5) III, xxiv-xxvi (224 lines); by **Joseph von Lassberg**, *Lieder saal, das ist: Sammelung altteutscher Gedichte* (Eppishausen 1820-5) I, 152-8 (#26, 182 lines); and by **Carl Haltaus**, *Liederbuch der Clara Hätzlerin*, Bibliothek der gesammten National-Literatur 8 (Quedlinburg and Leipzig 1840, repr. Berlin 1966) pp 168-70 (#21, 212 lines).

An 84-line poem on colours appears as #19 in the Hätzlerin collection (ed. Haltaus, *Liederbuch* pp 165-6), and a 133-line poem on the colour green as #20 (*ibid.* pp 166-8).

Wilhelm Seelmann, '**Farbendeutung**,' *Jahrbuch des Vereins für niederdeutsche Sprachforschung* 8 (1882) 73-85, prints 540 lines of a

Middle Low German poem on colours, of which the first 40 lines are missing.

A 171-line poem on the significance of the colours of flowers is edited by **Herman Brandes**, '**Der guden farwen krans**,' *Jahrbuch des Vereins für niederdeutsche Sprachforschung* 10 (1884) 54-8. And an 18-line poem on colours (2 lines per colour) is edited by **Franz Stark**, '**Zur Farbensymbolik**,' *Germania: Vierteljahrsschrift für deutsche Alterthumskunde* 9 (1864) 455-6.

Further references to poems and plays, some unprinted, are assembled by **H. Niewöhner**, '**Farben, Die sechs**,' in *Die deutsche Literatur des Mittelalters: Verfasserlexikon* ed. **Wolfgang Stammler** (Berlin 1933-53) I, 602-6 (not repeated in the rev. ed. of 1977ff).

The fourteenth-century French poet **Watriquet de Couvin**, in an incomplete poem of 558 lines, #23 '**Li dis des .VIII. couleurs**,' ed. **Auguste Scheler**, *Dits de Watriquet de Couvin* (Brussels 1868) pp 311-28, expounds the eight colours of the peacock – gold, blue, silver/white, green, vermilion, red, tan/russet, and black – according to their amorous and chivalric significance.

MISCELLANEOUS

There are of course innumerable brief medieval interpretations of colours which do not fit into any of the categories already mentioned. I list a few examples in chronological order.

Rabanus Maurus, in *De universo* 21.10 'De coloribus,' PL 111, col. 563, interprets the colours as various virtues, giving several brief examples; in 21.14 'De vestibus sacerdotum,' PL 111, cols 568-9, he allegorizes the four colours of Exodus 25:4 (though without reference to the elements; see p. 176 above); and in 20.35 'De coloribus equorum,' PL 111, cols 552-3, he allegorizes the colours of horses.

The *Clavis scripturae,* ed. Pitra in *Spicilegium Solesmense,* includes interpretations of the colours of Exodus 25:4 (10.52-4; *Spic. Sol.* III, 154-6) and of the lily, rose, and violet along with their colours (7.49 and 59-60; *Spic. Sol.* II, 406-9 and 414-18), all with extensive parallel extracts from later writers; in the version of the *Clavis* edited by Pitra in the *Analecta sacra,* the corresponding interpretations (though without the accompanying extracts) appear in 4.20-4 (*Anal.* II, 58) and 3.4-6 (*Anal.* II, 41).

A brief commentary on Matthew 13:45-6, included in a Celtic manuscript possibly of the tenth century, ed. **André Wilmart**, *Analecta Reginensia*, Studi e testi 59 (Vatican 1933), ch. III 'Catéchèses celtiques,' pp 85-93, expounds the meanings of the colours of various kinds of pearls, including (pp 88-9) a pearl that is *multicolor* and its changing colours, red, hyacinth, black, and white.

The prologue of an *Expositio in Cantica canticorum* once attributed to Honorius Augustodunensis, PL 172, col. 519, briefly allegorizes several colours.

Hugh of Folieto (ps.-Hugh of St Victor, 12th C), in *De bestiis* (see p. 138 above) 1.1-10, PL 177, cols 15-19, presents an extended allegorization of the colours of the dove; in his *De claustro animae* (also ps.-Hugh of St Victor) 4.23-4, PL 176, cols 1162-4, he expounds the significance of green and white in the heavenly Jerusalem.

Pierre Bersuire (Petrus Berchorius) includes in his *Reductorium morale* bk 13, chs 1-5 (*Opera omnia* II, 539-44) entitled 'De colore,' 'De albedine,' 'De rubeo colore,' 'De viriditate,' and 'De nigredine.'

Allegorical significances of colours can also be found by looking up individual colours in the alphabetical *distinctiones* described above in chapter 1.

Finally, it may be worth adding that certain Renaissance treatises on the significance of colours, though their references are mainly to Classical and Renaissance authors, can sometimes be of marginal importance for our subject. I mention by way of example **Fulvio Pellegrino Morato**, *Del significato de' colori, e de' mazzoli* (Venice 1558), with a subject-index on fols 25v-31v; **Lodovico Dolce**, *Dialogo nel quale si ragione delle qualità, diuersità, e proprietà de i colori* (Venice 1565), with indices of colours, their significances, and other subjects on fols 87r-88r; and **Giovanni de' Rinaldi**, *Il mostruosissimo mostro* (Venice 1611), I 'Del significato de i colori,' fols 3r-33r, with a table at the end of the volume listing 20 colours and their significances. An often-cited nineteenth-century work by **Frédéric Portal**, *Des couleurs symboliques dans l'antiquité, le moyen-âge, et les temps modernes* (Paris 1857), contains almost no relevant references and can be considered worthless for our purposes.

Appendix
Medieval Encyclopedias

by MICHAEL W. TWOMEY

Introductory

The type of medieval encyclopedia of concern here views natural phenomena allegorically as well as scientifically. In its classic form, it follows a hexaemeral scheme, treating natural subjects in order of their appearance in the biblical account of the six days of Creation; see, for examples, Zahlten's *Creatio mundi* (discussed on p. 140 above), a richly illustrated study of the hexaemeral tradition in biblical commentary and in medieval encyclopedias. Since their purpose is mainly instructional, encyclopedias collect a great deal of *exemplum* material, which, especially from the thirteenth century on, makes them influential on sermons and other didactic literature; see Welter, *L'Exemplum dans la littérature religieuse* (discussed on p. 88 above), passim; and **Christian Hünemörder, 'Antike und mittelalterliche Enzyklopädien und die Popularisierung naturkundlichen Wissens,'** *Sudhoffs Archiv* 65 (1981) 339-65. Encyclopedias frequently duplicate material found elsewhere, such as in lapidaries and bestiaries. Since manuscripts and early printed editions vary, it is often well to consult as many versions of an encyclopedia as possible for the odd but potentially useful variant.

The following list contains the medieval encyclopedias most likely to yield literary imagery. It therefore does not include strictly scientific, philosophical, or technical/domestic-arts literature (called *Fachliteratur* in German). Since this listing focusses only on treatments of natural phenomena, it also does not include works whose primary subject matter is spiritual or moral (e.g. Hugh of St Victor's *Didascalicon*,

Peter of Limoges's *De oculo morali,* and Radulfus Ardens's *Speculum universale* are not included here for this reason, even though their scope makes them in some sense encyclopedic), nor does this listing include the vices and virtues tradition. The one exception to this general rule is Uguccione's *Magnae derivationes,* which is included because it is in the tradition of Isidore's *Etymologiae* and because it is known to have influenced Dante.

For the reader's convenience the encyclopedias are divided into groups of 'major' and 'minor' encyclopedias: that is, those that are broad, rich in allegory, and widely-disseminated as opposed to those that are narrower, more strictly scientific, and local. Within these large divisions, the encyclopedias are arranged in order of composition. Only encyclopedias which originated before 1400 and versions of these which were made before 1500 are included. For each encyclopedia are cited the most recent and best editions, the major secondary literature, and other scholarship which bears directly on research for imagery. Wherever possible, for texts which lack modern editions, information concerning the manuscripts and early printed editions is provided. Thus, although not every edition and study of every encyclopedia is cited, by consulting this list one should very quickly find one's way in any given encyclopedia and in the entire field of medieval encyclopedias. One should of course use this listing along with the brief discussion of encyclopedias in the final part of chapter 1 above.

Should one wish to know more about the allegorical method of medieval encyclopedias, the best general studies are **Michel de Boüard, 'Encyclopédies médiévales: Sur la "connaissance de la nature et du monde" au moyen âge,'** *Revue des questions historiques* 112 (1930) 258-304; and *Cahiers d'histoire mondiale* 9/3 (1966), the pertinent essays from which have been reprinted separately as **Maurice de Gandillac** et al., *La Pensée encyclopédique au moyen âge* (Neuchâtel and Paris 1966). The latter contains authoritative articles by several hands covering Isidore of Seville, Rabanus Maurus, Alexander Neckham, Bartholomaeus Anglicus, Thomas of Cantimpré, Vincent of Beauvais, and others.

Three major studies of medieval science which can be of use for general orientation and for locating some manuscripts and early printed editions are **Lynn Thorndike,** *A History of Magic and Experi-*

mental Science, History of Science Society Publications N.S. 4 (New York 1923-58), 8 vols; **George Sarton**, *Introduction to the History of Science* (Baltimore 1927-48), 3 vols in 5; and **Pierre Duhem**, *Le Système du monde: Histoire des doctrines cosmologiques de Platon à Copernic* (Paris 1913-65), 10 vols.

Finally, for identifying manuscripts there is **Lynn Thorndike** and **Pearl Kibre**, *A Catalogue of Incipits of Mediaeval Scientific Writings in Latin*, Mediaeval Academy of America Publications 29 (rev. and augmented ed. Cambridge, Mass. 1963), updated and corrected in *Speculum* 40 (1965) 116-22 and 43 (1968) 78-114. At this writing, Linda Ehrsam Voigts, University of Missouri, is preparing a catalogue of incipits of scientific and medical writings in Old and Middle English.

Current research can be followed in the annual bibliography on the history of science published in the December issue of *Isis: An International Review Devoted Mainly to the History of Science and Its Cultural Influences*, as well as in the sections on authors and on the sciences in the annual bibliography *Medioevo latino*.

Major Encyclopedias

Isidore of Seville, *Etymologiae* (*Origines*)

The *Etymologiae* of Isidore of Seville (early 7th C) is unquestionably one of the basic texts of the Middle Ages, examining fallen nature through etymology in an attempt to recapture original, unfallen nature embodied in each word's earliest form: for example, 'Asinus et asellus a sedendo dictus, quasi asedus' (12.1.38). The *Etymologiae* added Christian signification to the Classical encyclopedic model of Pliny to become the prototypical medieval encyclopedia. Appropriately, the *Etymologiae* begins with grammar, rhetoric, and dialectic, then continues with mathematics, medicine, scripture and liturgy, God and the angels, the Church, languages, men, the animal and mineral worlds, and man's works.

There are two complete editions generally available in North America. 1/ The edition in PL 82, cols 19-728, is taken from the edition of Isidore's *Opera omnia* by **Faustino Arévalo** (Rome 1797-1803), 7 vols, and is followed by appendices, *variae*, and notes (including

Arévalo's) in cols 729-1054; contents are in cols 1053-60. 2/ **W.M. Lindsay's** edition, *Etymologiarum sive originum libri XX*, Scriptorum classicorum bibliotheca Oxoniensis (Oxford 1911), 2 vols, is a critical edition with a good index at the end of vol. II. However, preferable to this is *San Isidro de Sevilla, Etimologías*, ed. **José Oroz Reta** and **Manuel-A. Marcos Casquero**, Biblioteca de autores christianos 433 (Madrid 1982-3), 2 vols; this edition contains Lindsay's text, corrected, together with a Spanish translation and thorough notes and indices by the editors, plus an excellent introduction by Manuel C. Díaz y Díaz in I, 7-257.

Even more important, when it is completed, will be the new critical edition (with translation) of the *Etymologiae* which is being prepared for the series Auteurs latins du moyen âge by an international team of scholars under the general editorial direction of **Jacques Fontaine** and **Yves Lefèvre**. It will comprise 20 volumes of text and a final volume of indices. So far, 4 volumes, each designated by book number, have appeared: *Isidore de Séville, Etymologies livre XVII: De l'agriculture*, ed. **Jacques André** (Paris 1981); ... *II: Rhetoric*, ed. **Peter K. Marshall** (1983); ... *IX: Les Langues et les groupes sociaux*, ed. **Marc Reydellet** (1984); and ... *XII: Des animaux*, ed. **Jacques André** (1986).

Several important studies are worth mentioning. **Jacques Fontaine,** *Isidore de Séville et la culture classique dans l'Espagne wisigothique* (Paris 1959-83), 3 vols, discusses Isidore's classical sources.

The manuscript dissemination of Isidore's work is charted by **Bernhard Bischoff,** 'Die europaeische Verbreitung der Werke Isidors von Sevilla,' in *Isidoriana*, ed. **Manuel C. Díaz y Díaz** (Léon 1961) pp 317-44 and reprinted in his *Mittelalterliche Studien* (Stuttgart 1966) I, 171-94; and by **Marc Reydellet, 'La Diffusion des Origines** d'Isidore de Séville au haut moyen âge,' *Mélanges d'archéologie et d'histoire de l'Ecole française de Rome* 78 (1966) 383-437, which is updated in **'Compte rendu du Colloque Isidorien tenu a l'Institut d'études latines de l'Université de Paris le 23 juin 1970,'** *Revue d'histoire des textes* 2 (1972) 282-8.

J.N. Hillgarth, 'The Position of Isidorian Studies: A Critical Review of the Literature 1936-1975,' *Studi medievali* 3rd ser. 24 (1983) 817-905, though it would now need updating, is the best survey of major scholarship, including some from before 1936; the same author's article on Isidore in the *Dictionary of the Middle Ages*, ed.

Joseph R. Strayer et al. (New York 1985) VI, 563-66, is an authoritative introductory treatment of Isidore in English.

Rabanus Maurus, *De rerum naturis* (*De universo*)

The *De rerum naturis* of Rabanus Maurus (early 9th C) adds further layers of Christian signification to Isidore's *Etymologiae*. A typical entry quotes Isidore, lists a series of figural meanings *in bono* and *in malo,* and may include a classical myth. By establishing a hexaemeral *ordo rerum,* Rabanus wrote the first fully achieved medieval encyclopedia. The text is printed in PL 111, cols 9-614, with a table of contents by book and chapter at cols 1617-21.

Two major studies worth mentioning insofar as they bear on the imagery of *De rerum naturis* are **Elisabeth Heyse, *Hrabanus Maurus' Enzyklopädie 'De rerum naturis': Untersuchungen zu den Quellen und zur Methode der Kompilation,*** Münchener Beiträge zur Mediävistik and Renaissance Forschung 4 (Munich 1969); and **Diane O. Le Berrurier, *The Pictorial Sources of Mythological and Scientific Illustrations in Hrabanus Maurus' De rerum naturis,*** Outstanding Dissertations in the Fine Arts (New York 1978).

Honorius Augustodunensis, *Elucidarium*

The *Elucidarium* (ca 1100) by Honorius Augustodunensis is a *magister-discipulus* dialogue which in three books covers God's works and biblical history, man in this world, and the future life.[1] A wealth of imagery is found in it; for instance:

D. Quare in aqua [homo] baptizatus est?

M. Aqua contraria est igni. Quid est peccatum nisi ignis? Sicut in animo ira, in carne concupiscentia; unde et igne supplicii punitur: ut hic ignis extinguatur, in aqua baptizatur. Est et aliud: aqua sordes abluit, sitim extinguit, imaginem reddit; ita gratia Spiritus Sancti in baptismate sordes peccatorum abluit, sitim animae verbo Dei restringit, imaginem Dei per culpam amissam restituit. (1.139)

---

1 Recently **Valerie I.J. Flint** has identified Honorius as one of two Henrys of Augsburg: **'Heinricus of Augsburg and Honorius Augustodunensis: Are They the Same Person?'** *Revue bénédictine* 92 (1982) 148-58.

There are two editions of the *Elucidarium*, one in PL 172, cols 1109-
1176, the other in **Yves Lefèvre, *L'Elucidarium et les lucidaires*,**
Bibliothèque des écoles françaises d'Athènes et de Rome 180 (Paris
1954) pp 359-477, which is also the major study. Sometimes manuscript versions contain more and different material. A manuscript survey is now underway: see **Mario Degli Innocenti, 'Per un cen-
simento completo dei manoscritti dell'*Elucidarium* di Honorius
Augustodunensis. I: Manoscritti in biblioteche italiane,'** *Scriptorium* 36 (1982) 269-80.

Vernacular translations are numerous. A very early English version of
1.23-5 and 2.1-6 is in MS. London, BL Cotton Vespasian D.XIV (ca
1125). It was published by **Max Förster, 'Two Notes on Old English
Dialogue Literature,'** in *An English Miscellany Presented to Dr.
Furnivall in Honour of His Seventy-Fifth Birthday* (Oxford 1901) pp
86-101; and **'Altenglische Predigtquellen,'** *Archiv für das Studium
der neueren Sprachen und Literaturen* 116 (1906) 312-14. This
twelfth-century English *Elucidarium* may be found with other items
from the same manuscript in *Early English Homilies from the
Twelfth Century MS. Vespasian D.XIV*, ed. **Rubie D.-N. Warner,** EETS
O.S. 152 (London 1917, repr. New York 1971) pp 140-5.

   A fifteenth-century version is found in *Die mittelenglische Version
des Elucidariums des Honorius Augustodunensis*, ed. **Friedrich
Schmitt,** Wissenschaftliche Beigabe zum Jahresberichte des königlichen humanistischen Gymnasiums Burghausen für das Schuljahr
1908/09 (Burghausen 1909). A new edition, by Michael W. Twomey,
Ithaca College, is in preparation.

The many French *Lucidaires*, for their part, fall into five main groups
distinguished by Lefèvre, *L'Elucidarium* pp 272-89; few are in print.
Manuscripts and Renaissance editions are noted by **Karl Schorbach,**
*Studien über das deutsche Volksbuch Lucidarius und seine Bearbeit-
ungen in fremden Sprachen*, Quellen und Forschungen zur Sprach-
und Culturgeschichte der germanischen Völker 74 (Strassburg 1894)
pp 231-68.

   A *Lucidaire* from the late twelfth or early thirteenth century is in
*Eine altfranzösische Übersetzung des Elucidarium: Edition des Elu-
cidaire der Handschrift Lambeth Palace 431*, ed. **Henning Düwell,**
Beiträge zur romanischen Philologie des Mittelalters 7 (Munich 1974).

Another is *Ung tres singulier et profitable livre appellé le Lucidaire*, ed. **J. Nachbin** (Paris 1938); but see Lefèvre, *L'Elucidarium* pp 304-5 for caveats concerning this edition.

A poetic translation of bk 3 by **Gillebert de Cambray** is unedited, but the text is described by **Paul Eberhardt**, *Der Lucidaire Gilleberts* (Halle 1884); this version was popular in northern France and in England ca 1250-1400. On this and other French adaptations, see Lefèvre, *L'Elucidarium* pp 292-323.

An Anglo-Norman expanded version from the last quarter of the thirteenth century is by **Peter of Fetcham** (or Peckham), *Lumiere as lais*, manuscripts of which are listed by **M. Dominica Legge**, 'Pierre de Peckham and his *Lumiere as lais*,' *Modern Language Review* 24 (1929) 37-47 and 153-71, esp. 42-3.

A Provençal version from a fifteenth-century manuscript is given by **Georges Reynaud**, 'Elucidarium sive dialogus summam totius Christianae theologiae breviter complectens,' *Revue des langues romanes* 33 (1889) 217-50 and 309-57.

Other translations exist in Italian, German, Dutch, Icelandic, Swedish, and Welsh. The Italian version (14th C and later) exists in manuscript only. For a study and manuscript inventory, see **Mario Degli Innocenti**, 'I volgarizzamenti italiani dell'*Elucidarium* di Onorio Augustodunense,' *Italia medioevale e umanistica* 22 (1979) 239-318; and 'La tradizione manoscritta dei volgarizzamenti italiani dell'*Elucidarium* di Onorio Augustodunense,' *Studi medievali* 3rd ser. 23 (1982) 193-229.

In German, there is a fifteenth-century High German translation, complete, in MS. Munich, Bayerische Staatsbibliothek Cgm. 224 fol.; and a Low German translation dated 1469 in MS. Strassburg, Universitäts- und Landesbibliothek, L germ. 177 4to.

The Dutch translation, which is in verse, is from the end of the fourteenth century: *Oudvlaemsche Gedichten der XIIe, XIIIe, en XIVe Eeuwen*, ed. **Philippe Marie Blommaert** (Ghent 1838-51) III, 1-74. Corrections are given by **J. Verdam**, 'Die dietsce *Lucidarius*,' *Tijdschrift voor nederlandsche Taal- en Letterkunde* 1 (1881) 232-57. Two articles by **R. Th. M. van Dijk** provide a study of the *Elucidarium* tradition in the Netherlands and an edition of a manuscript fragment: '**Middelnederlandse Lucidariusboeken**,' and '**De Kampse Fragmenten van de dietsche Lucidarius**,' *Tijdschrift voor nederlandse Taal- en Letterkunde* 89 (1973) 275-91 and 90 (1974) 106-31.

An Icelandic version of the *Elucidarium* (which includes only 1.1-106 and 140-6, and 3.57-120) is available in an excellent facsimile edition of a clearly written thirteenth-century manuscript: *The Arna-Magnœan Manuscript 674 A, 4to: Elucidarius*, ed. **Jón Helgason**, Manuscripta Islandica 4 (Copenhagen 1957). A transcription of the manuscript is in **Konrað Gíslason**, 'Brudstykker af den islandske *Elucidarius*,' *Annaler for nordisk Oldkyndighed og Historie* for the year 1858, pp 51-81. Another Icelandic version (up to 2.75) is in *Hauksbók*, ed. **Eiríkur Jónsson** and **Finnur Jónsson** (Copenhagen 1892-6) pp 470-99.

Of the two Swedish versions, both from the fifteenth century, one is fragmentary (bk 1 only), the other complete. Both are in *Svenska Kyrkobruk under Medeltiden*, ed. **Robert Geete**, Samlingar utgifna af svenska fornskriftsällskapet 119 (Stockholm 1900) pp 95-246.

The Welsh translation is from the mid-fourteenth century: *The Elucidarium and Other Tracts in Welsh from Llyvyr Agkyr Llandewivrevi*, ed. **J. Morris Jones** and **John Rhŷs**, Anecdota Oxoniensia: Medieval and Modern Series 6 (Oxford 1894) pp 2-76.

Honorius Augustodunensis, *Imago mundi*

Another of Honorius's works, *Imago mundi*, which he issued several times between about 1110 and 1139, covers the following large subjects: bk 1, the creation and shape of the world, the elements, geography, the oceans, the weather, cosmology; bk 2, time and its calculation; and bk 3, the six world ages up to the Holy Roman Empire. Like the *Elucidarium*, the *Imago mundi* is etymological as well as rich with metaphorical meanings. Until recently, the handiest edition was PL 172, cols 115-88; there is now an edition by **Valerie I.J. Flint**, 'Honorius Augustodunensis: *Imago mundi*,' *Archives d'histoire doctrinale et littéraire du moyen âge* 49 (1982) 7-153, fn. 2 of which lists the major scholarship. Honorius's cosmology is studied in **Barbara Maurmann**, *Die Himmelsrichtungen im Weltbild des Mittelalters*, Münstersche Mittelalter-Schriften 33 (Munich 1976) passim.

There are adaptations of the *Imago mundi* in Old French, Anglo-Norman, Italian, and Welsh. The prose *Imago mundi* by **Gossouin** (or Gautier) **of Metz** is actually four separate redactions of a greatly expanded adaptation of the *Imago mundi* done in 1245-50. Gossouin dropped bk 2, expanded bk 1 into two books, and devoted bk 3 almost exclusively to astronomy. The resulting version is edited by **O.H. Prior**, *L'Image du monde de maître Gossouin* (Lausanne and Paris 1913). Similar in content to the prose redaction are three as yet unedited verse redactions, on the relationship of which to each other and to the prose redaction one should consult both the introduction to Prior's edition and **Ch.-V. Langlois**, *La Connaissance de la nature et du monde*, La Vie en France au moyen âge du XIIᵉ au milieu du XIVᵉ siècle 3 (2nd ed. Paris 1927) pp 135-48. Extracts from the historical section may be found in **Paul Meyer**, '*L'Image du monde*, rédaction du MS. Harley 4333' and 'Les Manuscrits français de Cambridge, IV. Gonville et Caius College [384, *Image du monde*],' *Romania* 21 (1892) 481-505 and 36 (1907) 517-22; also **Alfons Hilka**, *Drei Erzählungen aus dem didaktischen Epos l'Image du monde (Brandanus – Natura – Secundus)*, Sammlung romanischer Übungstexte 13 (Halle 1928). The prose redaction was accurately translated into English and printed by Caxton in 1480 or 1481 and reissued in 1490: *Caxton's Mirrour of the World*, ed. **Oliver H. Prior**, EETS E.S. 110 (London 1913 for 1912).

An Anglo-Norman verse adaptation dating from ca 1230 renders about three quarters of bk 1, with interpolations from the *Elucidarium;* it may be found in *A Critical Edition of La Petite Philosophie, an Anglo-Norman Poem of the Thirteenth Century*, ed. **William Hilliard Trethewey**, Anglo-Norman Text Society 1 (Oxford 1939). Another Anglo-Norman verse adaptation, of 1.1-33, was done by **Perot de Garbelei** (probably early 14th C): 'Divisiones mundi,' ed. **Oliver H. Prior** in *Cambridge Anglo-Norman Texts* ed. O.H. Prior (Cambridge 1924) pp 33-62.

Of the two published Italian adaptations, both fourteenth century, one (with commentary) is in **Vittorio Finzi**, ed., 'Di un inedito volgarizzamento dell'*Imago mundi* di Onorio d'Autun,' *Zeitschrift für romanische Philologie* 17 (1893) 490-543 and 18 (1894) 1-73. The other covers only 1.1-76: *L'Ymagine del mondo (Firenze, Bibl. naz. cod. palat. 703)*, ed. **Francesco Chiovaro**, Quaderni partenopei 1 (Naples 1977).

The Welsh adaptation, found in the Llyfr coch Hergest and two other manuscripts, also renders only bk 1: *Delw y Byd = Imago mundi*, ed. **Henry Lewis** and **P. Diverres** (Caerdydd 1928), with glossarial indices at the back.

Lucidarius

Lucidarius, sometimes titled *Elucidarius* or *Kleine Cosmographia* in printed editions down through the eighteenth century, is a Middle High German prose compilation of extracts from the *Elucidarium, Imago mundi,* and *Gemma animae* of Honorius Augustodunensis; from the *Philosophia mundi* of Guillaume de Conches; and from the *De divina officiis* of Rupert of Deutz. Written ca 1190-5 as a guide for the laity, it enjoyed immense popularity in German and in other vernaculars. Its scheme is eschatological; hence bk 1 concerns Creation, heaven and hell, early biblical history, geography, the cosmos, and the weather; bk 2 concerns Christ, the mass, and the liturgical year; and bk 3 concerns death and the end of the world.

There are three editions, each based on a different text: 1/ in *Volksbücher von Weltweite und Abenteuerlust,* ed. **Franz Podleiszek,** Deutsche Literatur: Sammlung literarischer Kunst- und Kulturdenkmäler in Entwicklungsreihen; Reihe Volks- und Schwankbücher 2 (Leipzig 1936) pp 99-149; 2/ *Lucidarius,* ed. **Felix Heidlauf,** Deutsche Texte des Mittelalters 28 (Berlin 1915), which is now easily searchable through the *Wortindex zur heidlaufschen Ausgabe des Lucidarius,* ed. **Ulrich Goebel,** Indices verborum zum altdeutschen Schrifttum 1 (Amsterdam 1975); 3/ in *Die deutschen Volksbücher,* ed. **Karl Simrock** (Frankfurt 1845-67) XIII, 375-442.

A fragmentary text of bk 3, in a version different from and earlier than any of the above, is given by **Volker Mertens,** 'Ein *Lucidarius-*Fragment des 12. Jahrhunderts,' *Zeitschrift für deutsches Altertum und deutsche Literatur* 97 (1968) 117-26.

The standard study of the *Lucidarius* tradition – a valuable guide to manuscripts, early printed editions, and translations of both the *Lucidarius* and Honorius's *Elucidarium* – is Schorbach, *Studien* pp 3-230 (see p. 187 above). However, for sources and influence, one should consult **Günter Glogner,** *Der mittelhochdeutsche Lucidarius, eine mittelalterliche Summa,* Forschungen zur deutschen Sprache und Dichtung 8 (Münster i.W. 1937).

Versions in other vernaculars are as follows. Dutch, early fourteenth century: in manuscript fragments and one partial version only, in MS. London, BL Add. 10286.

Danish, ca 1300: *En Klosterbog fra Middelalderens Slutning (AM 76 8°)*, ed. **Marius Kristensen**, Samfund til Udgivelse af gammel nordisk Litteratur (Copenhagen 1933) pp 53-115; perhaps more readily available in *Lucidarius, en Folkebog fra Middelalderen*, ed. **Johannes Knudsen**, Folkelaesning 88 (Copenhagen 1909), which is based on **C.J. Brandt**'s edition by the same title, Nordiske Oldskrifter 7 (Copenhagen 1849) and on the early edition of **Gotfred of Ghemen** (Copenhagen 1510).

Swedish, fourteenth century: part of the cosmological section from bk 1, in *Fragment av fornnordiska Handskrifter*, ed. **Ragnar Lindstam** (Huskvarna 1922) pp 27-39.

Bohemian, ca 1400: *Staročeský Lucidář: Text Rukopisu Fürstenberského a Prvotisku z Roku 1498*, ed. **Čeněk Zíbrt**, Sbírka Pramenů ku Poznání Literárního Života v Čechách, na Moravě a v Slezsku, 1.2.5 (Praze 1903).

There is a Spanish *Lucidario* from the late thirteenth century, but like many medieval works named after the *Lucidarius* it borrows only the title. Nevertheless, it is worth mentioning since it is an 'original' compilation from other major encyclopedias: see *Los Lucidarios españoles*, ed. **Richard P. Kinkade** (Madrid 1968).

Alexander Neckham, *De naturis rerum* and *Laus sapientie divine*

Alexander Neckham (Nequam, Alexander of St Albans, 1157-1217) wrote two encyclopedic works: *De naturis rerum*, which in the manuscripts has added to it a commentary on Genesis and Ecclesiasticus; and *Laus sapientie divine*, a metrical adaptation of *De naturis rerum*. Though brief, *De naturis rerum* is comprehensive, covering Creation, the heavens, time, birds, fish, geology, plants, animals, the arts, and society. Alexander makes frequent use of etymologies, exempla, and anecdotes, and his work is heavily imbued with classical and patristic learning. For example, concerning ploughs he says (2.169):

> Aratrum, opus divinum, ingenii coelestis inventioni se debet, cujus utilitas stili officio comprehendi non potest. Diximus tibi Dodona, vale, regnat longe lateque Cereris gratiosa munificentia. Desiderat autem aratrum ad sui constitutionem burim, stivam, temonem, aures binas, cultrum, vomerem. Aratro praedicationis et doctrinae coluerunt terram sanctae ecclesiae orthodoxi patres.

The only edition remains that of Thomas Wright (see p. 43 above). There is a critical edition of bks 1, 2.1-216 and 405-84, and 4.252-435 of *Laus sapientie divine* in **Gregory Leo Berry**'s 1978 Yale University dissertation, '**A Partial Edition of Alexander Neckham's *Laus sapientie divine*,**' which also includes a discussion of the sources, style, and genre.

The only complete study of Neckham, **R.W. Hunt**'s 1936 Oxford dissertation, has at last been published: *The Schools and the Cloister: The Life and Writings of Alexander Nequam (1157-1217)*, ed. and rev. **Margaret Gibson** (Oxford 1984). In his chapter on Neckham's scientific knowledge (pp 67-83), Hunt discusses the sources of *De naturis rerum* and *Laus sapientie divine;* he lists manuscripts on pp 134-6 (*DNR*) and p. 138 (*LSD*). The only other thorough study of Neckham is **George Francis Wedge**'s 1967 University of Minnesota dissertation, '**Alexander Neckham's *De naturis rerum*: A Study, together with Representative Passages in Translation,**' which also includes notes on the sources and a discussion of the tropological theme of *De naturis rerum.*

Bartholomaeus Anglicus, *De rerum proprietatibus*

The most popular encyclopedia in England and France, even into the Renaissance, was the *De rerum proprietatibus* (ca 1225) of Bartholomaeus Anglicus (sometimes erroneously called Bartholomaeus Glanville), which today is most accessible in the edition of Frankfurt 1601 (repr. Frankfurt 1964). The edition has a small but useful index. Bks 3 and 4 have been edited by **R. James Long** under the title, *On the Properties of Soul and Body*, Toronto Medieval Latin Texts 9 (Toronto 1979). Bartholomaeus provides an authoritative description of each subject, often relying on an etymology, and then draws a concise moralization from it. In 19 books Bartholomaeus treats God, the angels, man, astronomy, the elements, meteorology, geography, precious stones, natural history, and a variety of minor subjects.

Edmund Voigt, 'Bartholomaeus Anglicus, *De proprietatibus rerum*,' *Englische Studien* 41 (1910) 337-59, provides a list of early editions in Latin, French, English, Dutch, and Spanish. **Gerald E. Se Boyar, 'Bartholomaeus Anglicus and his Encyclopaedia,'** *Journal of*

English and Germanic Philology 19 (1920) 168-89, is still the standard study. Se Boyar is complemented by **Thomas Plassmann,** 'Bartholomaeus Anglicus,' *Archivum Franciscanum historicum* 12 (1919) 68-109, which also summarizes the contents of Bartholomaeus on pp 108-9. These three studies should be updated with **M.C.** Seymour, 'Some Medieval English Owners of *De proprietatibus rerum*,' *Bodleian Library Record* 9 (1974) 156-65, and 'Some Medieval French Readers of *De proprietatibus rerum*,' *Scriptorium* 28 (1974) 100-3. The *Liber de moralitatibus* is a moralization of Bartholomaeus's bks 8, 4, 12, 13, 18, 17, and 16 (in that order) compiled in 1281-91; see the discussion on pp 45-6 above.

Bartholomaeus's influence was extended by translations into several European vernaculars. There is a complete English translation (finished in 1398) by **John Trevisa,** *On the Properties of Things: John Trevisa's Translation of Bartholomaeus Anglicus, De proprietatibus rerum,* ed. **M.C.** Seymour et al. (Oxford 1975), 2 vols; the third volume of this heavily emended text, with introduction, commentary, and glossary, is promised. Until then, the most up-to-date treatment of Trevisa's translation is in **Anthony S.G. Edwards,** 'John Trevisa,' in *Middle English Prose: A Critical Guide to Major Authors and Genres* ed. **A.S.G. Edwards** (New Brunswick, N.J. 1984) pp 133-46. There are also anonymous Middle English abstracts of bk 7, a standard medieval medical text, and of bk 17, on plants: **M.C. Seymour,** 'A Middle English Abstract of Bartholomaeus, *De proprietatibus rerum*,' *Anglia* 87 (1969) 1-25 and 91 (1973) 18-34. A brief but thorough study of specific allusions to Bartholomaeus in Middle English is in **A.S.G. Edwards,** 'Bartholomaeus Anglicus' *De proprietatibus rerum* and Medieval English Literature,' *Archiv für das Studium der neueren Sprachen und Literaturen* 222 (1985) 121-8.

The French translation, *Le Propriétaire des choses*, done in 1372 by **Jean** (Jehan) **Corbichon** (Corbechon/de Corbichon), has no complete modern edition, but incunabula editions (e.g. Lyons 1485, 1486, 1487, etc.) are available in America and European libraries. An edition of the chapters on the sun and moon from bk 8 is found in **Michel Salvat,** ed., 'Barthélemi l'Anglais, "Traités du soleil et de la lune," traduits par Jean Corbechon (1372) (édition et commentaire),' in *Le Soleil, la* *lune, et les étoiles au moyen-âge,* Sénéfiance 13, Publications du Centre universitaire d'études et de recherches médiévales aixois, Université de Provence (Marseilles 1983) pp 339-57. A brief study, together with a list of manuscripts, is in **Donal Byrne, 'Rex imago Dei: Charles V of France and the *Livre des propriétés des choses,' Journal of Medieval History** 7 (1981) 97-113. Reproductions from several pages of MS. Amiens, Bibl. municipale 399 may be found in **Jean Desorby, 'Le Livre des propriétés des choses de Barthélemi l'Anglais – manuscrit de la Bibliothèque municipale d'Amiens,'** in *Les Quatres Elements dans la culture médiévale: Actes du colloque des 25, 26, et 27 mars 1982* ed. **Danielle Buschinger** and André Crepin, Göppinger Arbeiten zur Germanistik 386 (Göppingen 1983) pp 299-308.

The Provençal translation, *Elucidari de las proprietatz de totas res naturals,* dated about mid-fourteenth-century, exists only in MS. Paris, Sainte-Geneviève 1029. A critical edition of the prologue and bks 1-7 is found in **Sharon Guinn Scinicariello, 'A Critical Edition of Books I-VII of the *Elucidari de las proprietatz de totas res naturals'** (University of North Carolina diss. 1982). Extracts from bks 15, 17, 18, and 19 are found in C. Appel, 'Der provenzalische Ludicarius,' *Zeitschrift für romanische Philologie* 13 (1889) 225-52, while an extract from 18.26 is in **Guy Raynaud de Lage, 'Le Livre de la chasse et l'***Elucidari,' Annales du Midi* 64 (1952) 355-6, repr. in his *Les Premiers Romans français et autres études littéraires et linguistiques,* Publications romanes et françaises 138 (Geneva 1976) pp 35-6. Other brief extracts from 6.22-3, 15.13, and 19.136 can be found in both *Provenzalisches Lesebuch,* ed. **Karl Bartsch** (Elberfeld 1855) pp 179-81, and (lacking 19.136) in *Chrestomathie provençale,* ed. **Bartsch,** rev. **Eduard Koschwitz** (6th ed. Marburg 1904) cols 393-8.

The Italian translation, done in the late thirteenth or early fourteenth century by **Vivaldo Belcalzer,** has no modern edition, but its three manuscripts are described in **Vittorio Cian, *Vivaldo Belcalzer e l'enciclopedismo italiano delle origini,*** Giornale storico della letteratura italiana, suppl. 5 (Turin 1902) pp 74-86, and extracts are given passim. The contents are listed by **Ghino Ghinassi, 'Nuovi studi sul volgare mantovano di Vivaldo Belcalzer,' *Studi di filologia italiana*** 23 (1965) 28-68.

The Spanish translation, done ca 1400 by **Vincent de Burgos**, has three incunabula editions: Toulouse 1494, Saragossa 1495, and Toledo 1529.

The only German translations of Bartholomaeus are partial ones. **Konrad von Megenberg**, *Von der Sel: Eine Übertragung aus dem Liber de proprietatibus rerum des Bartholomäus Anglicus*, ed. **Georg Steer**, Kleine deutsche Prosadenkmäler des Mittelalters 2 (Munich 1966), is an adaptation of 3.2-7. On the unedited fifteenth-century translation of bks 1 and 2 by Michael Baumann, see **Georg Steer, 'Die Gottes- und Engellehre des Bartholomäus Anglicus in der Über-tragung des Michael Baumann,'** *Würzburger Prosastudien I*, ed. Forschungsstelle für deutsche Prosa des Mittelalters am Seminar für deutsche Philologie der Universität Würzburg, Medium Aevum philologische Studien 13 (Munich 1968) pp 81-101.

The Middle Dutch version is *Van den Proprieteyten der Dinghen* (Haarlem 1485).

Thomas of Cantimpré, *Liber de natura rerum*

The *Liber de natura rerum* of Thomas of Cantimpré (or of Brabant, ca 1240) was vastly influential as a sourcebook for preachers down through the fifteenth century, but was only recently edited for the first time by Helmut Boese (see p. 44 above). Thomas collects much *exemplum* material, explaining what something is, what it is used for, and how it functions. There are three versions, of 19, 20, and 18 books; Boese's edition presents the 20-book version. The topics covered are man, the soul, monsters, animals, plants, geology, meteorology, and cosmography. Until Boese's critical introduction and notes appear, information on the three versions must be pieced together out of the following: **John Block Friedman, 'Thomas of Cantimpré, *De naturis rerum*: Prologue, Book III and Book XIX,'** in *La Science de la nature: Théories et pratiques*, Cahiers d'études médiévales 2 (Montreal and Paris 1974) pp 107-54; **Helmut Boese, 'Zur Textüber-lieferung von Thomas Cantimpratensis'** *Liber de natura rerum,'* *Archivum fratrum praedicatorum* 39 (1969) 53-68; **Christian Hüne-mörder, 'Die Bedeutung und Arbeitsweise des Thomas von Can-timpré und sein Beitrag zur Naturkunde des Mittelalters,'** *Medizinhistorisches Journal* 3 (1968) 345-57; and **G.J.J. Walstra**,

'Thomas de Cantimpré, *De naturis rerum:* Etat de la question,' *Vivarium* 5 (1967) 146-71 and 6 (1968) 46-61.

De natura rerum also circulated in French, German, and Dutch translations. The French (14th C) is a moralized and expanded version of bk 3: *Eine altfranzösische moralisierende Bearbeitung des Liber de monstruosis hominibus orientis aus Thomas von Cantimpré, De naturis rerum,* ed. Alfons Hilka, Abhandlungen der Gesellschaft der Wissenschaften zu Göttingen, philologisch-historische Klasse 3/7 (Berlin 1933), which contains an outline and running table of correspondences on pp 11-22.

A German translation by Konrad von Megenberg (ca 1350) was extremely popular in fourteenth- and fifteenth-century Germany; *Das Buch der Natur,* ed. Franz Pfeiffer (Stuttgart 1861, repr. Hildesheim 1962); table of contents on pp liii-lxii and glossarial index on pp 553-807. The best recent study is Uwe Ruberg, 'Allegorisches im *Buch der Natur* Konrads von Megenberg,' *Frühmittelalterliche Studien* 12 (1978) 310-25, which also refers to all earlier scholarship. Konrad divides the text into eight books with interpolated sections on physiognomy and the divine, the latter of which are also found in his *Von der Sel,* ed. Steer (for which see previous page).

There are also two fifteenth-century German versions of *De natura rerum,* each in a unique manuscript. 1/ Michael Baumann's *Buch von der natur und eygenschaft der dingk,* dated 1478, is found in MS. Wertheim, Fürst. Löwenstein-Wertheim-Freudenbergsches Archiv (no catalogue number). It includes bks 1-18 of *De natura rerum,* bks 1 and 2 of Bartholomaeus's *De proprietatibus rerum,* the *Commentarius symbolum apostolorum* of Rufinus Tyrannius of Aquileia, and a collection of eucharistic prayers. On Baumann, one should consult the article by Steer mentioned above (previous page). 2/ Peter Königschlaher's translation of *De natura rerum,* dated 1472, is found in MS. Stuttgart, Landesbibliothek Cod. med. et phys. fol. 15; it is briefly discussed in Peter Assion, *Altdeutsche Fachliteratur,* Grundlagen der Germanistik 13 (Berlin 1973) p. 57.

The Dutch version of *De natura rerum,* 16,000 lines of verse, was done in the mid-thirteenth century by Jacob von Maerlant: *Naturen bloeme,* ed. Eelco Verwijs, Bibliotheek van middelnederlandsche

Letterkunde 7, 8, 14, 18, 21 (Groningen 1872-8); this omits most of bk 1 and all of bks 2 and 18-20.

Also worth mentioning is Thomas's *Bonum universale de apibus* (Cologne 1478-80, Douai 1627; etc.), the definitive medieval study of bees, which develops an extended allegory of spiritual authority. Contents are listed in **Alexander Kaufmann**, *Thomas von Chantimpré* (Cologne 1899) pp 21-6. A Middle Low German version (bk 1 only) is in *Die mittelniederdeutsche Version des Bienenbuches von Thomas von Chantimpré*, ed. **Nils Otto Heinertz** (Lund 1906); this version has recently been given critical examination by **Manfred Misch**, *Apis est animal – apis est ecclesia: Ein Beitrag zum Verhältnis von Naturkunde und Theologie in spätantiker und mittelalterlicher Literatur*, Europäische Hochschulschriften 1/107 (Bern and Frankfurt 1974) pp 70-103.

Vincent of Beauvais, *Speculum maius*

The largest of all medieval encyclopedias is the one known as the *Speculum quadruplex* or *Speculum maius* (ca 1256-9) by the Dominican Vincent of Beauvais. Vincent attempted to treat 'all things' in the *Naturale*, 'all arts' in the *Doctrinale*, and 'all times' in the *Historiale* (prologue, ch. 16); hence the *Speculum maius* borrows freely from the best Classical and medieval authorities. The sections most relevant to this discussion are the *Naturale* and the *Doctrinale*. The *Naturale*, which is based on Thomas of Cantimpré's *De natura rerum*, employs a hexaemeral plan, often obscured, combined with a governing eschatological interest. Besides natural things, it treats God and the angels, theology, and history. Likewise, the *Doctrinale* covers not only language, ethics and politics, mechanics, medicine, natural philosophy, mathematics, and theology, but a broad range of ancillary subjects within these categories. The fourth mirror, the *Morale*, is in fact a pastiche of extracts from Aquinas and others added by an anonymous late thirteenth-century forger. The most readily available edition of the whole *Speculum* remains that of Douai 1624 (repr. Graz 1964-5); this edition contains superb indices, but is otherwise inferior to the incunabula: e.g. Strassburg ca 1473-6 and Venice 1493-4. These are discussed briefly in **B.L. Ullman, 'A Project for a New Edition of Vincent of Beauvais,'** *Speculum* 8 (1933) 312-26.

Ullman's article should be considered alongside **Serge Lusignan,** *Préface au Speculum maius de Vincent de Beauvais: Réfraction et diffraction,* Cahiers d'études médiévales 5 (Montreal and Paris 1979), the best recent discussion of the date and inauthenticity of the *Morale* and of the date, stages of composition, and plan of the *Speculum maius.* This work also includes studies of the *Libellus apologeticus* and prologue attached to the *Speculum maius,* an edition of the *Libellus,* and a brief bibliography. The *Apologia actoris* of the *Historiale,* edited from thirteenth- and fourteenth-century manuscripts, may be found together with a study of the *Historiale* in **Anna-Dorothee v. den Brincken, 'Geschichtsbetrachtung bei Vincenz von Beauvais: Die** *Apologia actoris* **zum** *Speculum maius,'* *Deutsches Archiv für Erforschung des Mittelalters* 34 (1978) 410-99. In addition, there is now a useful anthology of studies about the *Speculum maius* and unpublished vernacular versions: *Vincent of Beauvais and Alexander the Great: Studies on the Speculum maius and Its Translation into Medieval Vernaculars,* ed. **W.J. Aerts, E.R. Smits,** and **J.B. Voorbij,** Mediaevalia Groningana 7 (Groningen 1986).

As evidence of Vincent's vast influence, one need only consider the half-dozen or so articles written in the 1930s, 40s, and 50s by **Pauline Aiken** on Chaucer's use of the *Speculum maius* in his *Canterbury Tales.*

Since 1974 there has been an Atelier Vincent de Beauvais at the Centre de recherches et d'applications linguistiques, Université de Nancy II, France. The Atelier publishes a journal called *Spicae,* vol. 1 of which (1978) contains a valuable **'Orientation bibliographique'** to Vincent by **Jean Schneider,** pp 6-30. The Atelier's work, plus the current state of Vincent studies (as of a few years ago), is described by **Monique Paulmier-Foucart, 'L'Atelier Vincent de Beauvais,'** *Le moyen âge* 85 (1979) 87-99.

Minor Encyclopedias

Isidore of Seville, *De natura rerum*

Isidore's *De natura rerum* (ca 612-14) is primarily scientific, but it is useful for its occasional allegorizations, such as this comment (borrowed from Gregory's *Moralia* 32.15.25) from the beginning of ch. 12, 'De caelo': 'Caelum spiritualiter ecclesia est, quae in huius vitae nocte sanctorum virtutibus quasi claritate siderum fulget.' *De natura rerum* treats time, the world, the heavens and heavenly phenomena, bodies of water, and land. Isidore's sources are about evenly distributed between Christian and pagan (e.g. Lucretius, Chalcidius). The *De natura rerum* was never as popular as the *Etymologiae,* but it was disseminated widely before about 800 and again after the twelfth century in a total of three recensions of 46, 47, and 48 chapters each. It is conveniently available in PL 83, cols 963-1018 (Table of contents in 1377-8) and in the critical edition (with French translation) of **Jacques Fontaine,** *Isidore de Séville, Traité de la nature*, Bibliothèque de l'Ecole des hautes études hispaniques 28 (Bordeaux 1960). Fontaine's introduction and notes discuss intellectual backgrounds, manuscripts and dissemination, and language. There are also a useful *index verborum* (pp 337-455) and examples of manuscript illustrations; source passages are included in the textual apparatus.

Pseudo-Isidore of Seville, *De ordine creaturarum*

Apparently an anonymous seventh-century Irish work, the *De ordine creaturarum* roughly follows the hexaemeral scheme of major encyclopedias, covering the Trinity, the angels, corporeal creatures, the heavens, the devil and demons, the waters, the earth and the earthly paradise, human nature and sin, hell, purgatory, and the future life, all of which are viewed in relation to the creation, temptation, and fall of man. *De ordine creaturarum* contains little metaphorical imagery *per se,* but it does contain typically 'Irish' material, sometimes presented in question-and-answer fashion. The authorship question is argued by the editor of the critical edition, *Liber de ordine creaturarum, un anónimo irlandés del siglo VII*, ed. **Manuel C. Díaz y Díaz,** Monografías de la Universidad de Santiago de Compostela 10 (Santiago de Compostela 1972) pp 13-28. This edition includes a facing-page Spanish translation, manuscript information, a table of biblical citations, an index of authors cited, and an *index rerum*. There is also a convenient edition, albeit without indices, in PL 83, cols 913-54.

Bede, *De natura rerum*

Bede wrote the *De natura rerum* at about the same time he was writing the *De temporibus* (703), taking for its base Isidore's *De natura rerum* and the pseudo-Isidorian *De ordine creaturarum* and supplementing them both with passages from Pliny. Thus the contents include the Creation, the elements, the heavens and heavenly bodies, meteorology, the seas, and the earth. The contents, textual history, and glosses are studied in the introduction to **Charles W. Jones's** edition of the *De natura rerum* in *Bedae Venerabilis opera, pars VI: Opera didascalica I*, CCSL 123A (Turnhout 1975) pp 173-88, which one should augment with the introduction to Jones's edition of Bede's *De temporum ratione*, CCSL 123B, pp 241-61. The edition in PL 90, cols 187-278, is based on the text from the Cologne 1537 edition of Bede's works; it contains extensive glosses, some of which are incorrectly ascribed to Byrhtferth of Ramsey; see **Jones, 'The Byrhtferth Glosses,'** *Medium Ævum* 7 (1938) 81-97, and *Bedae pseudepigrapha: Scientific Writings Falsely Attributed to Bede* (Ithaca, N.Y. 1939) pp 10 and 21-38. Some of these glosses, now included in Jones's edition as part of the textual apparatus, seem to have been from a common body of computistical lore available in the ninth century. Bede used parts of *De natura rerum* when he revised *De temporibus* into *De temporum ratione*. In this fashion, *De natura rerum* made its way into Ælfric's adaptation into Old English (ca 993) of *De temporum ratione:* **Heinrich Henel,** ed., *Ælfric's De temporibus anni*, EETS O.S. 213 (London 1942), with Latin source passages as a running accompaniment to the Old English text.

Summarium Heinrici

The *Summarium Heinrici*, whose title comes from an acrostic contained in its verse prologue, was composed in or near Worms between 1007 and 1022 by an unknown author. It is a revision, in 10 books arranged by subject, of Isidore of Seville's *Etymologiae* (with borrowings from Priscian, Cassiodorus, and Bede), to which is appended an 11th, original book of alphabetically organized glosses. Other German glosses are found throughout, whence its importance to German lexicography. The *Summarium* exists in the original 10-book version and in an abridged 6-book version from the twelfth century. The 10-book version covers language, time, music, God, angels, man, animals, fish, birds, plants, the earth, astronomy, the seas, geography, stones and minerals, human society, clothing, vessels, war, and tools. The 6-book version, which is devoid of imagery and is barely more than a set of glosses from Latin to German, covers the same material. There is a critical edition, *Summarium Heinrici*, ed. **Reiner Hildebrandt**, 2 vols, Quellen und Forschungen zur Sprach- und Kulturgeschichte der germanischen Völker N.F. 61 [185] and 78 [202] (Berlin 1974-82), which offers bks 1-10 of the 10-book version in vol. I, and bk 11 and the 6-book version in II.

Werner Wegstein, *Studien zum Summarium Heinrici: Die Darmstädter Handschrift 6*, Würzburger Forschungen, Texte und Textgeschichte 9 (Tübingen 1985), offers a critical review of previous scholarship and editions, a review of the authorship question, a survey of the manuscripts, a study of the manuscript transmission, and a transcript of MS. Darmstadt, Hessische Landes- und Hochschulbibliothek, 6, together with a study of this manuscript. There are indices of German glosses (pp 235-43) and of Latin *lemmata* (244-60).

Lambert of St Omer, *Liber floridus*

The *Liber floridus*, compiled by Lambert of St Omer from about 1112 through 1121, was popular from the time of its composition, although modern readers have faulted it for its apparent lack of organization. Indeed, its randomness makes it virtually impossible to describe adequately, since material on the same topic (e.g. the world-ages) may be found scattered throughout the text. Fortunately, a thorough description of the contents is available in the table of contents (pp xix-xliii) to the diplomatic edition of Lambert's autograph manuscript by **Albert Derolez**, *Liber floridus* (Ghent 1968). This edition contains excellent colour reproductions of the manuscript illustrations (table of illustrations, pp xvi-xvii); a bibliography of major scholarship is on p. xlvii.

This bibliography may be supplemented with that found on pp xi-xvi of **Albert Derolez**'s study of Lambert's autograph manuscript: *Lambertus qui librum fecit: Een codicologische Studie van de Liber floridus-autograaf*, Verhandelingen van de Koninklijke Academie voor Wetenschappen, Letteren en Schone Kunsten van België; Klasse der Letteren 40/89 (Brussels 1978). The contents include sections on history, cosmology, meteorology, geography, natural history, precious stones, genealogy, virtues and vices, chronology, language, astrology, the Bible and biblical personages, Antichrist, the Crusades, and plants, along with poems, legends, marvels, miracles, and other miscellanea – even the romance of Apollonius of Tyre.

Consulting the manuscripts, which accumulated much extra material over time, is possible with the aid of **J.P. Gumbert's** list of additions in '**Recherches sur le stemma des copies du** *Liber floridus*,' in *Liber floridus Colloquium: Papers Read at the International Meeting Held in the University Library, Ghent, on 3-5 September 1967*, ed. **Albert Derolez** (Ghent 1973) pp 45-50, which is augmented by a list of manuscripts on p. 87. The other essays in this richly illustrated volume are also authoritative.

Finally, **Virginia Grace Tuttle's** 1979 Ohio State University dissertation, '**An Analysis of the** *Liber floridus*,' through an examination of the pictorial programme and contents of Lambert's manuscript, argues for a twelve-part ecclesiological structure that imitates the form of Beatus of Liébana's commentary on the Apocalypse.

Hildegard of Bingen, *Physica* and *Causae et curae*

Although Hildegard is famous for her mystical visions, her two small encyclopedias, *Physica* (or *Liber simplicis medicinae*) and *Causae et curae* (both mid-12th C) were also widely read. It is now thought that Hildegard intended them to constitute one encyclopedia, *Liber subtilitatum diversarum naturarum creaturarum:* see **Helmut Schwitzgebel**, '**Die Überlieferung der Werke der Hildegard von Bingen und die heute noch vorhandenen Handschriften**,' *Blätter der Carl-Zuckmeyer-Gesellschaft* 5/2 (1979) 133-50, esp. 145-6. Both books are concerned with the medicinal properties of objects in the natural world, but both are also fond of allegories. The topics covered in the *Physica* are: plants, elements, trees, stones, fish, birds, animals, reptiles, and metals. The most readily available modern edition of the *Physica* remains PL 197, cols 1117-1352, which has a table of contents in cols 1379-84.

There is a German translation by **Peter Riethe**, *Naturkunde: Das Buch von dem inneren Wesen der verschiedenen Naturen in der*

Schöpfung (Salzburg 1959); German-Latin indices are on pp 147-69. Riethe has also translated bk 4, on stones, into German under the title *Das Buch von den Steinen* (Salzburg 1979), which has large colour photographs, linguistic and lapidary notes, and a good bibliography of primary and secondary literature.

Causae et curae regards illnesses as the result of the Fall, and accordingly begins with two ontological books on the Creation and Fall, linking man to the macrocosm through the elements and humours; the following three books focus on diseases and cures. The best edition is by **Paul Kaiser**, *Hildegardis causae et curae*, Bibliotheca Teubneriana (Leipzig 1903, repr. Basel 1980), which has an index to Latin words and names on pp 244-51 and an index to German words on pp 252-4. The edition of *Causae et curae* by Pitra in *Analecta sacra* VIII [*Analecta Sanctae Hildegardis opera spicilegio solesmensi parata*] pp 468-82, where it is called *Liber compositae medicinae de aegritudinum causis, signis, atque curis*, is abridged, and so should be avoided.

A good introduction to *Causae et curae* may be found on pp 14-46 of **Heinrich Schipperges's** translation, *Heilkunde: Das Buch von dem Grund und Wesen und der Heilung der Krankheiten* (Salzburg 1957), which contains excellent indices at the back. **Schipperges's** recent critical study, '**Heilkunde und Lebenskunst im Weltbild Hildegards von Bingen,**' *Blätter der Carl-Zuckmeyer-Gesellschaft* 5/2 (1979) 79-94, is also worth consulting. Thorndike, *History of Magic* II, 124-54, remains a valuable introduction to Hildegard's work. Hildegard's cosmology is studied in Maurmann, *Himmelsrichtungen* (for which see p. 189 above), passim. The standard bibliography, **Werner Lauter,** *Hildegard-Bibliographie: Wegweiser zur Hildegard-Literatur*, Alzeyer Geschichtsblätter, Sonderheft 4 (Alzey 1970 and 1984), 2 vols, is also worth mentioning.

Pseudo-Hugh of St Victor, *De bestiis et aliis rebus*

De bestiis et aliis rebus, in manuscript attributed to Hugh of St Victor, is a compilation of four books apparently made in the twelfth century. Bks 1-3 treat birds (1), beasts (2), fish, plants, and man (3); bk 4 is an alphabetical *De proprietatibus rerum*. A typical chapter contains some scientific data plus a figurative interpretation, as for instance this observation on apes from bk 2:

Cujus figuram diabolus habet qui caput habet, caudam vero non habet, et licet totus turpis sit, tamen posteriora ejus impense turpia et horribilia sunt. Diabolus enim initium habuit cum angelis in coelis, sed quia hypocrita fuit et dolosus intrinsecus, perdidit caudam, quia totus in fine peribit, sicut dicit Apostolus: 'Quem Dominus Jesus interficiet spiritu oris sui' [2 Thess. 2:8].

The only edition of *De bestiis* remains PL 177, cols 13-164; index in cols 9-14. Through ch. 56, bk 1 is considered to be the *De columba argentata* (or *De avium natura, De tribus columbis, Liber avium*) of Hugh of Folieto (Hugues de Fouilloy, ca 1100-72) since the findings of **Henri Peltier, 'Hugues de Fouilloy: Chanoine regulier, prieur de Saint-Laurent-au-Bois,'** *Revue du moyen âge latin* 2 (1946) 41-2. Bk 2 has been assigned to **Alain de Lille** and has been considered a version of the *Physiologus,* while the authorship of bks 3 and 4 remains uncertain. For a concise summary of these questions one should see **N. Häring, 'Notes on the** *Liber avium* **of Hugues de Fouilloy,'** *Recherches de théologie ancienne et médiévale* 46 (1979) 56.

Secretum secretorum

The *Secretum secretorum* is a pseudo-Aristotelian epistle to Alexander the Great that can be traced to the *Kitāb Sirr al-asrār,* an Arabic rule for princes; it may originate further back, but its claims of Greek origin and Syriac translation have been neither proved nor disproved. (On the Arabic source, one should consult **Mahmoud Manzalaoui, 'The Pseudo-Aristotelian** *Kitāb Sirr al-asrār,'* *Oriens* 23-4 [1974] 147-257.) In its long history of translation, expansion, and abridgment, the *Secretum* accrued layers of encyclopedic learning on alchemy, precious stones, medicine, astrology, and physiognomy. The *Secretum* has neither the range nor the depth of natural subjects covered by major encyclopedias, yet it was so popular that it was one of the main sources for the material that it does cover; moreover, many manuscripts are augmented with extra material. Indeed, the *Secretum* tradition is so vast and complex that if one suspects its influence, it is advisable to consult as many texts of it as possible.

The *Secretum* reached the West in two Arabic versions. 1/ The Short (or Western) Form was translated into Latin ca 1150 by John of Spain (of Toledo/of Seville, Johannes Hispalensis/Hispaniensis). It may be found in *Denkmäler provenzalischer Literatur*, ed. **Hermann Suchier** (Halle 1883) I, 473-80; and in **Johannes Brinkmann,** *Die apokryphen Gesundheitsregeln des Aristoteles für Alexander den Grossen in der Übersetzung des Johann von Toledo* (Leipzig 1914) pp 39-46. 2/ The Long (or Eastern) Form, translated into Latin early in the thirteenth century by Philippus Tripolitanus, is available in Roger Bacon's edition, complete with Bacon's notes: *Opera hactenus inedita Rogeri Baconi,* ed. **Robert Steele** (London 1920) v, 1-175. Steele provides an English translation of the Arabic original, pp 176-266.

Steele's introduction is still an excellent guide to the *Secretum* tradition, but now one should consult **Mario Grignaschi, 'L'Origine et les métamorphoses du** *Sirr al asrâr,*' and 'La Diffusion du *Secretum secretorum (Sirr-al-'Asrar)* **dans l'Europe occidentale,'** *Archives d'histoire doctrinale et littéraire du moyen âge* 43 (1976) 7-112 and 47 (1980) 7-70. In addition, *Pseudo-Aristotle, The Secret of Secrets: Sources and Influences,* ed. **W.F. Ryan** and **Charles B. Schmitt,** Warburg Institute Surveys 9 (London 1982), contains recent, authoritative articles by Grignaschi and others on the Arabic, Hebrew, Latin, French, and Russian versions.

The major surveys of the manuscripts and early editions are 1/ **Richard Förster, 'Handschriften und Ausgaben des pseudo-Aristotelischen** *Secretum secretorum,*' *Zentralblatt für Bibliothekswesen* 6 (1889) 1-22 and 57-76 (additions on 218-19); and 2/ **Friedrich Wurms,** *Studien zu den deutschen und den lateinischen Prosafassungen des pseudo-Aristotelischen Secretum secretorum* (Hamburg diss. 1970) pp 25-126; this includes corrections for, but does not entirely supersede, Förster's list.

Vernacular versions of the *Secretum* are numerous. *Three Prose Versions of the Secreta secretorum,* ed. **Robert Steele,** EETS E.S. 74 (London 1898) contains three fifteenth-century English texts of the Long Form. *Lydgate and Burgh's Secrees of Old Philisoffres,* ed. **Steele,** EETS E.S. 66 (London 1894) is a metrical paraphrase of the Long Form by John Lydgate up to line 1491 which was completed by an anonymous versifier whom Steele believed to be Benedict Burgh. *Secretum secretorum: Nine English Versions,* ed. **M.A. Manzalaoui,** EETS O.S. 276 (Oxford 1977) presents seven texts from before 1500; one is of the Short Form. Also worth mentioning is **Thomas Hoccleve's** *Regement of Princes,* ed. **Frederick J. Furnivall,** EETS

E.S. 72 (London 1897), which is largely based on the *Secretum*. A Scottish *Secretum* by **Gilbert of the Haye** (ca 1456) may be found in *Gilbert of the Haye's Prose Manuscript*, ed. **J.H. Stevenson**, Scottish Text Society 20-1 (Edinburgh 1901-14) II, 71-165.

Of the three different Anglo-Norman versions of the *Secretorum*, only the one of **Peter of Fetcham** (or Peckham), a thirteenth-century versification containing only the material on the rule of princes and health, has been edited: *Le Secré de secrez by Pierre d'Abernun of Fetcham*, ed. **Oliver A. Beckerlegge**, Anglo-Norman Text Society 5 (Oxford 1944); another edition is in *Opera ... Baconi* ed. Steele, V, 287-313. The two other Anglo-Norman versions are described by Beckerlegge, pp xxii-xxiii.

The earliest Old French translation is by **Jofroi de Waterford** and **Servais Copale**, from about 1290, of the Long Form; extracts of the manuscript (MS. Paris, BN fr. 1822) are in the *Histoire littéraire de la France* XXI, 217-25. Another version (late 14th C) was printed by Antoine Vérard, Paris 1497; a third (also late 14th C) is in MS. Paris, BN fr. 562. The Provençal version (in verse; 13th C), based on the Short Form, is in Suchier's *Denkmäler* I, 201-13.

A Castilian version of the Short Form apparently was made directly from the Arabic *Sirr al-asrār* in about 1300: *Poridat de las poridades*, ed. **Lloyd A. Kasten** (Madrid 1957). Kasten's *'Secreto de los secretos, translated by Juan Fernández de Heredia'* (University of Wisconsin diss. 1931) presents the fourteenth-century Aragonese adaptation of the Long Form. The Catalan *Secretum* is a translation of the *Poridat: Libre de saviesa del rey en Jacme I d'Arago*, ed. **Gabriel Llabrés y Quintana**, Biblioteca catalana (Santander 1908); another edition is by **J.M. Castro y Calvo**, Publicaciones de la sección de filología románica del Consejo superior de investigaciones científicas, Delegación de Barcelona, Instituto Antonio de Nebrija (Barcelona 1946). A brief study is **Kasten, 'Several Observations Concerning** *Lo libre de saviesa* **Attributed to James I of Aragon,'** *Hispanic Review* 2 (1934) 70-3.

The German prose translation of the Long Form by **Hiltgart von Hürnheim** (ca 1282), together with a Latin text, may be found in *Mittelhochdeutsche Prosaübersetzung des Secretum secretorum*, ed. **Reinhold Möller**, Deutsche Texte des Mittelalters 56 (Berlin 1963); but for caveats concerning this edition see Wurms, *Studien* pp 133-6. Other German translations are listed and discussed by Wurms, *Studien* pp 127-33 and 136-42, and by Möller, pp lxvi-lxxiv. Two texts of the Short Form are given by Brinkmann, *Apokryphen Gesundheitsregeln* pp 47-55. The Dutch translation is by **Jacob von Maerlant, *Heimlijkheid der Heimlijkheden*,** ed. **Andries Anton Verdenius** (Amsterdam 1917).

Uguccione da Pisa, *Magnae derivationes*

Although it has yet to be edited and published, and although it is not strictly speaking an encyclopedia but an etymological dictionary with an encyclopedic range, the *Magnae derivationes* of Uguccione da Pisa ([H]ugutio Pisanus) deserves mention at least for its influence on Dante, which was demonstrated by **Paget Toynbee, 'Dante's Latin Dictionary,'** in ***Dante Studies and Researches*** (London 1902; repr. Port Washington, N.Y. and London 1971) pp 97-114. Main entries are Latin words from which Uguccione (often following Isidore's *Etymologiae*) derives other words by etymology. For example, from *Ge,* Greek for *terra* 'earth,' Uguccione derives *gehenna, igneus, genesis, genus, genealogia, gens, gigno, gigas, gemini,* and other words. Occasionally he uses a name-etymology. According to **Claus Riessner,** *Magnae derivationes* (see below) p. xviii, one third of Uguccione's text comes from Isidore's *Etymologiae;* in **'Quale codice delle *Etymologiae* di Isidoro di Siviglia fu usato da Uguccione da Pisa?'** *Vetera Christianorum* 13 (1976) 349-65, Riessner argues that Uguccione used one of three manuscripts of the *Etymologiae* now kept in the Vatican Library. The chief difficulty in using the *Magnae derivationes* is that whereas the main entries are alphabetically organized, the derivations themselves are not; thus the text is searchable only in manuscripts that contain indices. For example, in MS. Oxford, Bodl. e Mus. 96 (3582), the derivations are listed alphabetically before Uguccione's prologue and cross-indexed by main entry; within the text itself, derivations are identified marginally.

The major tools for studying the *Magnae derivationes* are **Giuseppe Cremascoli, 'Uguccione da Pisa: Saggio bibliografico,'** *Aevum* 42 (1968) 123-68, which lists citations and studies beginning with Salimbene da Parma; **Claus Riessner, *Die 'Magnae derivationes' des Uguccione da Pisa und ihre Bedeutung für die romanische Philologie*,** Temi e testi 11 (Rome 1965), which is the major study and includes numerous selected entries as an appendix; and **Aristide Marigo,** *I codici manoscritti delle 'Derivationes' di Uguccione Pisano: Saggio d'inventorio bibliografico con appendice sui codici del 'Catholicon' di Giovanni da Genova* (Rome 1936). The *Magnae derivationes* forms the basis for the alphabetically organized *Catholicon* by Giovanni da Genova (Joannes de Balbis), completed in 1286, which despite its searchability did not supersede the *Derivationes* in importance.

Arnoldus Saxo, *De finibus rerum naturalium*

Arnoldus Saxo's mid-thirteenth-century encyclopedia *De finibus rerum naturalium* contains five books treating the heavens and earth, corporeal creatures, stones, the supposed powers of natural things, and ethics. The only complete edition remains *Die Encyklopädie des Arnoldus Saxo*, ed. **Emil Stange**, Programmschrift des Königlichen Gymnasiums zu Erfurt (Erfurt 1905-7), 3 vols in 1. The best first recourse to Arnoldus is now **F.J. Worstbrock**'s article in *Die deutsche Literatur des Mittelalters: Verfasserlexikon*, ed. **Kurt Ruh** et al. (2nd ed. Berlin 1978 ff) I, 485-8.

Brunetto Latini, *Trésor* and *Tesoretto*

Brunetto Latini wrote two encyclopedic works, both during the decade 1260-70. The *Trésor*, written in Old French, covers the following subjects: bk 1, theology, universal history, the elements, the heavens, geography, agriculture, and the bestiary; bk 2, ethics, vices and virtues; bk 3, rhetoric and government. The *Tesoretto* is an Italian précis of the *Trésor* in heptasyllabic couplets.

Brunetto wrote two versions of the *Trésor*, the chief difference between them being the addition of historical chapters on Frederick II and Manfred and the omission of four chapters from the bestiary. Both versions are represented in the critical edition of **Francis J. Carmody,** *Li Livres dou Tresor*, University of California Publications in Modern Philology 22 (Berkeley 1948). Though editorially unsound, the earlier edition by **P. Chabaille**, Collection de documents inédits sur l'histoire de France, 1. sér. (Paris 1863), records interesting and potentially useful *variora*.

The *Trésor* achieved its widest circulation in the Italian translation called the *Tesoro*, attributed to Bono Giamboni. The most readily available modern editions are 1/ *Il Tesoro di Brunetto Latini, volgarizzato da Bono Giamboni*, ed. **Luigi Gaiter** (Bologna 1878-83), 4 vols, on which one should consult the review by **Thor Sundby** in *Romania* 9 (1880) 469-72; and 2/ same title, ed. **L. Carrér**, Biblioteca classica italiana di scienze, lettere, ed arti 2/1-2 (Venice 1839). An edition of bk 1 by **Roberto de Visiani**, *Del Tesoro volgarizzato di Brunetto Latini, libro primo*, Scelta di curiosità litterarie inedite o rare dal secolo XIII al XVII, dispensa 104 (Bologna 1869), is based on a different manuscript tradition, and therefore contains potentially useful variants.

The best guide to the manuscripts is **Adolfo Mussafia**, 'Sul testo del *Tesoro* di Brunetto Latini,' in *Denkschriften der kaiserlichen Akademie der Wissenschaften*, philosophisch-historische Klasse 18 (Vienna 1869) pp 265-334, repr. as an appendix to the major study of Brunetto, **Thor Sundby**, *Della vita e delle opere di Brunetto Latini*, trans. **Rodolfo Renier** (Florence 1884); however, it should be supplemented by **Carla Mascheroni**, 'I codici del volgarizzamento italiano del *Trésor* di Brunetto Latini,' *Aevum* 43 (1969) 485-510. It is from the *Tesoro* that **Jean Corbichon** (last quarter, 14th C) produced the French *Trésor qui parle de toutes choses* (Lyon 1491, Paris 1539).

In addition to the *Tesoro*, there are other Italian versions of the *Trésor*. A verse rendering (ca 1310) possibly by one Mauro da Poggibonzi, is in two manuscripts in the Biblioteca nazionale centrale, Florence: MS. Pal. 807 (not 679, the number given by d'Ancona, below) and MS. Panc. 28. Each represents a different version and contains material not found in Brunetto's original. For extracts from the historical chapters in bk 1 see **Alessandro d'Ancona**, 'Il *Tesoro* di Brunetto Latini versificato,' *Atti della Reale Accademia dei Lincei: Classe di scienze morali, storiche, e filologiche* ser. 4, 4/1 (1888) 122-60, 228-9, and 240-59. There is also a fifteenth-century translation of the bestiary section, which may be found in **Milton Garver**, 'Some Supplementary Italian Bestiary Chapters,' *Romanic Review* 11 (1920) 308-27. A version in the Bergamo dialect by **Raimondo da Bergamo** is in MS. Venice, Bibl. nazionale Marciana It. II, 54.

Finally, there are versions of the *Trésor* in Spanish, Catalan, and Latin. The Spanish, still unpublished, is by **Alfonso de Paredes** (ca 1290). Two manuscripts are listed in Carmody, *Livres dou Tresor* p. xxi; a table of contents from a third, together with a brief discussion of the considerable popularity of the *Trésor* in Spain, may be found in **Francisco López Estrada**, 'Sobre la difusión del *Tesoro* de Brunetto Latini en España,' in *Gesammelte Aufsätze zur Kulturgeschichte Spaniens* ed. **Johannes Vincke**, Spanische Forschungen der Görresgesellschaft 1/16 (Münster i.W. 1960) pp 137-52.

The best guide to the Catalan versions is in the edition of bks 1 and 2 of the 1418 translation by **Guillem de Copons**, *Llibre del tresor*, ed. **Curt J. Wittlin**, Els nostres clàssics A/102, 111 (Barcelona 1971-6).

Of the two Latin versions mentioned by Carmody, *Livres dou Tresor* p. xxi, apparently only one, MS. Paris, BN lat. 6556, actually exists, and whether it is a source or a translation has not been established with certainty.[1] It contains fourteenth-century fragments corresponding to *Trésor* 1.100-25 which **L[éopold] D[elisle]** published under the title, '**La Source des chapitres C-CXXV du livre I du** *Trésor* **de Brunetto Latini**,' *Bibliothèque de l'Ecole des chartes* 54 (1893) 406-11.

The *Tesoretto* uses a frame modelled after Boethius's *De consolatione philosophiae*. There is now a convenient edition with facing-page English translation by **Julia Bolton Holloway**, *Il Tesoretto (The Little Treasure)*, Garland Library of Medieval Literature A/2 (New York 1981); one should also consult the standard editions of **Giovanni Pozzi** in *Poeti del Duecento*, ed. **Gianfranco Contini**, La letteratura italiana, storia e testi 2 (Milan 1960) pp 169-277; and of **B. Wiese**, *Il Tesoretto e Il Falvolello*, Bibliotheca Romanica 94-5 (Strasbourg and New York 1909).

---

1 Carmody cites MS. Florence, Bibl. Medicea-Laurenziana Plut. XLII, 31, from *Dictionnaire des manuscrits*, ed. Comte Louis de Mas-Latrie, Nouvelle encyclopédie théologique 40-1 (Paris 1853) II, 580. However, according to **A.M. Bandini**, *Catalogus codicum Italicorum bibliothecae Mediceae Laurentianae, Gaddianae, et Sanctae Crucis*, Catalogus codicum manuscriptorum bibliothecae Mediceae Laurentianae 5 (Florence 1778) p. 195, this manuscript contains only a panegyric to Cosimo de'Medici. The other versions of the *Trésor* in this catalogue are the Italian *Tesoro*.

Book of Sidrach

The *Book of Sidrach* (mid-thirteenth-century; also called the *Fountain of All Knowledge*) is a popular adaptation of an Old French *Lucidaire* (see Lefèvre, *L'Elucidarium* pp 323-6), though it poses as an ancient Eastern dialogue between Bactus, king of Bactriane, and Sidrach, a wise man, on God, the angels, the devil, man, the soul, and the world. Before 1500, translations were made into Provençal, Italian, English, Dutch, Ripuarian, and German. The versions vary in length from about 400 questions (in the Dutch text) to about 1200 questions (in the French original).

The only modern edition of the complete Old French *Sidrach* must be pieced together out of two University of North Carolina dissertations which edit and study MS. Paris, BN fr. 1160, the earliest and best manuscript: **Honoria Sapelo Treanor, 'Le Roman de Sydrac, fontaine de toutes sciences'** (1939), and **William McFall Holler, 'Le Livre de Sydrac, fontaine de toutes sciences, Folios 57-112'** (1972). Extracts are given in *Histoire littéraire de la France* XXXI, 285-318. Printed editions (e.g. *Fontaine de toutes sciences* [Paris 1528]) are listed for the French, English, and Dutch versions by **William E.A. Axon, 'On a Fourteenth Century Fragment of the *Book of Sidrach*,'** *Transactions of the Royal Society of Literature* 2nd ser. 30 (1910) 189-205. A partial list of manuscripts and printed editions for the French, Provençal, Italian, English, and Dutch versions may be found in Parlangèli (see next page), pp 146-8. A convenient synopsis and study is in Langlois, *Connaissance* pp 198-275.

Provençal versions of *Sidrach* exist in two independent adaptations: MS. Paris, BN fr. 1158 (ca 1300; 535 questions), and a privately owned manuscript copied by Bertrand de Boysset in 1372 (prologue and first 47 questions only); the manuscripts are described by **Robert Marichal, 'La Langue de la traduction provençale du *Livre de Sidrach* (Paris, Bibl. nat. MS. fr. 1158),'** in *Recueil de travaux offert à M. Clovis Brunel*, Mémoires et documents publiées par la Société de l'Ecole des chartes 12 (Paris 1955) II, 205-6.

An Italian rendering of 557 questions (early 14th C) may be found in *Il Libro di Sidrach*, ed. **Adolfo Bartoli**, Collezione di opere inedite o rare dei primi tre secoli della lingua 25 (Bologna 1868). A fifteenth-century Italian version of 562 questions is given in **Oronzo Parlangèli**, '**Un codice Ambrosiano del** *Sidrac*,' *Rendiconti dell'Istituto lombardo di scienze e lettere: Classe di lettere e scienze morali e storiche* 83 (1950) 148-218.

Extracts from a fragmentary fifteenth-century Salentino version (MS. Milan, Bibl. Ambrosiana I, 29) are given in **V. de Bartholomaeis**, '**Un'antica versione del** *Libro di Sydrac* **in volgare di terra d'Otranto**,' *Archivio glottologico italiano* 16 (1902) 28-68; plans for a complete edition have been anounced by **Paola Sgrilli**, '**Preliminari all'edizione del** *Sidrac* **salentino**,' *Studi mediolatini e volgari* 25 (1977) 171-200.

Middle English translations of *Sidrach* take two forms. One, a rhymed version of 365 questions from the fifteenth century, may be found in *The History of Kyng Boccus and Sydracke ... by Hugo de Caumpeden* (London [ca 1510]). It is edited in **Robert Edward Nichols, Jr**, '*Sidrak and Bokkus,* **Now First Edited from Manuscript Lansdowne 793**' (University of Washington diss. 1965), which also surveys manuscripts and printed editions, discusses the author, and surveys versions in Danish, Dutch, Italian, French, and Provençal. The other is a prose version from a fragmentary mid-fifteenth-century manuscript, Oxford, Bodl. Digby 194. These two versions, together with French and Italian manuscripts of *Sidrach* located in British libraries, are described by **Karl D. Bülbring**, '**Sidrac in England**,' in *Beiträge zur romanischen und englischen Philologie: Festgabe für Wendelin Foerster zum 26. Oktober, 1901* (Halle 1902) pp 445-78. A brief and convenient survey of Middle English versions is in **Francis Lee Utley**, '**Dialogues, Debates, and Catechisms**,' in *Manual of Writings in Middle English* ed. Severs et al. (for which see p. 84 above), III, 744-5, with a bibliography of manuscripts, printed editions, and studies on pp 900-1.

A Dutch translation of *Sidrach* (early 14th C) may be found in *Het Boek van Sidrac in de Nederlanden*, ed. **J.F.J. Van Tol** (Amsterdam 1936). Further manuscript fragments are given by **Hartmut Beckers**, '**Bruchstücke unbekannter** *Sidrac*-**Handschriften aus Münster, Düsseldorf, und Brüssel**,' *Amsterdamer Beiträge zur älteren Germanistik* 1 (1972) 89-110.

From a Dutch version or versions were made Ripuarian and Middle Low German versions. The Ripuarian version (mid-15th C), still unedited, is described by H. Niewöhner, 'Eine ripuarische Handschrift des Buches Sidrach,' *Zeitschrift für deutsche Philologie* 57 (1932) 183-93. The Middle Low German version, dated 1479 and containing 388 questions, is in *Das Buch Sidrach*, ed. H. Jellinghaus, Bibliothek des litterarischen Vereins in Stuttgart 235 (Tübingen 1904). The Danish version is in *Sydrak efter Haandskriftet Ny Kgl. Saml. 236 4^{lo}*, ed. Gunnar Knudsen (Copenhagen 1921-32), 3 pts.

Placides et Timéo

Placides et Timéo, also called *Li secrés as philosophes*, is an Old French imitation of a Platonic dialogue written between about 1250 and 1304. It survives in two redactions, possibly by one Jehan Bonnet. Much of its material derives from the *Image du monde* and the *Secretum secretorum*. Its contents include: God and the Creation, man, human reproduction, atmospheric phenomena, history, and government. There is now a critical edition with an introduction (pp vii-cii), notes (pp 328-37), glossary (339-81), table of names (383-91), and subject index (393-401): *Placides et Timéo, ou Li secrés as philosophes*, ed. Claude Alexandre Thomasset, Textes littéraires français 289 (Geneva and Paris 1980). Since the manuscripts do not entirely agree, it is well to consult the editor's analyses of the contents of the manuscripts (pp xxviii-lxii) and of the manuscript variants (277-328). The review by Françoise Fery-Hue in *Romania* 105 (1984) 142-54, provides corrections to typographical errors and describes a manuscript unknown to Thomasset when his edition went to press. The sources of and scientific lore in *Placides et Timéo* are studied in Thomasset, *Une vision du monde à la fin du XIIIe siècle: Commentaire du dialogue Placides et Timéo*, Publications romanes et françaises 161 (Geneva and Paris 1982).

Dialogus creaturarum (Contemptus sublimitatis)

The *Dialogus creaturarum*, called *Contemptus sublimitatis* in six of its nine manuscripts, follows a roughly hexaemeral plan which covers the cosmos, precious stones, metals, plants, animals (some fabulous), and man. Most subjects are handled in pairs (e.g. 'De verbena et lupo,' dial. 30) in chapters revolving about a fable but also including scientific lore, etymologies, and moralizations. The *Dialogus* draws from a wide variety of named Classical and medieval sources. It exists in short and long redactions found in manuscripts from the late fourteenth century onwards in Italy, France, Spain, and Germany. The only modern edition is of the short redaction: *Die beiden ältesten lateinischen Fabelbücher des Mittelalters: Des Bischofs Cyrillus Speculum sapientiae und des Nicolaus Pergamenus Dialogus creaturarum*, ed. **J. G. Th.** Grässe, Bibliothek des litterarischen Vereins in Stuttgart 148 (Tübingen 1880) pp 127-280 [the *Speculum sapientiae* is not included here because it is strictly a collection of *fabulae*]. Grässe's edition is defective, and should be used only in the light of the criticisms presented by **Pio Rajna**, *Intorno al cosiddetto Dialogus creaturarum ed al suo autore* (Torino 1888) pp 1-26; Rajna offers a critical edition for the Prologue and first dialogue of the short redaction and of dialogues 20, 22, 42, 90, 100, and 103 of the long redaction. Rajna's study is also available in *Giornale storico della letteratura italiana* 3 (1884) 1-26, 4 (1884) 337-60, 10 (1887) 42-113, and 11 (1888) 41-73.

A French translation of the short redaction was done in 1482 by **Colart Mansion:** *Le Dialogue des créatures: Traduction par Colart Mansion (1482) du Dialogus creaturarum (XIVᵉ siècle)*, ed. **Pierre Ruelle**, Académie royale de Belgique, Classe des lettres et des sciences morales et politiques, Collection des anciens auteurs belges, N.S. 8 (Brussels 1985).

Grässe believed the *Dialogus* to have been written by Nicolaus Pergamenus; Rajna (see esp. pp 55-65) argued for the authorship of Mayno de' Mayneri; Ruelle agrees with Rajna that the author was from Milan but maintains (p. 31) that he is otherwise unidentifiable given the present evidence. Ruelle dates the text (p. 22) between 1326 and the end of the fourteenth century. Ruelle helpfully lists manuscripts of the Latin original's two redactions on pp 7-8 and describes early printed editions (all of the short redaction), with their present locations, on pp 8-15. Early printed editions of late medieval translations of the *Dialogus* into Dutch (e.g. Gouda 1482), French (Gouda 1482), and English (London, n.d.) are listed by Grässe, pp 307-8.

Indices

Index of Subjects, Medieval Authors, and Texts

This index lists the subjects, medieval authors, and texts found throughout the book, including major collections and series, together with some libraries, museums, and other institutions (indexed by location). Headings are in the usual language found in the text (e.g. Wisdom for Sapientia). As far as possible, headings and subheadings are those of chapter headings and sub-headings in the text. Wherever possible, entries have been simplified; thus, medieval texts often have abbreviated titles. The references are to page numbers, where the indexed items will be found sometimes in boldfaced bibliographical entries and sometimes in standard entries and/or discussions.

Index of Modern Authors, Editors, and Translators

This index lists all instances of modern authors, editors, and translators. Note: Icelandic names have been treated as European and American names (e.g. Jón Helgason will be found under H). Semicolons separate references to different works; where there are multiple references to the same work these are separated by commas and the number of the page which carries the full bibliographic citation is in boldface. Some pages carry full bibliographic citations for more than one work by the same author or editor; where this fact is not made clear by the use of boldface and/or repetition the page number is followed by a number in parentheses which indicates how many full citations to look for. Thus, for example, 'André, J. 185 (2)' means that there are two different works by André cited in full on p. 185.

Index of Manuscripts

In this index a page number in boldface indicates that the manuscript cited there is referred to only in a boldfaced title.

Index of Modern Translations

This index lists main citations of modern translations, in any language, of medieval authors and texts, including anthologies and series. Bibliography is listed on p. 12.

Toronto Medieval Bibliographies

Editor: John Leyerle
Centre for Medieval Studies, University of Toronto

1   Hans Bekker-Nielsen, *Old Norse-Icelandic Studies* (1967) o/p

2   Fred C. Robinson, *Old English Literature* (1970) o/p

3   James J. Murphy, *Medieval Rhetoric* (1971)

4   Andrew Hughes, *Medieval Music: The Sixth Liberal Art* (1973)

5   Rachel Bromwich, *Medieval Celtic Literature* (1974)

6   Giles Constable, *Medieval Monasticism* (1976)

7   Robert A. Taylor, *La Littérature occitane du moyen âge* (1977)

8   Leonard E. Boyle, O.P., *Medieval Latin Palaeography* (1984)

9   Richard W. Pfaff, *Medieval Latin Liturgy* (1982)

10   John Leyerle and Anne Quick, *Chaucer* (1986)

11   R. E. Kaske, with Arthur Groos and Michael W. Twomey, *Medieval Christian Literary Imagery* (1988)